Jonathan Garner

The Rise of the Chinese Consumer

THE RISE OF THE CHINESE CONSUMER

Theory and Evidence

Jonathan Garner
Managing Director, Global Strategist and Global Co-ordinator
of China research, Credit Suisse First Boston

With contributions from Vincent Chan, Marisa Ho, Dong Tao and CSFB's
global sector research teams

John Wiley & Sons, Ltd

Disclaimer

Other Wiley Editorial Offices

John Wiley & Sons Inc., 111 River Street, Hoboken, NJ 07030, USA

Jossey-Bass, 989 Market Street, San Francisco, CA 94103-1741, USA

Wiley-VCH Verlag GmbH, Boschstr. 12, D-69469 Weinheim, Germany

John Wiley & Sons Australia Ltd, 42 McDougall Street, Milton, Queensland 4064, Australia

John Wiley & Sons (Asia) Pte Ltd, 2 Clementi Loop #02-01, Jin Xing Distripark, Singapore 129809

John Wiley & Sons Canada Ltd, 22 Worcester Road, Etobicoke, Ontario, Canada M9W 1L1

Wiley also publishes its books in a variety of electronic formats. Some content that appears in print may
not be available in electronic books.

British Library Cataloguing in Publication Data
A catalogue record for this book is available from the British Library

ISBN 13 978-0-470-01869-9 (HB)
ISBN 10 0-470-01869-0 (HB)

Typeset in 10/12pt Times by TechBooks, New Delhi, India
Printed and bound in Great Britain by TJ International Ltd, Padstow, Cornwall, UK
This book is printed on acid-free paper responsibly manufactured from sustainable forestry
in which at least two trees are planted for each one used for paper production.

I dedicate this book to my wife Helen and our children Alice, Charles, Rosalind, Edward and Benjamin

Contents

Foreword

CSFB views the economic resurgence of China as a key investment theme of our times. Three years ago we took the decision to appoint Jonathan Garner to coordinate our worldwide research on this topic. This book is the fruit of the efforts he and his CSFB colleagues have put in to understanding the role China is playing as a source of structural change in the global economy and financial markets. We are happy to present this work to the broader public, with the hope that the ideas discussed reach a wider audience.

Paul Calello

Chairman and Chief Executive Officer of the Asia Pacific Region,
Credit Suisse First Boston

Stefano Natella

Global Head of Equity Research, Credit Suisse First Boston

Preface

'*There lies a sleeping giant, let her sleep for when she wakes up she will shake the world,*' Napoleon Bonaparte on China, early nineteenth century.

'*The Chinese have always been a great courageous and industrious nation; it is only in modern times that they have fallen behind . . . Ours will no longer be a nation subject to insult and humiliation. We have stood up,*' Mao Zedong, 1 October 1949.

'*It is time to prosper. China has been poor a thousand years . . . to get rich is glorious,*' Deng Xiaoping, 1982

The message of this book is that Chinese consumers have not only woken up and stood up but that in increasing numbers they are getting rich and starting to spend. The impact is likely to be felt in dramatically enhanced opportunities and challenges for consumer-facing companies worldwide over the next 10 years and beyond. The impact of Chinese consumers on these companies is likely to be as significant as the impact of Chinese producers on manufacturing and resources companies in the last 10 years. Indeed, on our base-case projections, the Chinese consumer is likely to have displaced the US consumer as the engine of growth in the global economy by 2014.

The book is divided into two major sections. In Section 1, we provide top-down scenario analysis for the likely development of aggregate US$ consumption expenditure in China over the medium term. We also put China into a global context by undertaking projections for other major economies using CSFB's macroeconomic team's forecasts for growth. We discuss the sustainability of the growth model followed by China in recent years and near-term business cycle issues arising from the government's efforts to combat overheating. There is then a detailed discussion of the impact of China's demographic trends on consumption spending as well as changes in the social and cultural context for consumption spending. We finish with projections for both China and other major countries of consumption spending by major product category type.

In Section 2, we provide conclusions from a proprietary consumer survey based on interviews with 2700 people in eight major Chinese cities in the second half of September 2004. The survey collected individual and household data on a range of products and services as well as general information on income and attitudes. Products and services covered were: Automobiles, Beverages, Electronic Goods, Food Producers, Food Retailers, Restaurant and Food Services, Household and Personal Care, Luxury Goods, Telecom Equipment, Tobacco and Transport and Travel. We then give comments on the implications of this survey for the opportunity facing major consumer stocks worldwide. We identify those global companies that are, in our view, best placed to benefit from the rise of the Chinese consumer. For some of these companies China currently represents only a small percentage of revenues. However, relative to their competitors, in our view they are making the strategic moves to benefit if the thesis of our piece is correct.

Acknowledgements

This book is an updated and revised version of a CSFB research note originally published in November 2004. Thanks are due in particular to Hotak Chow who worked for six months at CSFB in 2004 as an intern on the original note, particularly in the design and implementation of the consumer survey that forms Section 2. He played a major role from inception to completion. Giles Lim also worked as an intern in 2005 revising certain elements for this publication. Research International's team, led by Xinwu Yao and Yue Zhou, conducted the survey on the ground in China in September 2004. The demographic projections in this book were made using the MarketEstimator Excel-based tool provided by Asian Demographics Ltd and inputting CSFB's own economic assumptions, as discussed in detail in the report. Thanks are due to Dr Clint Laurent of Asian Demographics Ltd for giving his permission for its use and for our discussions on Chinese demography. Andrew Glyn was kind enough to read the manuscript in its entirety and to offer comments while Alexander Redman and Sophie Biro helped keep CSFB's emerging market strategy product on track during the time it took to put this book together. Thanks to all three.

I have benefited enormously from discussions on matters China related with my senior CSFB research colleagues Vincent Chan, Marisa Ho and Dong Tao who helped in the drafting of key parts of the original report. Many other CSFB colleagues past and present also contributed their sector expertise to this project and, in particular, Bill Stacey, Chris Ceraso, Harald Hendrikse, Koji Endo, Jeannie Cheung, Andrew Conway, Michael Bleakley, Guillaume Dalibot, Shuichi Shibanuma, Michelle Yan, Nathalie Wan, Michael Masdea, Robert Semple, Koya Tabata, Kunihiko Kanno, David Nelson, Andrew Kasoulis, Janice Meyer, Lauren Lieberman, Yukiko Oshima, Kulbinder Garcha, Mike Ounjian, Pieter Vorster, Chris Reid, Karen Chan, William Drewry, Julia Pennington, James Higgins and Neville Pike.

Finally, I would like to thank all of those institutional clients of CSFB and business persons and officials in China and the wider Asian region who offered their comments on the original note and shared our curiosity about the implications of the re-emergence of China on to the global economic stage. All errors and omissions remain my own.

Jonathan Garner
May 2005

Section 1
THEORY

1
Top-Down Projections of Consumption Growth in China

In this chapter, we provide a top-down view on Chinese household consumption spending growth, projecting ahead in both absolute terms and relative to key country peers for the period from 2004 to 2014.

We make the following conclusions. For 2004, we estimate the US$ value of aggregate household consumption spending in China as US$704bn. This represents around only 9 % of US consumption spending and 3 % of our estimate of global consumption spending. Thus currently, in US dollar terms, Chinese consumers are only a marginal force in global consumption spending.

However, major undervaluation of the Renminbi versus its purchasing power parity (PPP) exchange rate means this figure significantly underestimates the underlying quantity of consumption activity within China in our view. For example, in 2003 China consumed 33 % of global rice production, 22 % of soy bean oil production and 12 % of global meat production (Figure 1.1).

Assuming as a base case: (a) that trend real gross domestic product (GDP) growth rises by 7 % per annum; (b) that there is a 5.5 % increase in the share of consumption spending within GDP; and (c) that the Renminbi rises from 0.2 of its PPP level to 0.55, we conclude that the US$ value of consumption spending in China in 2014 will amount to US$3726bn (in 2004 US$). This represents a compound annual growth rate (CAGR) of 18 % for the 10-year period 2004 to 2014.

Our base-case projection is that by 2014 the US$ value of consumption spending in China will represent 37.3 % of US consumption spending and 10.5 % of our estimate of global consumption spending. Incremental additional annual US$ consumption spend in China will most likely be larger than that in the US by this time. We estimate that China will have an incremental spend of US$524bn (in 2004 US$) per annum 10 years from now compared with the US with US$262bn. The Chinese consumer is therefore likely to have displaced the US consumer as the engine of growth in the global economy.

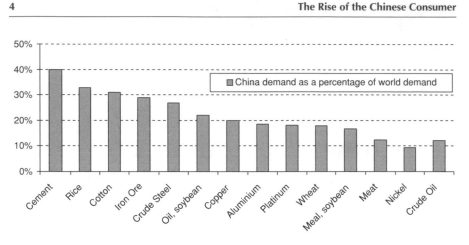

Source: Bloomberg, World Bank and CSFB research
Figure 1.1   China demand as a percentage of world demand, 2003

However, our scenario analysis indicates that there is a wide range of possible outcomes around our base case. In our best-case scenario, the US$ value of China consumption spending will reach 98.0 % of US consumption spending while the incremental US$ spend will be four times that of the US by 2014. In our worst-case scenario, China consumption spending will stagnate at only 11 % of US consumption spending.

HOW BIG IS CHINA'S ECONOMY?

Current US dollar comparisons lead, in our view, to significant understatement of the true size of China's economy. China's GDP ranks only seventh in the world in current US dollar terms. However, in PPP terms using International Monetary Fund (IMF) estimates, it is already the second-largest economy in the world and 62 % the size of the US economy, as shown in Figures 1.2 and 1.3.

PPP is a rate of exchange that accounts for price differences across countries, allowing international comparisons of real output and incomes. Proponents of using PPP exchange rates argue that market exchange rates are based on short-term factors and subject to substantial distortions from speculative movements and government interventions. By establishing purchasing power equivalence, where one PPP US dollar purchases the same quantity of goods and services in all countries, PPP conversions allow cross-country comparisons of economic aggregates based on physical levels of output, free of price and exchange-rate distortions.

In this chapter, we provide some aggregate projections for the size and relative importance globally of China's GDP both currently and in 10 years' time. We have used CSFB's economic team's views on trend real CAGRs of GDP (see Figure 1.4) to

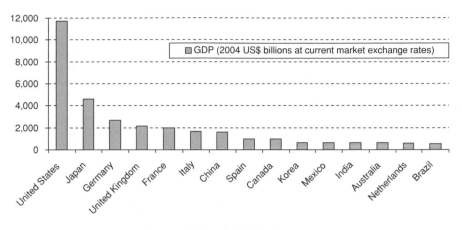

Source: IMF and CSFB estimates
Figure 1.2 Largest 15 global economies by 2004E (estimate) GDP (2004 US$ and current market exchange rates)

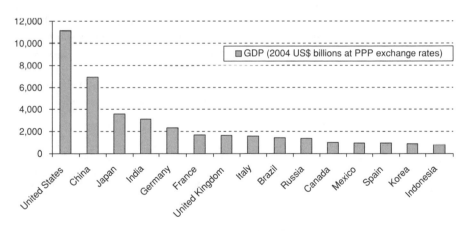

Source: IMF and CSFB estimates
Figure 1.3 Largest 15 global economies by 2004E GDP (2004 US$, PPP exchange rates)

project the sizes of various economies over the 10-year time horizon. These economies are the largest and most relevant global economies for comparison with China in our view. We project that real GDP growth in China will average 7 % over the cycle for the next 10 years, which would be the highest in the group of countries illustrated. At the other end of the spectrum the lowest trend GDP growth of below 2 % is anticipated in Italy and Germany. In the next chapter we explain why it is reasonable to assume that China's economy will be growing at such a rate.

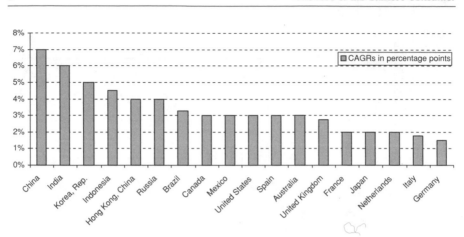

Source: CSFB estimates
Figure 1.4   CSFB assumptions for real CAGRs of GDP for what we view as the largest and most relevant global economies over the next 10 years

Given China's faster growth rate, how will its share of the world economy change in the next 10 years? Figure 1.5 shows that, assuming no exchange-rate changes, China's economy would reach 20 % of the size of the US economy in current US$ terms by 2014. On this measure, China would be the fourth-largest global economy at that time, slightly behind Germany. However, Figure 1.6 shows that in PPP terms, the Chinese economy would be 90 % of the size of the US in 10 years' time and almost six times the size of the German economy, while India's economy would be larger than Japan's.

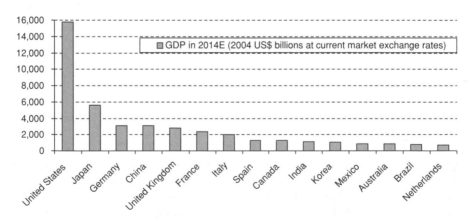

Source: IMF and CSFB estimates
Figure 1.5   Largest 15 global economies currently by GDP (2004 US$), projected to 2014E using CSFB estimated CAGRs and assuming no exchange-rate changes

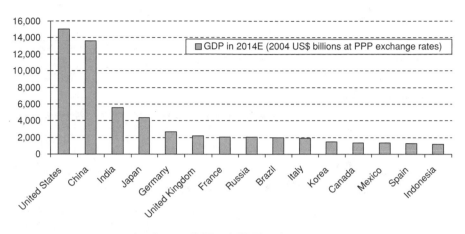

Source: IMF and CSFB estimates

Figure 1.6 Largest 15 global economies currently by GDP (2004 US$, PPP), projected to 2014E using CSFB estimated CAGRs

Which is the correct view: China's GDP at 20 % the size of the US in 10 years' time or China at 90 %; China's GDP slightly behind that of Germany or almost six times the size? The answer is that either outturn or neither is possible, depending on the level of the exchange rate. From the perspective of a US$-based investor interested in US$ earnings streams from investments in Chinese or foreign companies servicing the China consumer market, much hinges on whether China revalues towards the PPP exchange-rate level. It is to that issue we now turn in order to form a base-case view of the likely size of the Chinese economy in 2014.

THE 'REVALUATION EFFECT'

For more than a decade, China has maintained its currency at a level well below its PPP exchange rate (see Figure 1.7). The IMF estimates that at the current pegged rate of RMB8.28/US$1, the Renminbi is valued at around only one-fifth of its PPP exchange rate.

In our view, exchange-rate undervaluation has been a conscious strategy from the Chinese leadership to stimulate export-led growth and inward foreign direct investment (FDI). It also allows China time to undertake important structural reforms in agriculture and financial services before allowing significant import competition. China is not unique in following this growth model. A similar strategy is currently followed by India and was followed by the fast-growing East Asian economies in the 1980s. As GDP per capita and total factor productivity rose in these countries, there was a tendency for policy to shift towards diversifying the sources of growth towards consumption. As a result, currencies in many of these countries have tended over time

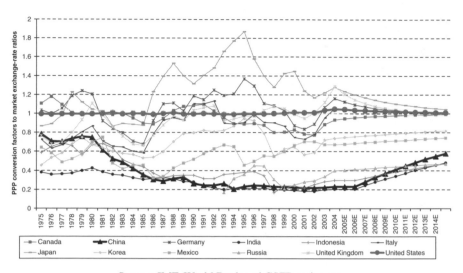

Source: IMF, World Bank and CSFB estimates
Figure 1.7   PPP conversion factors to market exchange-rate ratios, 1975–2014E

to appreciate towards their PPP exchange rate (see Figure 1.8). This has particularly been seen in the East Asian export-led economies including Japan and South Korea.

China's GDP per capita and total factor productivity are rising steadily, although in CSFB's view imminent major revaluation of the Renminbi is unlikely. However, we anticipate that China may move to a Singaporean nondisclosed currency basket with an accompanying moderate revaluation as early as H2 (second half) 2005. For some time we have expected major revaluation of the Renminbi to begin during the period 2006 to 2008 with a target exchange rate of RMB5.00/US$1.

Figure 1.8 shows our projected path for exchange-rate revaluation in China as PPP GDP per capita rises. We project that the Renminbi will reach 0.55 of its PPP level by 2014. [For a recent summary discussion on the choices facing China with respect to adjusting its currency regime and the likely scale of revaluation see Frankel (2005).] Figure 1.9 shows the global tendency for PPP appreciation as real GDP per capita increases. In our view, as China either switches to a floating currency or exhibits faster inflation than developed countries, it will tend to follow the same tendency. This would equate, were the current US$ peg regime to remain unaltered, to an exchange rate of RMB3/US$1 by 2014. The methodology used to estimate the convergence rate towards PPP is explained in detail in Appendix A. It draws on the academic literature on the determinants of convergence of exchange rates to their PPP levels. In particular, we make the key assumption of nonlinearity in the mean reversion process: 'the rate of convergence to PPP is faster when initial deviations are large' (Rogoff, 1996). The developed countries and the emerging markets were modelled independently, as were the Asian countries within the emerging markets.

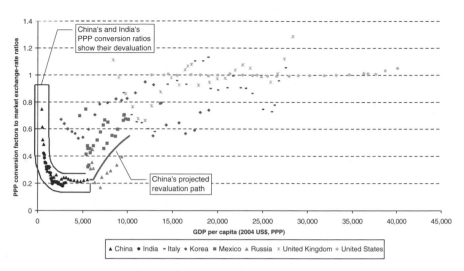

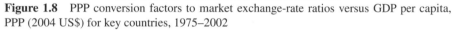

Source: IMF, World Bank and CSFB estimates

Figure 1.8 PPP conversion factors to market exchange-rate ratios versus GDP per capita, PPP (2004 US$) for key countries, 1975–2002

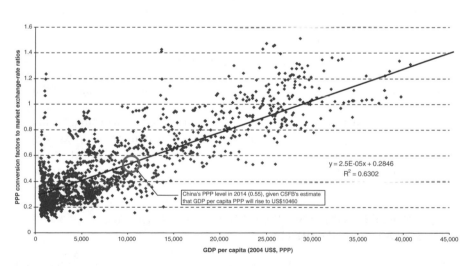

Source: IMF, World Bank and CSFB estimates

Figure 1.9 PPP conversion factors to market exchange-rate ratios versus GDP per capita, PPP (2004 US$) for 177 countries, 1980–2004E

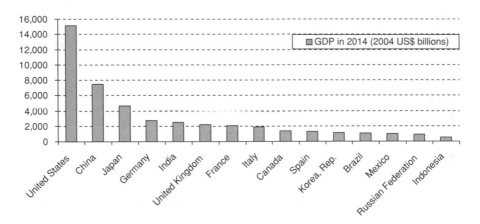

Source: IMF, World Bank and CSFB estimates
Figure 1.10   Largest 15 global economies by GDP (2004 US$), projected to 2014 using CSFB estimated CAGRs and convergence towards PPP in China and other countries with undervalued exchange rates

Our projected path for Renminbi convergence with its PPP level implies that by 2014 China's GDP economy would amount to US$7508bn (in 2004 US$ terms) or 49 % the size of the US. This is our base case and, in our view, a more realistic scenario than those given in Figures 1.5 and 1.6.

In Figure 1.10, we show China alongside the other major economies. Exchange rates for the other emerging market countries have been revalued (and for developed countries in some instances devalued) towards their PPP levels using the methodology described in Appendix A. The path for the exchange rates relative to their PPP levels is shown in Figure 1.8.

We therefore conclude that the US$ size of China's economy will almost quintuple via the combined effect of underlying growth and revaluation over the next 10 years. This would have major implications for multinational firms with growth strategies and exposure in China.

ECONOMIC GROWTH AND ITS EFFECTS ON AGGREGATE HOUSEHOLD CONSUMPTION

We now turn to analyse the relationship between economic growth and household consumption. Figure 1.11 shows the relationship between household consumption as a percentage of GDP and PPP GDP per capita for the largest economies. We would draw three conclusions.

First, higher-income countries tend to consume a higher proportion of GDP. This is particularly true of the US and UK where the consumption to GDP ratio has drifted

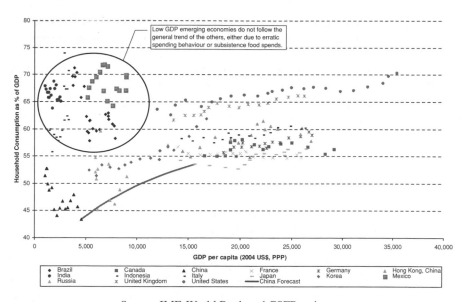

Source: IMF, World Bank and CSFB estimates
Figure 1.11 Household consumption as a percentage of GDP versus GDP per capita (2004 US$, PPP)

higher (and savings rates lower) as incomes rise. In these countries, investment is funded by foreign savings rather than those of domestic households. However, an upward movement in consumption to GDP is also observable from a lower base in the high-income/high-savings economies of East Asia as typified by Japan.

Second, very low income countries such as India and Indonesia (and to a lesser extent Brazil) tend if anything to consume an even higher proportion of GDP than the first category. This is owing to the urgent need of households to meet basic needs. Here savings rates also tend to be low.

Third, we can identify a group of intermediate income countries, including China and Korea, where the consumption to GDP ratio is much lower than in the case of the other two categories. Savings rates are high, which funds domestic investment, and – as long as that investment is productive – there is more rapid than average GDP growth.

It is clear from Figure 1.11 that China represents an outlier in the consumption to GDP ratio. Using official sources, we estimate a figure of 44 % in 2004, which is low by peer group standards. In our view, there may be significant underestimation of true consumption expenditure (and overestimation of the savings rate) owing to well-documented inadequacies in China's national statistics. We would note the retreat from state provision in the educational and health spheres and the rise of informal private sector provision, which may not be captured in the official data.

For the time being, we propose to take the Chinese data at face value. China thus appears to be following an extreme version of the path originally taken by Korea.

Over time, as PPP GDP per capita in Korea has risen from US$5000 (where China is today) to US$15 000, so the consumption to GDP ratio has risen by 10pp (percentage points) from 50 % to 60 %.

We project that the consumption to GDP ratio in China will rise by 5.5pp by 2014 as PPP GDP per capita rises from US$5299 to US$10 460. Appendix B explains in detail the methodology used in making this projection. In essence, we assume that the consumption to GDP ratio increases at a rate proportional to its deviation away from the long-term developed world average of 60 %. (We assume a structurally higher long-term ratio of 65 % for the consumption-prone economies of the US and the UK.)

BASE CASE FOR EVOLUTION OF US$ VALUE OF CHINA HOUSEHOLD CONSUMPTION SPENDING

We estimate that in 2004, at the current pegged exchange rate, the US$ value of household consumption spending in China is US$704bn. This represents 9 % of US consumption spending and 3 % of our estimate of global consumption spending, as shown in Figure 1.12.

Looking ahead to 2014, we use the three steps summarised below to form a base case for China:

- CSFB's Asian economics team's estimates for trend real GDP growth of 7 % over the 10 years to 2014;
- convergence in exchange rate to 0.55 of its PPP level (see Appendix A); and
- a rise in the consumption to GDP ratio of 5.5pp (see Appendix B).

Using these three steps, we conclude as a base case that the US$ value of consumption spending in China in 2014 would be around US$3726bn (in 2004 US$) (see Figure 1.13). This represents a CAGR of 18 % for the 10-year period 2004 to 2014. However, please note that the scenario analysis below indicates that there is a wide range of possible outcomes around this base case.

In order to put China into a global context, we have made similar projections globally for more than 175 countries. PPP GDP per capita starting values were calculated using CSFB economists' projections for trend real GDP growth where available and where not we use those of the IMF.

We conclude as a base-case projection that in 2014 the US$ value of consumption spending in China will represent 37.3 % of US consumption spending and 10.5 % of our estimate of global consumption spending. While the CAGR for the US$ value of consumption spending in China is likely to be 18 %, it is likely to be 11 % on a global basis. By contrast, we project a CAGR of just 2.1 % in the US. This results from making the assumption that the US consumption to GDP ratio declines to 65 % over the medium term from the current elevated level of over 70 %. Note that this assumption (which we also make for the UK) would still leave the US with a 5pp

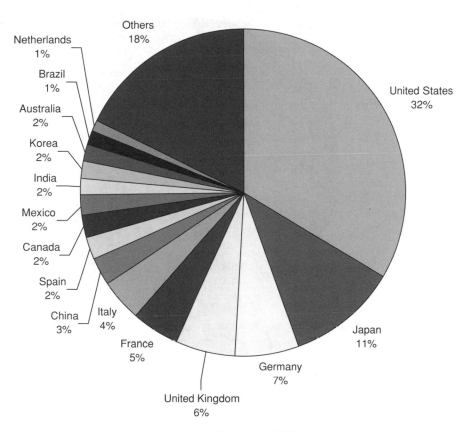

Source: IMF, World Bank and CSFB estimates

Figure 1.12 CSFB estimates for global aggregate household consumption US$ spend in 2004E

higher consumption to GDP ratio than the global mean. It would of course imply a rise in the domestic savings ratio and some decline from the current high levels of the US budget and current account deficits. We consider this assumption appropriate to make within an overall global scenario, which encompasses exchange-rate revaluation and rising consumption to GDP ratios in the emerging world in general and hence less availability of savings globally to plug the US fiscal and current account deficits.

On this basis, we project that by 2014–5 incremental additional annual US$ consumption spend in China is most likely to be larger than that in the US by a significant margin. We estimate that China will have an incremental spend of US$524bn (in 2004 US$) per annum 10 years from now compared with the US with US$262bn. Other countries' outturns are illustrated in Figure 1.14. If these projections are accurate, the locomotive of the global economy in terms of incremental annual consumption demand will have changed from the US consumer to the Chinese consumer.

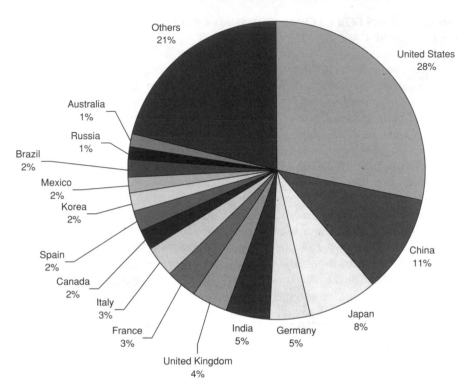

Source: IMF, World Bank and CSFB estimates

Figure 1.13   CSFB forecasts for global aggregate household consumption spend in 2014E

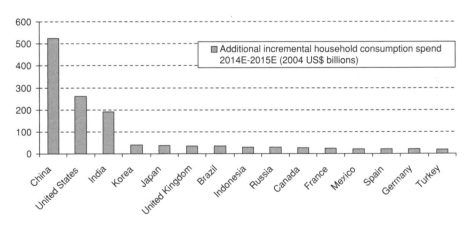

Source: IMF, World Bank and CSFB estimates

Figure 1.14   CSFB estimates for top 15 global additional incremental household US$ (2004 values) consumption spends between 2014E and 2015E

IMPLICATIONS FOR GLOBAL CONSUMER PRODUCT COMPANIES OF OUR BASE CASE

Our base case scenario implies that a global consumer products company operating in China whose business is performing in line with that of a market as a whole might anticipate top lines sales growth of 18 % year-on-year (yoy) compound on a sustained basis. Such a figure seems *a priori* to be high and obviously disguises a complex situation where some sectors are likely to grow more rapidly than others and where some companies are able to achieve a dominant position and earn strong margins while others fail to do so. It is for this reason that we undertook the detailed consumer survey that comprises Section 2 of this book.

At this stage we would simply note that, where the evidence is disclosed, major consumer product companies operating in China do indeed currently appear to be generating sales growth at or in excess of our base case of 18 % yoy. Moreover, it appears that sales growth from their Chinese operations is significantly outstripping their overall sales growth and in some cases is no longer being achieved from a small base. For Nokia, China is already its second largest market for sales behind the US. Figure 1.15 shows that for a group of 15 leading multinationals for which China sales data for 2004 have been disclosed, all but one – Volkswagen – achieved more rapid sales growth in China than they did globally. For all 15 companies the average sales growth in China was 29.5% versus 10.5 % globally.

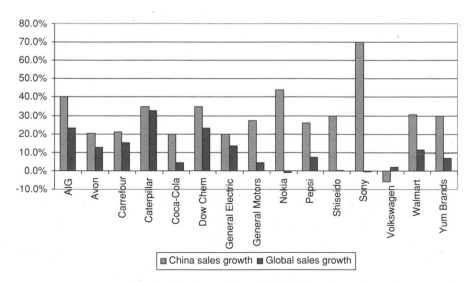

Source: Company data and CSFB estimates

Figure 1.15 China and global sales growth for leading multinational companies with operations in China (US$ terms, 2004 yoy)

OTHER SCENARIOS

Our base case for China rests on three assumptions: (a) that trend real GDP growth rises by 7 % per annum; (b) that there is a 5.5 % increase in the share of consumption spending within GDP; and (c) that the Renminbi rises from 0.2 of its PPP level to 0.55. Using other assumptions, we have calculated other scenarios for our projections: a best case and a worst case (see Table 1.1). The following chapter discusses in much more detail whether, in the context of the academic literature on economic growth, China is in a position to achieve our base-case outcome.

Table 1.1   China 2014E GDP and consumption spending scenario analysis (in 2004 US$).

	Units	Base case	Best case	Worst case
China's US$ GDP	US$ billions	7508	16365	2579
China's US$ GDP % USA	%	49	108	17
China's US$ consumption spend	US$ billions	3726	9819	1147
China's US$ consumption spend / % USA	%	37	98	11
CAGR 2004 to 2014	%	18	30	5
China's incremental annual additional US$ consumption 2014	US$ billions	485	884	57
Assumptions				
GDP growth (%)		7	9	5
Share of GDP (%)		50	60	44
Revaluation		0.55	Full: 1	None

Source: CSFB estimates.

In our best case, we have assumed: (a) that trend real GDP growth rises by 9 % per annum, which is similar to the growth rates achieved in recent boom years; (b) that there is a 15.5 % increase in the share of consumption spending within GDP so that full convergence to the global mean of 60 % is reached; and (c) that the Renminbi rises from 0.2 of its PPP level to 1, that is, full revaluation.

In our worst case, we have assumed: (a) that trend real GDP growth rises by 5 % per annum owing to failure to fix the financial system or the maintenance of other institutional impediments to growth; (b) that there is no increase in the share of consumption spending within GDP; and (c) that the Renminbi experiences no revaluation.

Our conclusion from the scenario analysis is that there is a wide range of outcomes around our base case, although we believe that 75 % of the probability distribution lies between the base case and the best case and only 25 % between the base case and the worst case, for reasons discussed in detail in the next chapter. In the best case, China's US$ GDP in 2004 US$ would rise to US$16.4trn while the US$ value of annual consumption spend would rise to 98 % of the US level. There would be a CAGR of 30 % in the US$ value of household consumption spend (mainly owing to the very rapid exchange-rate revaluation). In the worst case, China's US$ GDP in 2004 US$ would rise to just US$2.6trn, while consumption spending would languish at just 11 % of the US total, which is little different to the current ratio.

REFERENCES

Frankel, J. (2005) On the Renminbi: the choice between adjustment under a fixed exchange rate and adjustment under a flexible rate, NBER Working Paper 11274.
Rogoff, K. (1996) The purchasing power parity puzzle. *Journal of Economic Literature*, **34**.

2
Drivers of and Constraints to China's Long-Run Economic Growth

Which of our three scenarios for the evolution of the China consumer theme in the next 10 years is most likely? In this chapter we explain why, in our view, an outcome between our base-case and best-case scenarios, where the Chinese consumer displaces the US consumer as the engine of the global economy over the medium term, has a 75 % likelihood. Meanwhile, in our estimation, scenarios between the base case and the worst case, where the Chinese consumer stagnates in relative importance, have a 25 % likelihood.

We come to these conclusions by placing China's past and likely future economic experience in the context of the academic literature on the determinants of economic growth over the longer term. This allows us to explore the likelihood that the Chinese economy and consumption spending power will indeed grow in the ways projected in the previous chapter.

DRIVERS OF LONG-RUN ECONOMIC GROWTH

We begin with the academic literature on the determinants of long-run economic growth. Professor Angus Maddison has provided the following useful summary of the four main quantifiable causal influences found in academic literature to explain the fact that world per capita income has risen eightfold since 1820 (Figure 2.1). They are: (a) technological progress; (b) accumulation of physical capital in which technological progress usually needs to be embodied; (c) improvement in human skills, education and organisational ability; and (d) closer integration of individual national economies through trade in goods and services, investment, intellectual and entrepreneurial interaction (Maddison, 1997).

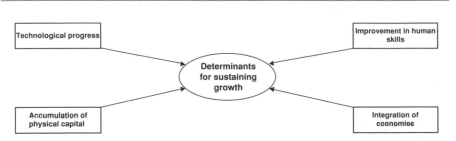

Source: Maddison, A. (1997), Causal influences on productivity performance 1820–1992: a global perspective, *Journal of Productivity Analysis*, pp. 325–360. Reproduced by permission of Springer Science and Business Media
Figure 2.1   Causal factors driving long-run economic growth

Technological progress and the increase in physical capital stock are crucial drivers of long-run economic growth. The major area of technological progress appears to have been in transport and communications. Passenger and goods transport moved from the age of the horse and the canal in 1820 to motor vehicle and airplane. Handwritten letters and the pigeon have been replaced with worldwide telecommunications and satellite networks. Electricity has also transformed production processes in manufacturing industries. These innovations have been embodied in successive waves of investment in physical capital stock. Over the period 1820 to 1992 the US stock of nonresidential structures increased nearly 800-fold or 21-fold per person employed (Figure 2.2). The ratio of machinery and equipment to GDP rose 13-fold

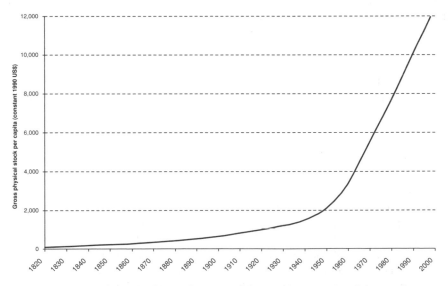

Source: Maddison, A. (2004), Contours of the world economy and the art of macro-measurement 1500 to 2001, Ruggles Lecture
Figure 2.2   US gross physical capital stock per capita (constant 1990 US$), 1820–1998

in both the US and UK between 1820 and 1998 and nearly 14-fold in Japan since 1890 (Maddison, 2004).

Technological innovation takes place worldwide but there is substantial evidence for a unique role played by 'leader' countries. In the nineteenth century, the UK consistently had the highest level of total factor productivity. It is possible to observe a 'leader / follower' process whereby innovations in the UK diffused gradually to the other advanced economies. In the twentieth century, from 1913 onwards the US took on the role of leader and until 1973, as measured by labour and total factor productivity performance, exhibited a rate of progress much faster than the UK ever achieved in the nineteenth century. This was a major reason why world economic growth was much faster in the twentieth century than in the nineteenth century. Since 1950, the margin of US productivity leadership has been substantially eroded as the advanced capitalist economies of Europe as well as Japan adopted successful 'follower' strategies.

Trade in capital goods is a major mechanism by which technological progress diffuses worldwide. It also prompts specialisation in the types of production in which individual countries and firms are most efficient. The benefits of this specialisation to long-run economic growth were first explained by Adam Smith in *An Inquiry into the Nature and Causes of the Wealth of Nations* (1776). Maddison (1997) calculates that in 1820 exports were only 1 % of world output. By 1913, this ratio had risen to 8.7 % before falling in the period of neomercantilism that lasted until 1950. A resurgence in international trade appears to have played a major role in the acceleration of economic growth in the 1950s and 1960s and by 1992 exports had risen to 13.5 % of world output, shown in Figure 2.3. Our own calculations indicate that recent trade liberalisation has led to the ratio climbing still further to 18.4 % in 2004 (constant 1990 US$).

We draw two other key conclusions from the literature on international trade and economic development. First, smaller countries appear to get proportionately bigger benefits from international trade than larger countries as it is easier for them to specialise in what they do best. Second, export orientation and openness to international FDI, which has characterised the faster-growing European and Asian countries, have been much more successful strategies at the country level than the import substitution approaches followed in Latin America.

Human capital development and improvements in organisational structures for the allocation of capital have also made a major contribution to long-run economic growth. In 1820, the vast majority of the population in the most advanced economies were illiterate. During the nineteenth century, universal primary education became compulsory in these countries. In the twentieth century, there was a major expansion in secondary and tertiary education. Maddison found, using a rough correction for the return achieved for each level of education, that the average person's human capital increased 10-fold from 1820 to 1992. The other major improvement in human capital has arisen from advances in medicine, which have led to a steady increase in life span and decrease in child mortality.

On the organisational side, one major advance identified in the academic literature is the transition from entrepreneurial capitalism to the development of the joint

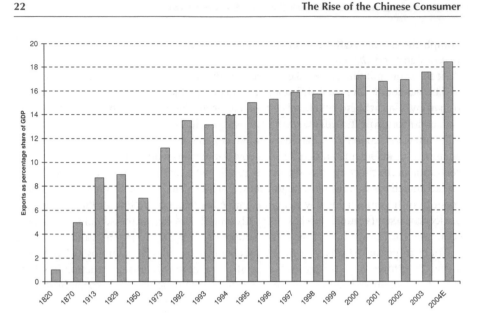

Source: Maddison, A. (1997), Causal influences on productivity performance 1820–1992: a
global perspective, *Journal of Productivity Analysis*, pp. 325–360, and CSFB research.
Reproduced by permission of Springer Science and Business Media
Figure 2.3   Global exports as a percentage share of GDP (constant 1990 US$ exports and
GDP), 1820–2004E

stock company and thereafter increasingly well-regulated public equity and debt markets. This has allowed the pooling of the risk of investment in new technologies or increases in physical capital investment in existing technologies. Another advance appears to have been the improved management of the banking system, both by regulatory agencies and bank managers themselves, which has reduced the risk of savings misappropriation and systemic failure.

CONSTRAINTS TO LONG-RUN GROWTH

The academic literature also dispels certain commonly held views on constraints to long-run economic growth, particularly in relation to natural resource scarcities and economies of scale. However, it has re-emphasised the importance of the institutional context.

Natural resource scarcities have not generally been a constraint although initial endowments (that is, US versus Japan) may have had an influence on the pattern of economic growth. Land area per capita has generally fallen over time (by as much as 14-fold in the US), while the increase in energy inputs has been relatively modest compared with the economic growth achieved. Maddison calculates only a threefold increase in per capita energy usage in the US since 1820, much smaller proportionally than the growth in the stock of machinery.

The academic literature thus strongly points against the pessimistic conclusions drawn by Malthus and others on the role of scarce natural resources as a constraint on economic growth. In fact, owing to technological progress, investment in physical capital stock (tractors, agrichemical plant) and international trade (ships able to transport nonrefrigerated and refrigerated agricultural goods), there has been a major reduction in the proportion of the human population employed in agriculture. Indeed, the advanced economies have been characterised by major migration from the countryside to the cities and now generally have less than 5 % of total employment in agriculture (see Figure 2.4).

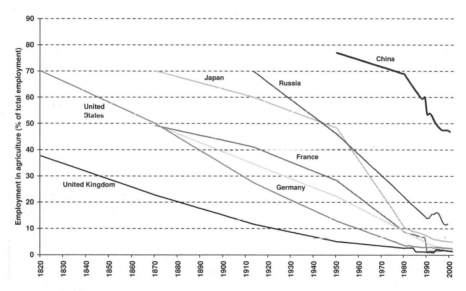

Source: Maddison, A. (1997), Causal influences on productivity performance 1820–1992: a global perspective, *Journal of Productivity Analysis*, pp. 325–360, and CSFB estimates. Reproduced by permission of Springer Science and Business Media
Figure 2.4   Employment in agriculture as a percentage share of total employment

Neither does there appear to be any evidence for economies of scale at the overall country level. It might be thought that total factor productivity would be higher and grow faster in larger economies that are more easily able to invest in new technologies. However, several small countries have very high levels of total factor productivity. Indeed, in the private sectors of the advanced economies, the average size of productive establishments is quite small. In 1990, in the private sector of the US economy there were about 6 million establishments employing on average 14 people. The median US manufacturing establishment at the time was no different in numbers of persons employed from the median establishment in the Netherlands.

Long-run economic growth does not appear to have been constrained by the need to put in more labour effort. Indeed, hours worked per head have generally decreased over time, particularly in the twentieth century.

The incidence of major wars between countries does not appear to have been an impediment to long-run economic growth. However, lower-level persistent conflict, particularly civil war, does appear to have been a major obstacle to growth in Africa and elsewhere.

Countries such as Germany and Japan, which suffered major short-term disruptions to economic growth owing to their involvement in major wars, appear to have been able to return relatively quickly to their longer-term growth trajectory. Indeed, strands of the academic literature emphasise the benefits that accrued to these countries in the destruction of obsolescent vintages of capital stock during the wars and the enhanced diffusion of technology from the US during the rebuilding process.

Despite the improvements made in recent years in growth accounting, which allows causality to be measurably assigned to the various factors just discussed, individual country outcomes are more highly varied than would be generally expected. This suggests the need for individual country studies and shows that the techniques of the historian may be as helpful as those of the economist.

In recent years, the academic literature and indeed the major development institutions such as the World Bank have placed a much greater emphasis on the constraints to growth posed by the institutional context at the country level. Apart from the importance of well-regulated banks and public equity and debt markets, the major areas where there are substantial country level differences and which appear to have been of importance in relative growth experience include, but are not limited to, the items discussed in Table 2.1.

Table 2.1 Determinants of growth in an institutional context.

Key institutions supporting growth
The free purchase and sale of property
Nondiscretionary legal systems that enforce private contracts and protect property rights
Accountancy and audit systems
The availability of insurance and development of non-life-insurance markets
The development of a welfare state, which has made market forces more legitimate versus the alternative methods of resource allocation (e.g. the socialist alternative)
A free press
An enabling role for national and local government characterised by smaller size and lower levels of government corruption, hence reducing the likelihood of arbitrary and nonpredictable taxation and regulation by the state

Source: CSFB research.

EVALUATING CHINA'S PERFORMANCE AND PROSPECTS

We now move on to evaluate China's performance and prospects in the light of what is known about the drivers of, and constraints to, long-run economic growth. We conclude that China is following a strategy that is likely to lead to sustained improvements in total factor productivity and hence economic success over the longer term.

China's major ongoing strengths, which should support economic success, are:

- major increases in the physical capital stock, particularly of machinery and equipment, and replacement of obsolescent vintages with those closer to the leading edge;
- a rural/urban migration pattern that mirrors that of other countries during the period when total factor productivity rose most rapidly;
- an increasingly successful execution of a 'follower' strategy in technological innovation via successful policies to attract FDI from the most advanced countries;
- export orientation and increases in global export market share and the trade share within China's GDP, particularly since 1990; and
- major gains in human capital in the education sphere.

China's major weaknesses, which could constrain economic success, are:

- the institutional context for growth, in particular in relation to the overdominant role played in resource allocation (land, labour and capital) by national and local government;
- corruption and other abuses, which act as an inhibition to entrepreneurial activity;
- a poor return on invested capital as a consequence of institutional weaknesses in its allocation and in particular owing to the lack of development of the banking sector and public equity and debt markets;
- weaknesses in the public health sphere that have a negative impact on human capital development;
- the fact that China is generally a price taker in world commodity markets but lacks pricing power in world export markets; and
- environmental damage associated particularly with weaknesses in planning and land use policy and the major technology currently used for power production.

Before dealing with these points in detail, we begin with a brief and necessarily selective review of China's economic development in the last two millennia before focusing in somewhat more detail on the period since 1990. Our discussion draws on the pioneering economic history work of Angus Maddison and in particular *The World Economy: A Millennial Perspective* (2001).

China achieved a level of economic performance in the first century under the Han Dynasty that equates to GDP of about US$450 per capita (on a PPP basis using 1990 US$), which was sufficiently above the basic subsistence level to sustain the ruling elite in some luxury. Unlike in Western Europe, where the fall of the Roman Empire led to a significant decline in GDP per capita from a similar level, China managed to sustain approximately the same level of economic performance until around 960 (Figure 2.5). For the following three centuries, under the Sung Dynasty, per capita income increased by about a third and population growth accelerated. This seems to have been owing to the economic development of the south of the country and improvements in agricultural productivity in rice production. These jointly stimulated increases in internal trade. China's meritocratic bureaucracy also appears to have been a distinctly positive feature driving economic growth compared with the more primitive feudal institutions present in Western Europe.

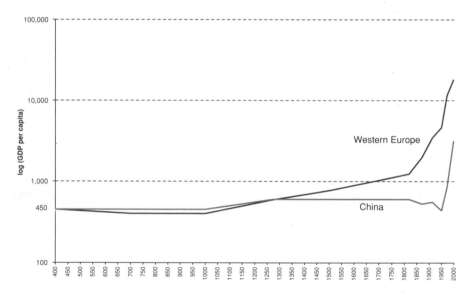

Source: Maddison, A. (2001), *The World Economy: A Millennial Perspective*, Copyright OECD, and CSFB research. Reproduced by permission

Figure 2.5   Comparative levels of GDP per capita PPP (constant 1990 US$) in China and Western Europe, 400–2000 AD

At the end of this period, China continued to enjoy a somewhat higher GDP per capita than Western Europe. However, the latter was gaining rapidly. There was a strong impetus from the Venetian Republic, which not only played a major leadership role in re-establishing trade within the Mediterranean basin but also created political and legal institutions that supported the development of commercial capitalism.

From a position where it was unquestionably the world's most advanced economy, China's GDP per capita stagnated between the end of the Sung Dynasty in the late thirteenth century and the beginning of the nineteenth century. In 1820, China's GDP per capita was US$600 (on a PPP basis using 1990 US$), which was around only one-half of the US$1270 level achieved in a group of 12 Western Europe countries. However, because China's population grew faster than that of Western Europe, China's total GDP in 1820 was still around 30 % higher than that of Western Europe and its offshoots in the Americas and Australasia.

Compared with Western Europe, it appears that China's weaknesses from the late thirteenth century to the early nineteenth century were concentrated in the areas of technological development and trade. In the early fifteenth century, China turned away from development of a maritime empire and a leading position in marine technology. At that time, the Ming navy consisted of over 3800 ships. The largest of these were five times the length of their Portuguese equivalents and used an advanced system of watertight compartments. Seven major expeditions commanded by Admiral Cheng-ho took place between 1405 and 1433 to the 'Western Ocean'. However, the costs of these expeditions and the lack of an immediate financial return exacerbated a domestic fiscal and monetary crisis, itself partly caused by the financing of the re-opening of the Grand Canal. China's focus shifted towards internal trade and by the 1470s the navy had dwindled and most of the shipyards were closed. In 1793, a British mission tried to establish diplomatic relations and demonstrate the attractions of Western technology to the Chinese and was strongly rebuffed.

In 1950, per capita GDP in China was less than three-quarters of its 1820s level. In Western Europe, it was more than three times higher and in the European offshoots in North America and Australasia on average almost eight times higher than its 1820s level. As a result of this and slower population growth, China's GDP was less than a twelfth of that of Western Europe and its offshoots by 1950. Hence a major collapse in absolute and relative economic performance took place.

A range of factors led to the virtual collapse of economic activity in China between 1820 and 1950. The slow decline of the Manchu Dynasty, the resulting institutional stagnation and substantial internal turmoil (which included several episodes of civil war) played a major role. Commercial penetration driven by imperialism and characterised by the forced expansion of the opium trade ensured that the benefits of expanded trade during this period accrued to foreign residents in China and foreign trading companies. In certain cities, most notably Shanghai, substantial economic development and inward investment did take place but there was no overall improvement in agricultural productivity for the majority of the country. Unlike in the case of the US or other offshoots of Western Europe during the nineteenth and first half of the twentieth century, large-scale technological transfer in manufacturing and the development of indigenous educational institutions at the secondary and tertiary level did not generally take place.

China's long-run economic performance began to turn the corner in the 1950s (see Table 2.2). From 1950 to 1973, GDP per capita rose by 2.9 % per annum versus –0.6 %

Table 2.2 Average growth rate of GDP per capita, 1913–2003 (%).

	1913–50	1950–99	1950–73	1973–90	1990–9	2000–3
Japan	0.9	4.9	8.1	3.0	0.9	−1.5
China	−0.6	4.2	2.9	4.8	6.4	7.6
Hong Kong	n.a.	4.6	5.2	5.4	1.7	−1.5
Malaysia	1.5	3.2	2.2	4.2	4.0	4.3
Singapore	1.5	4.9	4.4	5.3	5.7	0.6
South Korea	−0.4	6.0	5.8	6.8	4.8	5.8
Taiwan	0.6	5.9	6.7	5.3	5.3	1.4
Thailand	−0.1	4.3	3.7	5.5	3.6	0.7
Seven country average	−0.4	4.4	3.4	5.1	5.8	2.7
Bangladesh	−0.2	0.9	−0.4	1.5	3.0	1.5
Burma	−1.5	2.0	2.0	1.1	3.8	0.6
India	−0.2	2.2	1.4	2.6	3.7	4.6
Indonesia	−0.2	2.7	2.6	3.1	2.1	9.4
Nepal	n.a.	1.4	1.0	1.5	1.9	2.0
Pakistan	−0.2	2.3	1.7	3.1	2.3	2.8
Philippines	0.0	1.6	2.7	0.7	0.5	0.1
Sri Lanka	0.3	2.6	1.9	3.0	3.9	2.4
Eight country average	−0.3	2.2	1.7	2.5	3.0	3.4
15 resurgent Asia	−0.3	3.4	2.5	3.9	4.6	3.0
Other Asia	1.8	2.3[a]	4.1	0.4	1.1[b]	4.2
Latin America	1.4	1.7	2.5	0.7	1.4	−0.7
Africa	1.0	1.0[a]	2.1	0.1	−0.2[b]	3.6
Eastern Europe and former USSR	1.5	1.1[a]	3.5	0.7	−4.8[b]	14.1
Western Europe	0.8	2.9[a]	4.1	1.9	1.4[b]	5.3
United States	1.6	2.2	2.5	2.0	2.1	3.0

[a] 1950–98.

[b] 1990–8.

Source: Maddison, A. (2001), *The World Economy: A Millennial Perspective*, Copyright OECD, Asian Development Bank and CSFB research. Reproduced by permission.

in the period 1913 to 1950. In the period until 1978, economic activity was dominated by the state and was characterised by major increases in physical and human capital inputs. At times, such as during the Great Leap Forward, there appear to have been major allocation inefficiencies in their application. Trade expansion, which proved to be a major engine of growth for other East Asian countries, was largely missing in the case of China. The US, the global 'leader', applied comprehensive trade and travel and financial sanctions on China from 1952 until 1973.

China's GDP per capita growth rate accelerated significantly between 1973 and 1990 to 4.8 % per annum. This represented not only an improvement in absolute but also in relative economic performance. In particular, China recorded a much faster growth rate in GDP per capita than India, Pakistan and Indonesia, the other large-population countries in Asia. The major driver of the process appears to have been successive waves of liberalisation initially focused on relaxation of the state control on agriculture from 1978 onwards. This led to significant expansion in small-scale industry, particularly in rural areas.

From 1978 onwards the state also moved away from monopolising foreign trade and devalued the currency in order to encourage exports. Inward FDI began to take place, albeit from a low base. However, capital controls remained in place and little attempt was made to reform the financial sector or restructure the major state-owned enterprises engaged in large-scale industrial production and manufacturing.

As shown in Table 2.2, between 1990 and 1999 the growth rate of GDP per capita in China surged again to 6.4 % per annum. We estimate a compound average growth rate of 7.6 % from 1999 to the end of 2003. However, it appears that there may have been smoothing of the official GDP statistics both during the 1995–8 slowdown and the more recent boom. However, considering the wealth of supporting evidence from the more reliable trade data, as well as trends in demand for key inputs to the growth process such as base metals and minerals, we conclude that most, if not all, of this improvement in the trend growth rate per capita is real.

As a result, China has gone from being a significant laggard in economic growth terms between 1913 and 1950 to being the fastest-growing major economy in the world in the last 15 years. However, per capita GDP on our estimates (using PPP exchange rates) remains only some 13.9 % on average of the level in the US. Moreover, there are significant disparities in income levels on a regional basis as the pattern of economic growth has been uneven.

HOW HAS CHINA'S RECENT GROWTH BEEN ACHIEVED AND IS THIS GROWTH RATE SUSTAINABLE?

We now turn to discuss how this growth was achieved using the framework of the academic literature on economic development. We consider in turn: (a) rural/urban migration; (b) investment in physical capital stock; (c) technological change and the role of FDI; (d) openness to trade and in particular exports; (e) development of human capital; and (f) the institutional context.

Rural/urban migration lies at the heart of the acceleration in growth rates world-wide in the last two hundred years. The introduction of machinery into agricultural production allows surplus labour to be redeployed to the cities where it can engage in manufacturing and services activities. This in itself leads to increased specialisation and enhances total factor productivity.

In China's case, there has been a 30pp fall in the proportion of the population working in agriculture since the Second World War (see Figure 2.4). This leaves the

proportion of the Chinese labour force working in agriculture at approximately the
same level as Japan in the mid-1950s or the US in the 1870s.

PHYSICAL CAPITAL STOCK ACCUMULATION

In recent years, China has made major investments in physical capital stocks in manufacturing and in some public goods areas such as road and air transport systems. China
has set up special enterprise zones to encourage FDI via supportive tax regimes and
other measures including substantial local government provision of support services.
However, there continues to be inadequate investment in electricity production, water
supply and rail infrastructure relative to the rate of demand growth.

Figure 2.6 charts total annual fixed investment spending and the annual growth
rate from 1985 onwards with CSFB's economics team's forecast for 2004 and 2005.
In real terms, annual investment spending has risen more than sevenfold since the
early 1990s, representing the same kind of acceleration in the size of the physical
capital stock that took place earlier in economic history in the US, Japan and other
advanced countries. However, also notable is the extreme degree of cyclicality in
investment expenditure. Booms in the real growth rate in excess of 20 % per annum

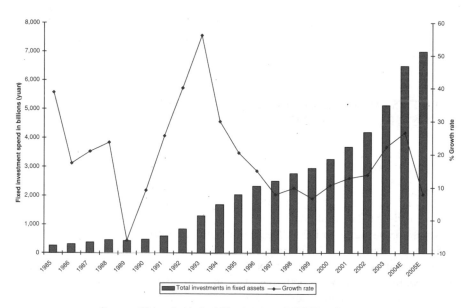

Source: China Statistical Yearbook and CSFB estimates

Figure 2.6   Total annual investment spend in fixed assets, constant 1985 yuan, 1985–2005E

were seen in the mid-1980s, early 1990s and again in the recent past. By contrast, there was a significant slump in the growth rate of investment spending in the late 1980s and mid-1990s. CSFB forecasts a similar slowing in the growth rate in the short to medium term. This extreme cyclicality in investment spending, together with the economy's increased openness to trade, drives China's volatile near-term business cycle.

Figure 2.7 shows that within total investment an increasing proportion has been made by nonstate-owned entities (that is, other collective entities, foreign or domestic private sector agents). The proportion of total investment made by the state has declined to just over 40 % of the total in recent years from more than 60 % of the total in the mid-1990s. This is, in our view, a welcome development, indicating at least prima facie increased private sector involvement in the economy.

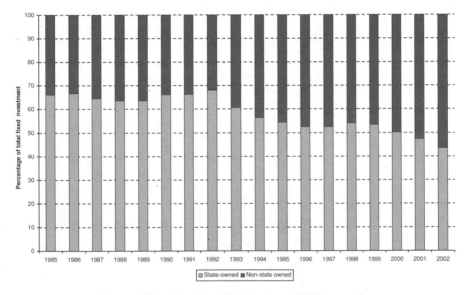

Source: China Statistical Yearbook and CSFB research

Figure 2.7   Percentage of total investments made by state and nonstate owners, 1985–2002

However, we note that the bulk of investment has been domestically funded with unprofitable state-owned enterprises still able – albeit to a lesser degree than previously – to obtain resources from the state-owned banking system on a nonmarket basis. Moreover, recent work by CSFB's head of China research, Vincent Chan, and his team shows that in recent years property investment has taken up a much higher share of investment than in other developing countries such as India (see Table 2.3).

Table 2.3 China, India and Vietnam investment by sector.

	China (1996–2003)			India (1995/96–2002/3)		Vietnam (1996–2002)	
	% of fixed investment[a]	% of fixed investment[b]	% of GDP	% of fixed investment	% of GDP	% of fixed investment	% of GDP
Agriculture	3.1	2.3	0.9	8.1	1.6	12.2	4.1
Industrial[c]	34.6	26.1	9.9	51.5	10.3	37.6	12.6
Services	62.4	47.1	17.9	40.4	8.1	50.2	16.8
Real estate, etc.	29.1	22.0	8.4	11.1	2.2	2.3	0.8

[a] The ratio is calculated based on fixed-asset investment of state-owned units and other enterprises over a designated size, which is about 75 % of total investment based on data between 1996 and 2003. Before 2004, data for fixed-asset investment by sector is only released for this group of enterprises.

[b] The ratio is calculated based on total fixed-asset investment, including urban collective enterprises and individual investment, apart from that by state-owned units and other enterprises over a designated size.

[c] Including mining, manufacturing, utilities and construction.

Source: CEIC and CSFB research.

POOR RETURN ON INVESTMENT

Weaknesses in the investment project appraisal and funding processes mean that China exhibits a low and declining overall economy return on investment. In Figure 2.8, we have constructed a series for the overall return on investment in China by plotting the ratio of GDP growth generated in a given year against the investment to GDP ratio in the preceding year. This is a somewhat artificial construct as in practice investment projects have payback periods lasting many years. However, the exercise is instructive as it clearly demonstrates that in recent years China has exhibited a declining overall economy return on investment relative to that which was achieved in the past.

This striking result may in part be owing to China classifying as investment expenditure items that would be treated as government current spending in other countries. China has very high whole economy investment and savings rates and apparently low fiscal deficit and government domestic debt burden relative to other emerging and developed economies. However, the state-owned banking system has accumulated very substantial nonperforming loans. In November 2003, Standard & Poor's (S&P), while launching its debt ratings for China's state-owned banks, estimated that impaired assets could account for up to 45 % of total system assets or around 60 % of GDP. At that time and subsequently, Standard & Poor's has argued that this overhang is a major reason why China's foreign currency debt rating ceiling was BBB+. At the time of the Standard & Poor's study, China's official statistics indicated a nonperforming

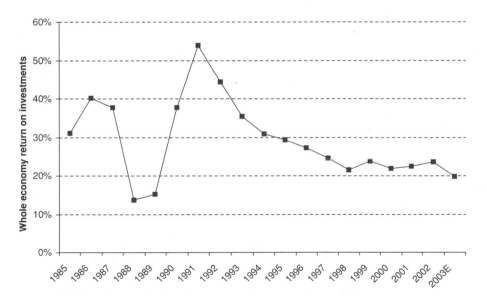

Source: China Statistical Yearbook and CSFB estimates

Figure 2.8   China whole economy return on investment proxy, 1985–2003E

loan ratio of 21.4 % (note that this is a narrower definition than that of Standard & Poor's). This ratio has fallen further as a result of loan growth and the US$45bn partial recapitalisation of Bank of China and China Construction Bank in January 2004.

These nonperforming loans appear mainly to be the result of lending to state-owned enterprises in manufacturing and local and regional infrastructure projects. It is impossible to disaggregate what proportion of this lending actually represents ongoing government current spending but we suspect that this phenomenon biases upwards China's reported whole economy investment and savings rates – perhaps by as much as 5–10 % of GDP – and biases downwards China's annual reported fiscal deficit by the same amount. As the government moves to restructure the state-owned banks via the introduction of foreign strategic capital and the writing-off of nonperforming loans, the true scale of this structural weakness is gradually being exposed.

The conclusion that return on investment is poor in absolute terms and relative to the advanced economies is confirmed by microlevel data on corporate profits performance. The profits performance of listed China equities is poor relative to peers in other countries. Table 2.4 shows that in 2003 annual net profits for the approximately 1400 stocks listed in the Shanghai A, Shenzen A and Hang Seng Mainland Composited Index amounted to US$37.4bn, which is only 7 % of the profits of the S&P 1500 Super Composite or 12 % of the profits of the Bloomberg European 500. Moreover, the profit distribution of China's listed companies is highly concentrated in the upstream resources/basic materials sector and government-protected industries, and not in downstream industries, where it would appear that the country's competitive advantages would lie (see Table 2.5).

CSFB HOLT cash flow return on investment (CFROI®) analysis also points to the same distinctions (Figure 2.9). The China H share index – mainly comprising businesses in the resources and telecoms sectors – has a relatively high CFROI® in a pan-Asian context in recent years, having significantly increased with the major listings of 1999–2000. Meanwhile, the more diverse local China A share index continues to have the second-lowest CFROI® in the region after Japan.

The key reason for the concentration of returns in a narrow range of sectors is that it is easier for excess capacity to emerge in downstream sectors owing to the lack of constraints from natural resources, technology or government administrative restrictions. Therefore, while upstream/government-regulated sectors benefit from a syndrome of 'China demand, China cost structure, but international (or government-protected) pricing/supply side discipline', downstream sectors have to face a syndrome of 'China demand, China cost structure and China pricing/supply side discipline', that is, little or no discipline in pricing and the supply side.

In our view, the status quo will not last as the high fixed investment ratio in China, which is driven largely by a low and declining cost of capital, is not likely to be sustainable. In addition to the bottoming out of the global interest rate cycle, other factors are also at work: (a) the Chinese population is ageing; (b) the much faster money supply growth compared with GDP growth over the last decade could create

Table 2.4 Profits in major listed equity markets in 2003.

	Reference index	Number of stocks	Net profits (US$bn)[a]
China	Shanghai A, Shenzhen A and Hang Seng Mainland Composited Index	1400	37.4
The Big 3			
US	S&P 1500 Super Composite	1498	514.1
EU	Bloomberg European 500	497	318.7
Japan	TOPIX Index (Tokyo)	1111	62.1
Other Asian countries			
Philippines	Philippines Composite Index	33	1.3
Malaysia	Kuala Lumpur Composite Index	98	6.4
Singapore	SES All Index	347	9.4
India	NSE S&P CNX 500 Equity Index and Bombay SE 500 Index	537	18.6
Indonesia	Jakarta Composite Index	339	5.0
Thailand	SE of Thailand SET Index	391	7.9
Australia	All Ordinaries Index	408	27.2
Korea	Korea Composite Index	664	21.3
Taiwan	Taiwan TAIPEX Index	649	20.3
Others			
Brazil	Brazil Bovespa Stock Index	54	16.9
Canada	S&P/TSX Composite Index	222	40.8
Mexico	Mexico Bolsa Index	33	7.4
Russia	Russian RTS Index $	65	15.4
South Africa	FTSE/JSE Africa All Share	155	16.5

[a] Last financial year – 2003 for most companies.
Source: Bloomberg.

long-term inflationary pressure; (c) banking reform will make banks more careful in granting credit; and (d) liberalisation and rationalisation of valuation in the domestic stock market.

The following changes could happen: (a) a structural rise in the cost of capital; (b) the role of investment in driving the economy will be reduced and gradually replaced by domestic consumption; (c) the profitability of downstream sectors could improve; and (d) the importance of the consumer goods and services sectors in driving the economy will increase. Indeed, if we define the 'postindustrial' era as 'an economy's growth being driven increasingly by services rather than by the industrial sector', China may enter this era earlier than the market expects owing to the correction of past 'overinvestment'. Table 2.6 provides our estimate of sector winners and losers within the Chinese economy based on these four likely structural changes in the Chinese economy.

Table 2.5 Profit distribution not reflecting China's competitive edge but rather its overinvestment problem.

(% of total, 2003)	Basic materials	Communications	Consumer, cyclical	Consumer, noncyclical	Diversified	Energy	Financial	Industrial	Technology	Utilities
China	12.8	20.7	6.0	6.4	2.4	35.3	2.4	6.6	1.0	6.3
US	1.5	9.0	11.5	19.1	0.0	9.0	30.5	9.1	7.3	3.1
EU	3.6	3.7	7.7	19.6	0.5	15.9	34.8	7.9	0.2	6.1
Japan	7.6	10.7	27.1	10.8	0.0	-0.8	3.6	21.5	8.5	11.0
India	19.3	1.5	6.5	10.4	0.6	24.8	21.0	7.4	4.8	3.7
Indonesia	2.7	18.5	10.8	20.7	0.6	1.0	39.1	5.3	0.0	1.2
Thailand	14.8	11.4	11.1	4.7	0.2	16.2	21.7	15.6	0.5	3.8
Australia	19.0	25.7	5.6	3.6	0.8	4.3	31.8	8.3	0.0	0.9
Korea	16.9	12.5	26.4	7.4	0.4	6.5	-18.4	42.2	-5.2	11.4
Taiwan	16.1	9.6	9.2	1.0	0.0	2.7	15.2	21.8	24.2	0.1
Brazil	24.7	6.3	0.0	4.5	3.0	36.7	16.0	1.2	0.0	7.7
South Africa	32.1	9.1	6.0	8.8	8.1	7.1	26.8	4.7	-2.7	0.0

Source: Bloomberg and CSFB estimates.

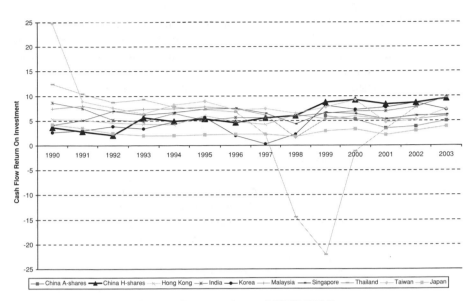

Source: Company data and CSFB HOLT

Figure 2.9 Cash flow return on investment from CSFB HOLT aggregator for select Asian countries, 1990–2003

Table 2.6 Winners and losers in the long term.

Sectors	Impact
Hard commodities	Negative. Demand for them is closely correlated with construction activity, which in turn depends on investment demand.
Power utilities	Negative, unless residential/services sector sales grow fast enough to compensate for industrial sales.
Insurance	Positive. The rising cost of capital will trigger an improving yield on investment.
Banks	Negative. The rising cost of capital will hinder loan growth, improve the quality of new loans, but worsen the quality of existing loans.
Telecommunication	Neutral. Demand for telecom services is geared more towards overall economic development and related technological changes.
Aviation/airports	Positive. Travelling will be a major beneficiary of rising consumption demand.
Ports	Neutral. More correlated with export activities.
Highway	Neutral. Demand will be more in line with overall economic growth.
Consumer services	Positive. Major beneficiaries of rising services consumption.
Property	Positive in the long term but likely to undergo some boom/bust cycle first.

Source: CSFB estimates.

We conclude that the declining whole economy return on investment and associated low level of corporate profitability in China are major areas of concern. If they are not addressed in a comprehensive manner by the current efforts at financial sector reform and consolidation in what – outside of the energy and telecoms sectors – is a highly fragmented local industrial sector, the likelihood of our worst-case scenario occurring rises significantly.

TECHNOLOGICAL CHANGE

China's strategy of opening to flows of FDI in recent years is leading to substantial ongoing technological transfer. It is allowing China to execute successfully a 'follower' strategy in relation to the most advanced countries in much the same way as was achieved by Japan and Korea in the earlier phases of their economic development. This is particularly so as in recent years China has moved up the value-added chain, with investment now taking place in areas such as automotive and semiconductors, which are more capital intensive. Furthermore, the sheer scale of the market opportunity in China for foreign multinationals increasingly ensures that the Chinese government is able to negotiate attractive technology transfer conditions in exchange for access to the local markets. Recent prominent examples include the aviation, rail transport and power generation industries.

Figure 2.10 shows that China's FDI inflows have risen dramatically since the early 1990s and in US$ terms now account for more than US$50bn per annum or around

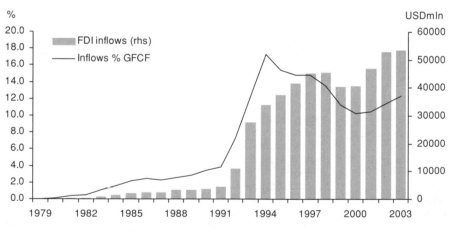

Source: Datastream and CSFB research

Figure 2.10   Foreign direct investment (absolute and as a percentage of gross fixed capital formation)

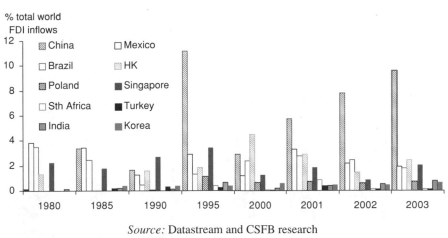

Source: Datastream and CSFB research
Figure 2.11   FDI inflows, emerging markets

18 % of gross fixed capital formation (GFCF). At this level, China has typically been one of the top three recipients of FDI inflows in recent years.

Relative to other emerging market countries, China is by far dominating FDI flows (Figure 2.11). Indeed there is some evidence that in other countries such as Mexico and Poland there has been a reduction in recent years, which has been blamed locally on competition from China. In India, FDI remains well below potential, still lagging in export-orientated manufacturing. India's services exports have expanded significantly despite the low levels of FDI and infrastructure and institutional impediments to inward investment, as services industries are labour rather than capital intensive and require relatively few capital inputs and imports.

Technological change is also helped by a rural/urban migration pattern that mirrors those of other countries during the period when their total factor productivity rose most rapidly. Academic evidence supports the thesis that innovation largely takes place in cities. The development and expansion of universities and other tertiary education institutions in cities is strongly correlated with acceleration of technological change in the advanced economies from the nineteenth century onwards.

In the absence of good data on plant vintage we find patent applications and expenditure on research and development to be useful indicators of China's participation in global technological change. Patent applications by residents of China, filed with a national patent office, have tended to run at around 10 000 per annum in recent years. While this is one-tenth of the number of patents received from residents of the US, China substantially outperforms India on this measure (Figure 2.12).

Figure 2.13 shows research and development expenditure as a percentage of GDP. While China's spending lags that of the US, it has almost doubled in recent years from 0.6 % of GDP to 1.1 % of GDP.

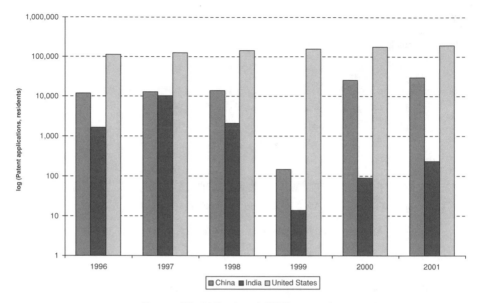

Source: World Bank and CSFB research

Figure 2.12   Patent applications in China, India and the US, resident only on a logarithmic scale, 1996–2001

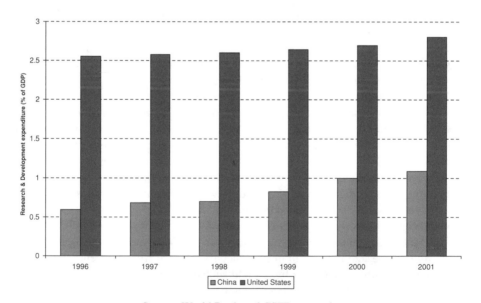

Source: World Bank and CSFB research

Figure 2.13   Research and development as percentage share of GDP, 1996–2001

Table 2.7 China's contribution to global trade growth (%).

	Global total trade growth	US	Asia	EU-12	Japan	Other	China	Asia except China
2003 trade share		**15.53**	**21.09**	**17.61**	**7.69**	**38.07**	**3.69**	**17.41**
1990	13.57	1.01	2.56	3.81	0.74	5.44	0.81	1.75
1995	18.95	2.08	5.13	3.26	1.52	6.96	1.06	4.07
2000	12.97	2.84	5.04	1.44	1.39	2.26	1.44	3.60
2001	−3.47	−0.76	−1.23	0.15	−0.84	−0.80	0.28	−1.51
2002	3.98	−0.07	1.68	0.69	0.05	1.64	2.02	−0.34
2003 average	13.41	1.25	4.06	3.26	0.81	4.04	1.09	2.97

Source: IMF and CSFB research.

TRADE

Global sourcing and the sharp rise in FDI flows by foreign multinationals into China has led to a complex pattern of trade and rising economic integration (particularly with Japan, other Asian countries and the US). One can no longer simply characterise China's role in exports as that of final goods assembler, or on the imports side as solely acting as a source of demand for raw materials and capital goods.

China is currently the world's fourth-largest exporter and seventh-largest importer of goods and services. On the import side, China is ranked in the top three in no fewer than 51 three-digit standard industry classifications (SICs) and on the export side in 52.

China's contribution to world trade growth varies substantially over time but the trend is towards increasing importance. Table 2.7 shows that China contributed 2pp or half of the estimated 4pp increase in world trade during 2002, offsetting a decline in contribution from the rest of Asia excluding Japan. In 2003, China's importance reduced as trade growth in the advanced economies recovered somewhat.

The wave of globalisation, first driven in the 1980s by the removal of barriers to trade and capital and then in the 1990s by the internationalisation of production processes to low-cost markets, has led to a sharp rise in trade competitiveness (market-share gains) (Figure 2.14). Changes in trade patterns ensued, with China standing first in global export market-share gains between 1985 and 2000 (from less than 1 % to 4 %), followed by the US, Korea and Mexico.

In 2003, China's total exports among the biggest 25 product groups traded world-wide were nearly $198bn, up 185.7 % from 1999 (Table 2.8). This represented 8.2 % of total world exports in these categories. Historically, China used to dominate lower value-added product groups such as textile, clothing and footwear. Over the past few years, however, China has expanded its exports into higher value-added product groups. Indeed, its exports grew the most in telecoms, computer and office equipment between 1999 and 2003, rising on average more than 340 % in those categories during

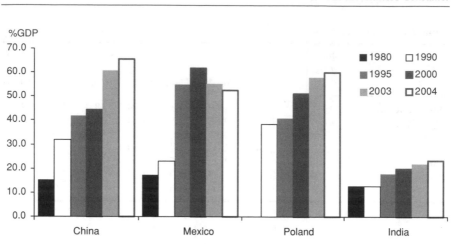

Source: IMF, Datastream and CSFB research
Figure 2.14   Merchandise trade openness – China gaining

that period. Other groups in which China's exports experienced strong growth were electrical equipment, furniture, apparels, articles of plastics and women/girls clothing. In these groups China's exports on average more than doubled during the same period. This has benefited the US, which is unsurprisingly and overwhelmingly the key import demand source, being the biggest importer in all eight product categories mentioned.

We find that Chinese exports have helped expand world exports in $ terms in all eight categories examined. This leads us to the conclusion that international trade does not follow a zero-sum game as assumed by many. The jump in China's exports has led to other major exporting countries encountering declining market share, particularly the US and to a lesser extent Japan and Singapore. However, it is corporations from these countries that have been highly active in shifting production to China. Hence, in our view it is firms who have not made the shift or moved up the value chain who have lost out while local consumers and firms who have made the move benefit. In this regard IBM's sale of its PC business to Lenovo is indicative of a wider trend.

Export prices dropped for telecoms, computer, office and electrical equipment as well as apparel and women and girls' clothing. However, export prices rose for furniture and articles of plastics, most likely as a result of higher input prices for wood and oil.

Trade leads to specialisation in areas of relative strength. Economic efficiency improves, there are overall gains in global output and average welfare but significant distributional issues arise.

In the mid-nineteenth century reductions in shipping costs (steam ships and then refrigeration) led the New World countries America, Australia and later Argentina and Brazil to enter the global market for agricultural production. They were relatively land abundant and labour scarce. Old Europe was relatively labour abundant and

Table 2.8 Details of China exports in selected product groups among the top 25 biggest sorted by the highest growth rate in Chinese exports between 1999 and 2003 and where China has become a major exporting country in 2003.

Product group	Exports in 2003 (in billion US$)		China exports increase 1999–2003 (%)	China's rank among exporters in 2003	Top ranked exporting country excluding China	Top ranked importing country	Change in worldwide export prices
	China	Worldwide					
Telecommunications equipment	27.8	194.4	248.9	1	South Korea	US	Down
Computer equipment	41.0	189.1	417.8	1	Netherlands	US	Down
Office equipment	19.1	124.7	361.8	1	Japan	US	Down
Electrical equipment	10.1	95.8	127.8	3	Japan	US	Down
Furniture	9.0	71.8	161.2	2	Italy	US	Up
Articles of apparel	15.0	63.9	67.3	1	Italy	US	Down
Articles of plastics	7.3	59.5	86.8	2	Germany	US	Up
Women/girl clothing	11.1	45.3	84.1	1	Italy	US	Down

Source: ITC and CSFB research.

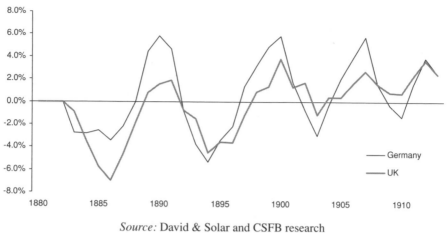

Source: David & Solar and CSFB research
Figure 2.15 Germany and UK inflation, 1880–1913

land scarce. Theory suggests that global economic integration hurts the owners of a country's relatively scarce resource (New World labour and Old World land in this case). Williamson (1995) finds that between 1870 and 1913 the ratio of wages to land rents in America fell by half and in Australia by three-quarters. In Britain and Sweden the ratio more than doubled in the same period.

There was massive convergence in the price of internationally traded goods. The amount by which grain prices in Chicago exceeded those in Liverpool fell from 60 % to 15 % from 1869–71 to 1911–13. Nominal prices of wheat collapsed worldwide (in the UK by two-thirds from 1870 to 1900). Substantial real wage convergence also took place. In the second half of the nineteenth century European real wages caught up with US real wages, which had been more than double in the 1850s. There was huge migration from Old Europe to the New World to work the land.

In the US the nominal price level declined almost continuously from 1866 to 1896 with the cost of living falling at an annual rate of 2 % per annum. The same was true of Germany and the UK with prices falling particularly rapidly in the late 1880s and late 1890s, as shown in Figure 2.15. The situation only changed with the discovery of huge amounts of gold in South Africa at the end of the 1890s. Commodity prices fell almost continuously apart from a brief boom at the end of the 1870s.

In the leading economy enormous gains accrued to stock market investors in this period. A deflationary boom with pronounced cyclicality proved fully consistent with major gains in real wealth. In the UK, the CSFB Equity Gilt study finds that with income reinvested Stg100 rose to Stg1548 from 1869 to 1913, representing a compound annual growth rate in real terms of 6.5 % per annum (Figure 2.16). The main sectors represented in the UK market in the CSFB Equity Gilt study in 1869 were banks, railways, insurance, shipping, iron, coal and steel producers. These industries were well able to reap returns from the simultaneous rise in real spending power at home, construction on infrastructure overseas and the rapid increase in international trade.

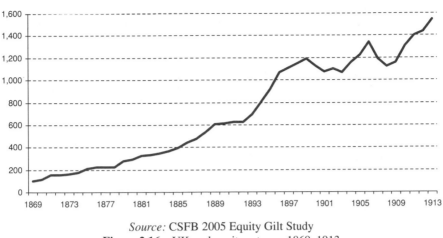

Source: CSFB 2005 Equity Gilt Study
Figure 2.16 UK real equity returns, 1869–1913

Today, China and other emerging markets are entering the global market for manufacturing and lower-end services production. Low- to mid-end skilled labour is relatively abundant in these countries versus their physical capital stocks. It is relatively scarce in the US, Europe and Japan.

Theory therefore suggests that real profit growth will exceed real wage growth over the cycle in the US, Europe and Japan. Meanwhile, real wage growth will be high in India and China relative to real profit growth. In Section 2 we find direct evidence from our consumer survey that significant real wage gains are indeed starting to be visible on the ground in China.

China's trade activity can be broadly characterised as being a price-taker in its imports of primary commodities but showing limited pricing power in its exports of low- to mid-end manufactures. A full assessment of China's natural resource endowments in a global context is beyond the scope of this book and we noted above that generally natural resource constraints have not been a major issue in holding back economic growth. However, in certain key commodity groups such as oil, alumina and iron ore and grain China in our view lacks the ability to expand domestic production and is becoming a structural global importer. Given the size of the population and the scale of the Chinese economy in PPP terms, as this takes place a significant deficit in its trade in these segments is starting to appear. As shown in Table 2.9, in H1 2004 China had a deficit in crude materials of 3.5 % of GDP, up from 1.4 % of GDP in 2000. Meanwhile, China's surplus in miscellaneous manufactured articles of 6.2 % of GDP was down marginally from 6.8 % of GDP in 2000. This speaks clearly to a need to move up the value chain into export markets with greater pricing power, in which regard China's gains in human capital and research and development expenditure should be a benefit.

Among the major commodities, China is most constrained in relation to oil reserves. As a result China has become in recent years the fourth largest net importer of oil

Table 2.9 China's trade pattern.

% of GDP	1980	1985	1990	1995	2000	2003	H1'04
Goods	−0.62	−4.98	2.28	2.38	2.23	1.74	−0.95
Food and live animals	0.02	0.75	0.85	0.55	0.70	0.79	0.60
Beverages and tobacco	0.01	−0.03	0.05	0.14	0.04	0.04	0.05
Crude materials, inedible, except fuels	−0.61	−0.19	−0.15	−0.83	−1.44	−1.98	−3.54
Mineral fuels, lubricants and related materials	1.34	2.32	1.04	0.03	−1.18	−1.23	−2.15
Animal and vegetable oils, fats and waxes·	−0.06	0.00	−0.21	−0.31	−0.08	−0.20	−0.30
Chemicals and related products	−0.59	−1.04	−0.76	−1.17	−1.68	−2.00	−2.64
Manufactured goods chiefly by materials (MG)	−0.05	−2.47	0.96	0.49	0.07	0.35	0.80
MG: textile yarn and fabrics				0.43	0.31	0.86	1.17
MG: iron and steel				−0.24	−0.49	−1.17	−1.26
MG: nonferrous metals				−0.11	−0.31	−0.32	−0.41
Machinery and transport equipment (MTE)	−1.41	−5.17	−2.94	−3.03	−0.86	−0.34	0.10
MTE: machinery specialised for particular industries				−1.73	−0.81	−1.16	−1.50
MTE: office machinery and automatic data processing machines				0.28	0.72	2.61	3.50
MTE: telecom and sound recording apparatus				0.11	0.66	1.74	2.44
MTE: electrical machinery, apparatus and appliances				−0.14	−1.08	−2.55	−3.29
Miscellaneous manufactured articles (MMA)	0.76	0.53	2.76	6.61	6.81	6.34	6.16
MMA: articles of apparel and clothing accessories				3.29	3.23	3.45	3.57
MMA: footwear				0.90	0.89	0.86	0.97
MMA: professional, scientific and controlling instruments				−0.18	−0.17	−0.96	−1.58
MMA: Miscellaneous manufactured articles				1.67	1.75	1.77	1.72
Commodities not classified elsewhere	−0.04	0.32	0.69	−0.10	−0.13	−0.02	−0.05
Services	0.00	0.18	0.39	−0.87	−0.52	−0.58	−0.83

Source: CSFB estimates and CSFB research.

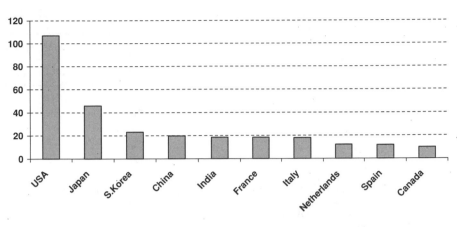

Oil imports by 10 biggest importers in 2003, in billion US$

Source: ITC and CSFB research

Figure 2.17 Oil imports by the 10 biggest importers (in billion US$)

globally (see Figure 2.17). We project further rises in imports over the medium term (see Figure 2.18).

Figure 2.19 shows that in 2003 China consumed 0.2 tonnes of oil per capita, well below the average for the group of emerging market countries illustrated and on a par with Ukraine. It is only one-tenth the level of developed countries in Europe and Asia. Currently, oil use in China is skewed to the industrial sectors with only limited

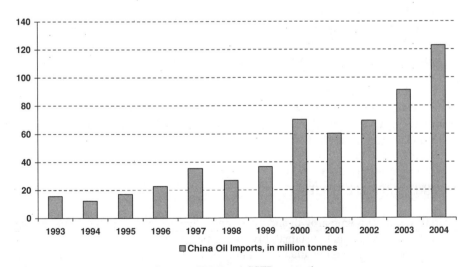

China Oil Imports, in million tonnes

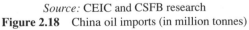

Source: CEIC and CSFB research

Figure 2.18 China oil imports (in million tonnes)

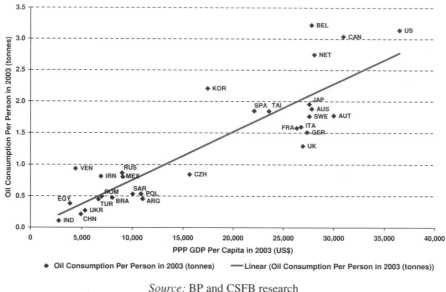

Source: BP and CSFB research
Figure 2.19 Oil consumption per person in 2003 (in tonnes)

usage in transportation. However, if our projections that auto usage will rise to close to 100 m by 2018 (see Chapter 6) are correct there are major challenges for China – and indeed the world – if technological innovation does not deliver vehicles with substantially more fuel efficiency than currently obtained.

China has become a large structural importer of iron ore in recent years as domestic steel production has surged. However, China's steel consumption per capita in 2003 – also at 0.2 tonnes – is already high by emerging market standards (Figure 2.20). It is on a par with Poland and Turkey and indeed certain advanced economies such as the UK and the Netherlands. This appears to be the result of a recent boom in property construction in China's major cities, particularly in mid- to high-end residential accommodation, which may not be sustained over the medium term. This segment of the economy has been explicitly targeted by policy makers in China's current campaign against overheating, as discussed in more detail below.

ENVIRONMENTAL ISSUES

China's rapid economic growth and associated urbanisation represents a major challenge for environmental sustainability. In particular, China currently suffers from major problems of water availability in the north of the country and loss of agricultural land to desertification. A recent report by China's State Environmental Protection

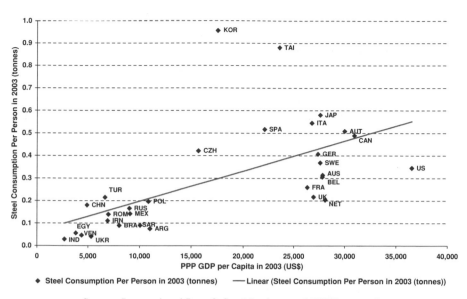

Source: International Iron & Steel Institute and CSFB research
Figure 2.20   Steel consumption per person in 2003 (in tonnes)

Administration (SEPA) states that areas suffering from soil erosion stood in 2004 at 3.56m km² or 37.1 % of the country's total land area. Forests cover only 16 % of China's land surface versus 74 % for Japan.

In an attempt to counteract declining land quality, China has become the world's largest producer and consumer of fertiliser, accounting for 20 % of world consumption, and now using three times the global average per acre. However, this has led to problems of water quality due to runoffs of fertiliser and pesticides.

There are very high levels of urban air pollution due to carbon dioxide, sulfur and nitrogen oxide emissions from China's predominantly coal-fired power stations. China is the world's largest producer and consumer of coal. This method of fuel production also yields high levels of acid rain, further impacting negatively on agriculture and human health. According to SEPA, acid rain occurred in 298 Chinese cities, or 56.5 % of the total. The number of cities with serious acid rain (lower than pH 5.6) reached 218, or 41.4 % of the total.

It is beyond the scope of this book to address this topic in any detail. However, we would note that in certain consumer product categories – most notably the projections for automobile ownership and air travel – the projections in this report may bump up against environmental and other infrastructure constraints in the medium term. The reader who wishes to explore this topic in further detail is referred to the excellent chapter on China in Diamond's (2005) book.

HUMAN CAPITAL

The development of human capital in China appears to be accelerating. China's secondary school enrolment record has improved significantly in recent years from 48.6 % of the relevant age cohort to 68.2 % from 1990 to 2000 (see Figure 2.21). There has been a much more substantial improvement than in the case of India and it is also interesting to note that in recent years secondary school enrolment has actually fallen by 4.5pp in the US between 1993 and 2000.

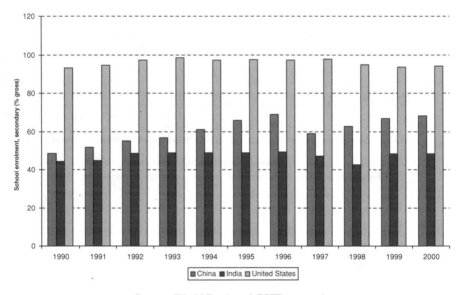

Source: World Bank and CSFB research
Figure 2.21   School enrolment, secondary (% gross), 1990–2000

In the tertiary sector, there has also been a significant increase in enrolment, but from a very low base. In 1990, 3.0 % of the relevant age cohort were receiving tertiary education in China, as shown in Figure 2.22. By 2000, this had more than quadrupled to 12.7 %. In this regard, India and China have kept pace with each other and gained substantially on the US, where tertiary education enrolment has actually fallen by over 10pp in recent years.

However, in health both China and India have failed to narrow the gap with the US (Figure 2.23). Health expenditure per capita in constant US$ terms has not risen in either country in recent years.

INSTITUTIONAL CONTEXT

Quantitative measures of absolute and relative institutional performance at the country level are hard to come by. The most useful for our purposes in analysing the

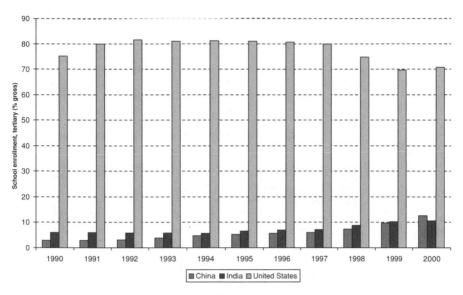

Source: World Bank and CSFB research

Figure 2.22   School enrolment, tertiary (% gross), 1990–2000

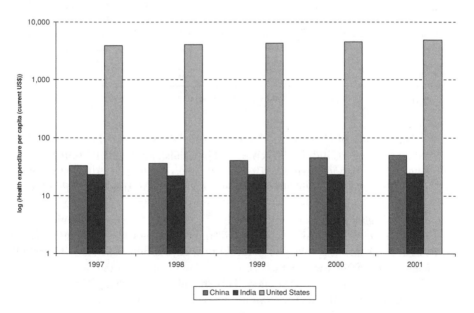

Source: World Bank and CSFB research

Figure 2.23   Health expenditure per capita (2004 US$) on a logarithmic scale, 1997–2001

Table 2.10   Transparency International Corruption Perception Index for leading emerging markets, 1995–2003.

	1995	1996	1997	1998	1999	2000	2001	2002	2003
Argentina	5.24	3.41	2.81	3	3	3.5	3.5	2.8	2.5
Brazil	2.7	2.96	3.56	4	4.1	3.9	4	4	3.9
Chile	7.94	6.8	6.05	6.8	6.9	7.4	7.5	7.5	7.4
China	2.16	2.43	2.88	3.5	3.4	3.1	3.5	3.5	3.4
Colombia	3.44	2.73	2.23	2.2	2.9	3.2	3.8	3.6	3.7
Czech Republic	5.37	5.2	4.8	4.6	4.3	3.9	3.7	3.9	n.a.
Egypt	n.a.	2.84	n.a.	2.9	3.3	3.1	3.6	3.4	3.3
Hungary	4.12	4.86	5.18	5	5.2	5.2	5.3	4.9	4.8
India	2.78	2.63	2.75	2.9	2.9	2.8	2.7	2.7	2.8
Indonesia	1.94	2.65	2.72	2	1.7	1.7	1.9	1.9	1.9
Israel	n.a.	7.71	7.97	7.1	6.8	6.6	7.6	7.3	7.0
Jordan	n.a.	4.89	n.a.	4.7	4.4	4.6	4.9	4.5	4.6
Malaysia	5.28	5.32	5.01	5.3	5.1	4.8	5	4.9	5.2
Mexico	3.18	3.3	2.66	3.3	3.4	3.3	3.7	3.6	3.6
Morocco	n.a.	n.a.	n.a.	3.7	4.1	4.7	n.a.	3.7	3.3
Pakistan	2.25	1	2.53	2.7	2.2	n.a.	2.3	2.6	2.5
Peru	n.a.	n.a.	n.a.	4.5	4.5	4.4	4.1	4	3.7
Philippines	2.77	2.69	3.05	3.3	3.6	2.8	2.9	2.6	2.5
Poland	n.a.	5.57	5.08	4.6	4.2	4.1	4.1	4	3.6
Russia	n.a.	2.58	2.27	2.4	2.4	2.1	2.3	2.7	2.7
South Africa	5.62	5.68	4.95	5.2	5	5	4.8	4.8	4.4
South Korea	4.29	5.02	4.29	4.2	3.8	4	4.2	4.5	4.3
Taiwan	5.08	4.98	5.02	5.3	5.6	5.5	5.9	5.6	5.7
Thailand	2.79	3.33	3.06	3	3.2	3.2	3.2	3.2	3.3
Turkey	4.1	4.54	3.21	3.4	3.6	3.8	3.6	3.2	3.1
Venezuela	2.66	2.5	2.77	2.3	2.6	2.7	2.8	2.5	2.4

Source: Transparency International, University of Goettingen and CSFB research.

likely sustainability of China's recent growth is the Transparency International (TI) Corruption Perceptions Index (CPI) compiled by Transparency International and the University of Goettingen, Germany. The TI CPI ranks countries in terms of the degree to which corruption is perceived by business people to exist among public officials and politicians.

A priori, a higher degree of corruption should have an effect on economic growth over the longer term. First, a more corrupt government process increases quite literally the costs of doing business through the necessity of paying bribes. Second, it increases the uncertainty over the way in which a country's laws and regulations may be applied to the business operating in that country. This should raise the required rate of return on equity as it increases the risk premium associated with the uncertainty of future cash flows accruing to investors rather than corrupt government officials. Over time this will depress investment spending and hence economic growth.

The CPI is a joint initiative of Transparency International and Goettingen University and has been updated once a year since 1995. The major operational work is conducted

Table 2.11 Transparency International Corruption Perceptions Index for the G3 countries, 1995–2003.

	1995	1996	1997	1998	1999	2000	2001	2002	2003
US	7.79	7.66	7.61	7.5	7.5	7.8	7.6	7.7	7.5
Germany	8.14	8.27	8.23	7.9	8	7.6	7.4	7.3	7.7
Japan	6.72	7.05	6.57	5.8	6	6.4	7.1	7.1	7

Source: Transparency International, University of Goettingen and CSFB research.

by Dr Johann Graf Lambsdorff of Goettingen University, Germany. The goal of the CPI is to provide data on extensive perceptions of corruption within countries. The CPI is a composite index, making use of surveys of business people and assessments by country analysts. It consists of credible sources using diverse sampling frames and different methodologies. These perceptions enhance our understanding of real levels of corruption from one country to another.

The index is a 'poll of polls'. In 2003, it was prepared using 17 sources, including surveys from the World Competitiveness Yearbook, Institute for Management Development, Information International, World Bank, Economist Intelligence Unit, Freedom House, World Markets Research Centre, Columbia University, Political & Economic Risk Consultancy, PricewaterhouseCoopers, Gallup International and EBRD, plus finally a survey conducted at Goettingen University that allows contributors the possibility for anonymous contributions and also directly approaches employees of multinational firms and institutions.

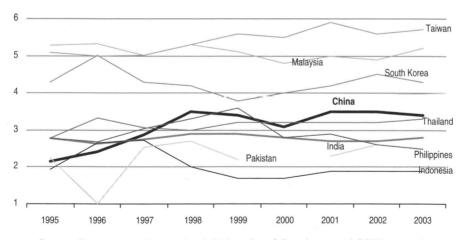

Source: Transparency International, University of Goettingen and CSFB research
Figure 2.24 Transparency International Corruption Perceptions Index for Asian countries, 1995–2003

The CPI index is scored out of ten. A ten equals a country perceived to be entirely clean while zero equals a country where business transactions are perceived to be entirely dominated by corrupt practices (including kickbacks and extortion by government officials). No country scores either ten or zero.

Table 2.10 shows the CPI scores for China and other countries in its peer group for the years 1995 to 2003. Of the 26 countries ranked in 2003 China ranked fifteenth on a par with Egypt, Morocco, Thailand and Turkey. This is one place lower than in 1998 when China ranked fourteenth.

In Asia, Taiwan and Malaysia currently have the best CPI score while the Philippines and Pakistan have the worst CPI score. Taiwan, Thailand and Korea have seen the best CPI score improvement between 1998 and 2003 in Asia while the Philippines and Pakistan have seen the worst deterioration during that period. China's absolute CPI score improved significantly in the 1995 to 1998 period but has remained constant since 1998 (see Figure 2.24).

Table 2.11 shows the CPI scores for the G3 countries: US, Japan and Germany. It is clear that there is a substantial gap between China's current performance on this measure and that of the other leading economies in the world.

REFERENCES

Diamond, J. (2005) *Collapse: How Societies Choose to Fail or Survive*, Allen Lane, pp. 358–78.

Maddison, A. (1997) Causal influences on productivity performance 1820–1992: a global perspective, *Journal of Productivity Analysis*, 325–60.

Maddison, A. (2001) *The World Economy: A Millennial Perspective*, OECD Development Centre, Paris.

Maddison, A (2004) Contours of the world economy and the art of macro-measurement 1500 to 2001, Ruggles Lecture, Cork, Ireland.

Smith, A. (1776) *An Inquiry into the Nature and Causes of the Wealth of Nations*, University of Chicago Reprint 1976, Chicago, Illinois.

Williamson, J.G. (1995) The evolution of global labour markets since 1830. *Explorations in Economic History*, **32**, 141–96.

3
Near-Term Risks to Consumption Arising from China's Efforts to Combat Overheating

What short-term risks arise for consumption spending from the Chinese government's move in 2004 to a policy tightening cycle? The Chinese economy appears to have exhibited significant business-cycle fluctuations in the past. These are not visible in official GDP growth statistics, particularly in recent years, although proxies for GDP growth such as electricity production (Figure 3.1) show significantly more volatility. Nor does official retail sales data (Figure 3.2) or household income growth data show significant variability with the cycle.

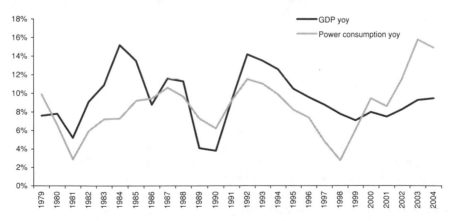

Source: China Statistical Yearbook, CEIC and CSFB research
Figure 3.1   China electricity demand growth (kilowatt bn) versus real GDP growth

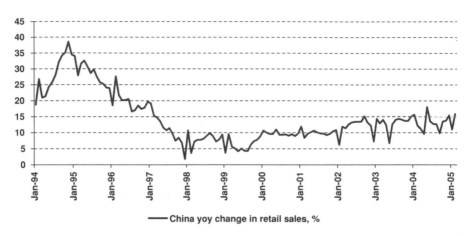

Source: CEIC and CSFB research
Figure 3.2   China real retail sales (yoy, % change)

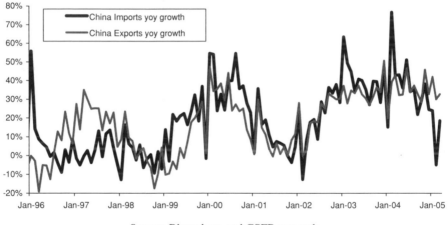

Source: Bloomberg and CSFB research
Figure 3.3   China imports and exports year-on-year growth

However, on the trade side major fluctuations in economic activity have clearly
taken placc in the past. There is evidence for a four-year business cycle. At the
peaks in the cycle in Q1 (first quarter) 1996, Q1 2000 and Q1 2004, import and
export growth have been rising at rates in excess of 50 % year-on-year (yoy) (Figure
3.3). At the troughs in the cycle in Q4 (fourth quarter) 1998 and Q4 2001, import and export growth have been falling at rates in excess of 10 % yoy. Note that
both of these latter two troughs in trade activity coincided with global industrial

production recessions, reflecting the extent to which China's economy was now becoming deeply integrated with the other major economies. Given that urban employment, particularly at higher incomes, has a heavy preponderance towards exports, it is reasonable to assume that earnings growth and employment growth would have been depressed at these times. Certainly the stock prices of Hong Kong listed companies with exposure to the China consumer performed relatively poorly during these downturns.

In our view, the aim of the current tightening cycle is to combat overinvestment, particularly in the property sector and capacity expansion in the aluminium, steel and cement sectors. The major exception has been auto financing, where the China Bank Regulatory Commission chose to act by requiring higher downpayments and shorter maturities. The result has been a virtual collapse in sales growth as shown in Figure 3.4, although the results of our consumer survey indicate that substantial pent-up demand for auto purchases remains.

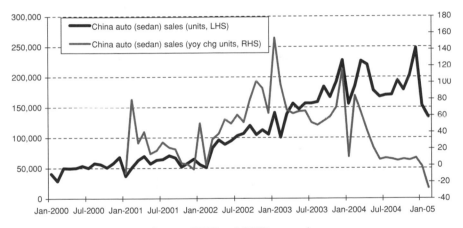

Source: CEIC and CSFB research

Figure 3.4 China auto (sedan) sales and sales growth (January 2000 to date)

Rebalancing aggregate demand away from investment spending towards consumption spending, while keeping the key engine of exports firing strongly through avoiding excessively rapid real appreciation of the currency, appears to us in general to be a sensible goal for policy at this stage of China's economic development. The measures that are being taken also contribute towards structural reform of the financial system.

The 27 bps (basis points) interest rate hike on 28 October 2004 marks the beginning of the second round of China's austerity programme. The first round of austerity, launched in late April featuring a drastic clampdown on loan growth through administrative intervention, was initially successful but lost its effectiveness when we believe the black market displaced the banking system for financing 'unwanted' steel and cement investments. We expect interest rates to rise by at least 200–300 bps over the next 12–18 months.

CONSUMPTION SPENDING SHOULD HOLD UP WELL

Although investment spending growth has already begun to slow markedly, local consumption has and should continue to hold up well for the following three reasons. First, Chinese consumers have relatively low leverage, as confirmed by our survey below. Interest rate hikes are likely to cause much less damage to consumption than investment. Generally, the household sector in China is a major net saver with little in the way of accumulated mortgage debt or consumer credit. It has been penalised by negative real interest rates in the deposit market and so benefits from the recent 27 bps increase in the official deposit rates. Meanwhile, the corporate sector and in particular state-owned enterprises in aggregate are probably a dis-saver and hence are penalised by the rise in official lending rates. Figure 3.5 illustrates the recent movements in real deposit and lending rates in China.

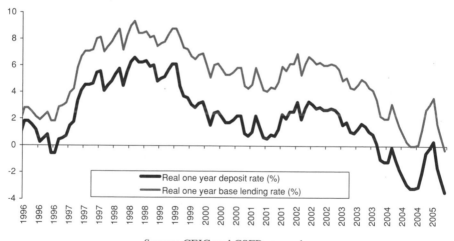

Source: CEIC and CSFB research

Figure 3.5   China real deposit and lending rates

Second, wage growth in the urban sector, where 80 % of total national spending is generated, is more correlated to service and export sectors rather than investment spending. Third, household formation is still strong and the younger generation is in our view happier to spend on borrowed finances while banks are happy to lend

Table 3.1 China key economic indicators (actual data and CSFB forecasts as of April 2005).

% yoy	2002	2003	2004E	2005E	2006E
GDP	8.0	9.3	9.5	8.6	7.2
Gross fixed investment	16.1	26.7	25.8	15.0	6.5
Real retail sales	8.8	9.1	13.3	11.2	10.0
CPI (year average)	−0.8	1.2	3.9	5.0	5.8
Exports	22.4	34.6	35.4	18.0	9.0
Imports	21.2	39.8	35.8	19.0	13.6
Trade balance (US$bn)	30.4	25.5	32.0	32.1	28.3
Current account (% of GDP)	2.7	3.1	3.5	2.9	2.0
Gross FX Reserves (US$bn)	286.4	403.3	609.9	781.4	880.2
Actual FDI (US$bn, YTD)	52.7	53.5	60.6	62.0	56.0

Source: CEIC and CSFB estimates.

(except for auto loans). We project retail sales growth to average 11.2 % for 2005 and 10.0 % for 2006, compared with an estimated 13.3 % for 2004.

Table 3.1 gives 2005–6 forecasts for GDP growth and other major macroeconomic variables as of April 2005.

4

China's Demographic Trends and Their Implications for Household Consumption

In this chapter, we analyse China's past and present demographic trends. They have major implications, not only for the development of aggregate household consumption but also for the product categories consumed.

In our view, four major features of China's changing demographics can be expected to affect consumption:

*   the age and gender distribution;
*   the urbanisation rate and the associated lifestyle change that goes with it;
*   income growth and changes in income distribution; and
*   changes in propensity to spend out of income (against the alternative of saving).

Assuming the base case we have defined above: (a) that trend real GDP growth rises by 7 % per annum; (b) that there is a 5.5 % increase in the share of consumption spending within GDP; and (c) that the Renminbi rises from 0.2 of its PPP level to 0.55, we provide consumption forecasts for individual product categories.

We conclude that:

*   The population is ageing rapidly. Unlike many emerging markets, China is not in essence a child or youth consumer market.
*   Population migration from the countryside to the cities has been and will be likely to remain huge and indeed involves unprecedented numbers of people and extreme changes in lifestyle within a single generation.
*   As people in urban regions are likely to continue to find better remunerating jobs in sectors that are integrated with the global economy, there are not only very rapid increases in average incomes but also significant increases in

income and wealth inequality underway. The number of households earning over US$5000 is growing nearly six times faster than the growth rate of average incomes. To that extent, the key segment of opportunity in China to address appears to be the older, more affluent urban consumer market.

• The savings rate is likely to increase further as household incomes increase and rural–urban migration takes place. However, owing to the projected overall growth rate of the economy, consumption expenditure still rises. There are also major changes underway within the consumption basket as consumers become open to new tastes and experiences for the first time.

POPULATION GROWTH STOPS IN TEN YEARS' TIME

We project that the total population in China will stop growing in 2014 at around 1.3bn people and will start to decline gradually thereafter (see Figure 4.1). China introduced its one-child policy in 1979. This policy has since changed the population profile of China dramatically and is likely to continue to do so. On 13 April 2004, Shanghai's municipal government announced that divorcees who remarry would be allowed to have a second baby. This relaxation of the one-child policy would allow couples to have a baby even if both partners already have one from previous marriages. It is unclear whether other local governments will follow suit and also relax their family planning policies, although at the national level commitment to the policy appears to remain strong.

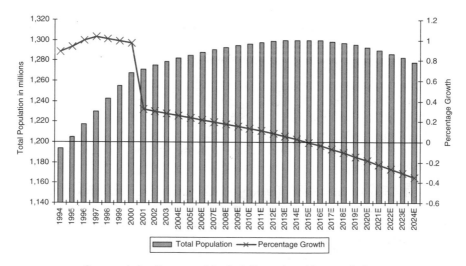

Source: Asian Demographics Ltd. Reproduced by permission
Figure 4.1   Total population and its percentage growth in China, 1994–2024E

Using a population model supplied by Asian Demographics Ltd, we have constructed past, present and projected data for age profiles of the population. The model uses education as a proxy for propensity to have children, urbanisation, earnings and death rates. Other factors are also taken into account, such as the age profile for women giving birth and deaths by age and gender showing trends in death rates. Validation is carried out by the comparison of the projected outcome for a census year with the actual census result from the Chinese government statistical agency. Accuracy is improving and in the case of the last round the mean average deviation of the age–gender profile was less than 2 %. For further details of this model contact Asian Demographics Ltd directly at www.asiandemographics.com.

Death rates are likely to continue to fall as wealth and urbanisation increases, but birth rates should fall significantly faster. This is owing to the reduced birth rate per woman and a fall in the number of women of a child-bearing age, which is explained in the ageing population section that follows. These are not new phenomena and have occurred since 1990. The reduced birth rate per woman is owing to the one-child policy and increased education and urbanisation. The fall in the number of women of a child-bearing age is owing to the bias of births in males and the shift in the age distribution, shown in Figure 4.2.

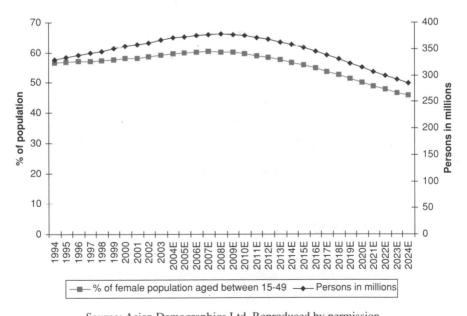

Source: Asian Demographics Ltd. Reproduced by permission

Figure 4.2 Percentage and absolute number of female population of child-bearing age in China, 1994–2024E

AN AGEING POPULATION

Figure 4.3 shows the changing age profile according to Asian Demographics' population model. In 1994, China had a young population, the majority of which were under the age of 29. Currently the majority of the population is between the ages of 15 and 44. In 2014, and even more so in 2024, the percentage of the population in the older age brackets increases significantly.

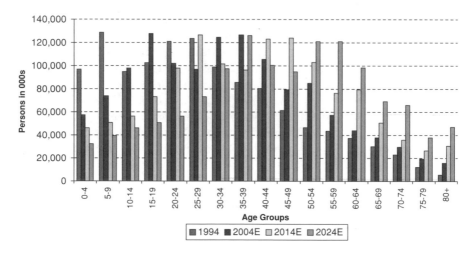

Source: Asian Demographics Ltd. Reproduced by permission
Figure 4.3   Age distribution of China in absolute population numbers, 1994–2024E

Figures 4.4 to 4.7 show the age distribution from 1994 to 2024 in percentages of population. Some of the changes in absolute numbers in various age brackets are striking. For example, the number of people in the 20–24 age bracket will almost halve from over 120m in 1994 to less than 60m in 2024. By contrast, the number of people in the 50–54 age bracket will almost triple from around 40m in 1994 to over 120m in 2024.

CHANGING LIFESTYLES

The combination of increased wealth and decreased rate of having children is dramatically altering the lifestyles of households and individuals. This is shown in Figure 4.8, which divides the population into various cohorts. Using the Asian Demographics dataset we project that:

• The delay in marriage offsets to some extent the decline in the proportion of young people within the total population. By 2013, we project that 29 % of the total population will be young singles versus 36 % currently.

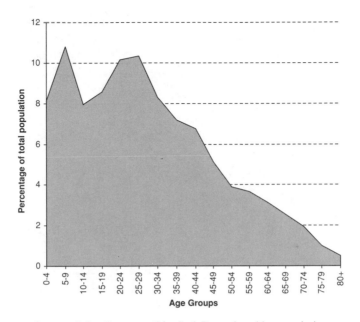

Source: Asian Demographics Ltd. Reproduced by permission
Figure 4.4   Age distribution of Chinese population in percentages, 1994

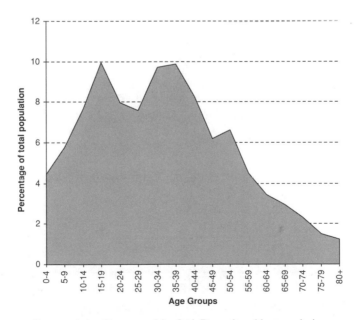

Source: Asian Demographics Ltd. Reproduced by permission
Figure 4.5   Age distribution of Chinese population in percentages, 2004E

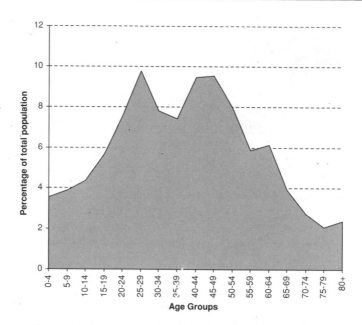

Source: Asian Demographics Ltd. Reproduced by permission

Figure 4.6   Age distribution of Chinese population in percentages, 2014E

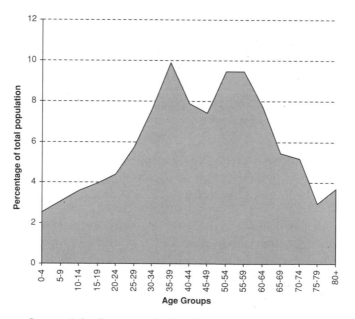

Source: Asian Demographics Ltd. Reproduced by permission

Figure 4.7   Age distribution of Chinese population in percentages, 2024E

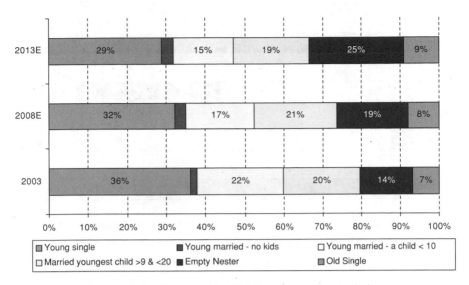

Source: Asian Demographics Ltd. Reproduced by permission

Figure 4.8   Percentage of population in defined lifecycle stages, 2003–2013E

- The proportion of the population who are young, married and with young children declines significantly from 22 % of the total to 15 % of the total.
- The proportion of the population married with older children grows for five years and then declines.
- The proportion of those of working age who have no children living at home with them and older single people grows dramatically from 21 % of the population currently to 34 % in 2013.

Figure 4.9 shows the breakdown by age group of those in each lifecycle stage while Figure 4.10 shows the average number of people in a household.

URBANISATION, POPULATION MIGRATION AND EDUCATION

China government statistics estimate that 39.1 % of the total population was urbanised in 2002. Using trends based on regressions from Asian Demographics and our own assumptions for underlying economic growth, we estimate that by 2014, 49.8 % of the population will be urbanised versus 40.2 % today. This proportion will rise to 58.2 % in 2024. This is shown in Figure 4.11.

The urbanisation process involves staggering numbers of people. In the 30 years from 1994 to 2024, China's urban population is likely to rise from 350m to 750m. This represents a net addition to the urban population of over 13m people a year (larger than the current population of Greece every year). The incentives for migration are obvious: to seek better remunerating jobs and achieve a higher standard of living.

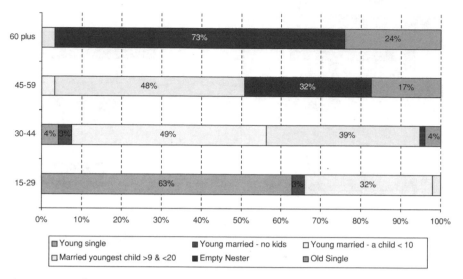

Source: Asian Demographics Ltd. Reproduced by permission

Figure 4.9   Percentage of age group in defined lifecycle stages, 2003

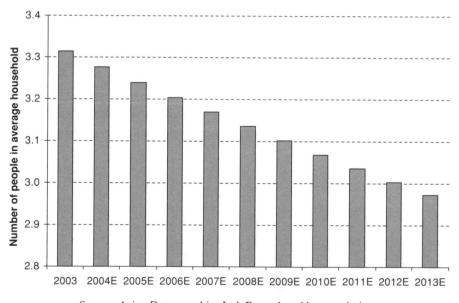

Source: Asian Demographics Ltd. Reproduced by permission

Figure 4.10   Average number of people in a household, 2003–2013E

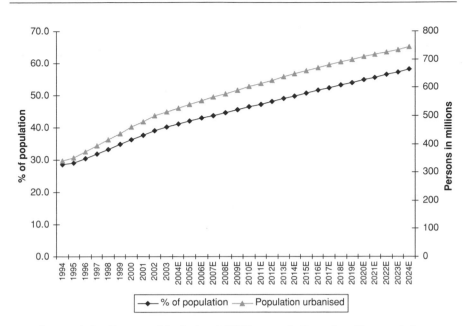

Source: Asian Demographics Ltd and CSFB research. Reproduced by permission
Figure 4.11 Percentage and absolute number of total population in urban areas in China, 1994–2024E

Rural and urban average household incomes are shown in Figure 4.12 (2002 values). Inequality in income between urban and rural citizens has been rising. Currently, average urban incomes are around three times higher than rural incomes versus a two times disparity 10 years ago. Average urban incomes have risen by 99.7 % in real terms in the last nine years versus a 53.1 % increase in rural incomes. We anticipate that average urban incomes will rise by a further 46.3 % over the next 10 years while rural incomes are likely to rise by around only 27.9 %.

We conclude that discretionary consumption spending – versus spending to meet basic needs – is likely to remain almost entirely an urban phenomenon in China; that is, the addressable market for most products, particularly those sold by foreign multinationals, is not the overall population but rather the urban population.

Figure 4.13 shows migration nationally and for three preferred migrant destinations. Beijing shows a huge amount of urban migration; 30.3 % of its population are immigrants with 2.3 % having migrated less than six months ago.

Urban migration is likely to be centred on regions that are already affluent, such as the provinces in the east and south-east (see Figure 4.14). The cities and industrial centres within these provinces are forming the nuclei attracting population from all over China. Over time we would expect the east and south-east of China, which are already evidently better lit than the rest of the country in NASA's view of the earth at night (see Figure 4.15), to become a mirror image of the eastern seaboard of the US.

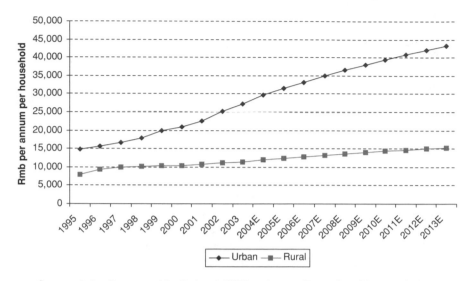

Source: Asian Demographics Ltd and CSFB estimates. Reproduced by permission

Figure 4.12   Rural and urban average annual household incomes in China, 1995–2013E

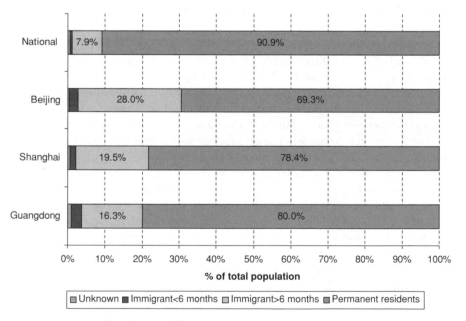

Source: Asian Demographics Ltd. Reproduced by permission

Figure 4.13   Residential status of population nationally and more prosperous areas, 2002

Figure 4.14   Map of China showing the preferred destinations for urban migration

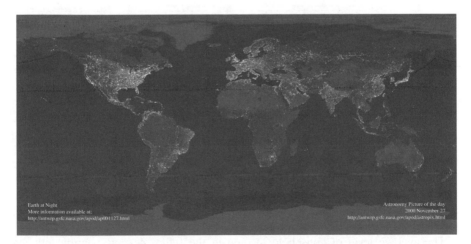

Source: NASA, National Environmental Satellite, Data and Information Service, National Oceanic and Atmospheric Administration
Credit: Data courtesy of Marc Imhoff of NASA GSFC and Christopher Elvidge of NOAA NGDC. Image by Craig Mayhew and Robert Simmon, NASA GSFC
Figure 4.15   Earth at night – the eastern half of China is likely to be as bright as the eastern half of the US in 10 years

CHANGES IN EDUCATIONAL STATUS

Figure 4.16 shows that 10 years ago, 56 % of the Chinese population had either completed primary education or partial attendance. Only 6.8 % had completed technical secondary or tertiary education. By 2014, using the Asian Demographics dataset, we project that only 21 % of the population will be in the former category while 29 % will be in the latter. With changes in education level come changes in consumer preferences and, in particular, openness to new tastes and experiences.

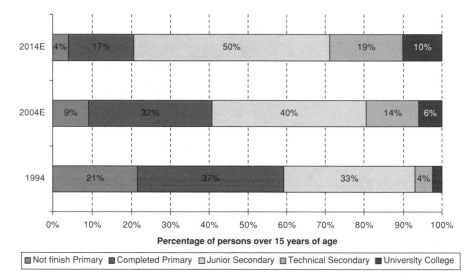

Source: Asian Demographics Ltd. Reproduced by permission
Figure 4.16   Education profile of persons over the age of 15 years, 1994–2014E

CHANGES IN INCOME DISTRIBUTION

Having discussed the basic issues of an ageing population, the rural/urban divide and the role played by migration to the cities and education, we now move on to look in more detail at the implications for income distribution.

The average level of household income in the future depends significantly on the GDP growth rate achieved and hence on which of the three scenarios for China's future economic growth occurs. Projections using the Asian Demographics income/expenditure model allow us to forecast changes in the income distributions and hence to calculate numbers in various income brackets over time. As a reminder, our base case used in the model is as follows: that trend real GDP growth rises by 7 % per annum and that the Renminbi rises from 0.2 of its PPP level to 0.55.

Figures 4.17 and 4.18 show both the income distribution of urban and rural China, historically and forecasted. For urban households, we project a significant thickening of the income distribution at the higher end for incomes of more than US$10 000 per household annually (2002 US$ values). We forecast the proportion of urban households earning more than US$10 000 per annum to rise from 3.0 % in 2004 to 64.8 % in 2013. By 2013, we estimate that 151m households will be in this relatively affluent bracket versus just 3.8m in 2003. For comparison purposes note that the total number of households in the US with income over US$10 000 per annum in 2003 was 102m with 91.0 % of all households having incomes above this level (US Census Bureau, 2004).

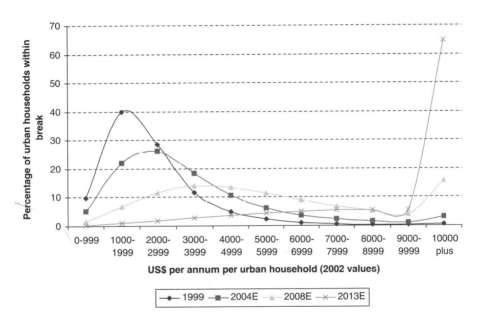

Source: Asian Demographics Income/Expenditure Model and CSFB estimates. Reproduced by permission of Asian Demographics Ltd

Figure 4.17   Income distribution of urban households using the base-case scenario

For rural areas we do not project that this will change to anything like the same extent. Therefore, as GDP increases, income inequality between the richest segment in the cities and households in rural areas is likely to become more acute.

We forecast that the proportion of the urban population earning over US$5000 – a level that can be associated with the transition to significant discretionary consumer spending (that is, 'new consumers') – will rise from 17.4 % to 90.6 % of the total from 2004 to 2013. The compound growth rate in the number of households earning more than this level is 24 % per annum. In total, over this period the number of households able to make discretionary consumer purchases beyond meeting basic needs will rise

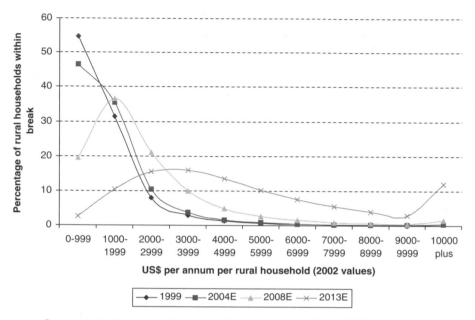

Source: Asian Demographics Income/Expenditure Model and CSFB estimates.
Reproduced by permission of Asian Demographics Ltd
Figure 4.18   Income distribution of rural households using the best-case scenario

from 31m to 212m. For comparison purposes note that the total number of households in the US with income over US$5000 per annum in 2003 was 108m, with 96.6 % of all households having incomes above this level.

A key conclusion from this analysis is that China is a volume not a margin market. The number of households earning over US$5000 rises more rapidly than the average income of the US$5000 plus household. However, most new consumers passing the hurdle will only just meet the income criteria. This is very different to the situation in the US, where the median income in 2003 was US$43 300 per head.

However, we can generate other scenarios using the cases described in the first chapter. These cases are:

- Best case. We assume that trend real GDP growth rises by 9 % per annum, which is similar to the growth rates achieved in recent boom years, and that the Renminbi rises from 0.2 of its PPP level to 1, that is, full revaluation (see Figures 4.19 and 4.20).
- Worst case. We have assumed that trend real GDP growth rises by 5 % per annum owing to failures to fix the financial system or the maintenance of other institutional impediments to growth and that the Renminbi experiences no revaluation (see Figures 4.21 and 4.22).

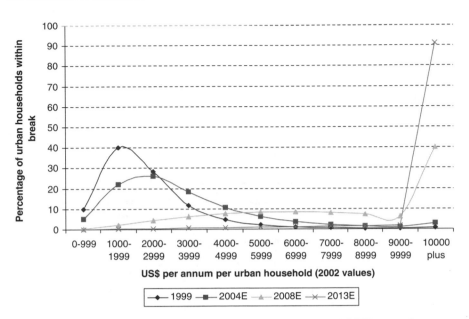

Source: Asian Demographics Income/Expenditure Model and CSFB research. Reproduced by permission of Asian Demographics Ltd

Figure 4.19   Income distribution of urban households using the best-case scenario

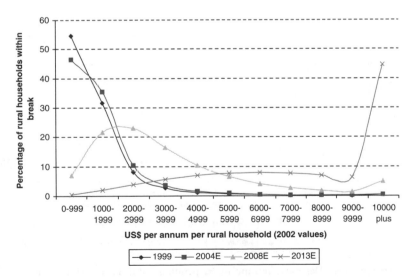

Source: Asian Demographics Income/Expenditure Model and CSFB research. Reproduced by permission of Asian Demographics Ltd

Figure 4.20   Income distribution of rural households using the best-case scenario

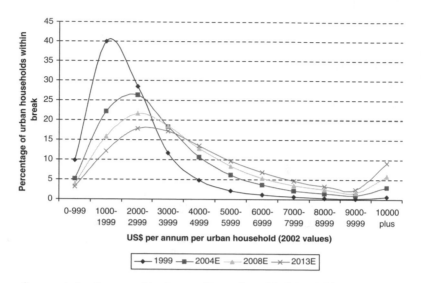

Source: Asian Demographics Income/Expenditure Model and CSFB research.
Reproduced by permission of Asian Demographics Ltd
Figure 4.21   Income distribution of urban households using the worst-case scenario

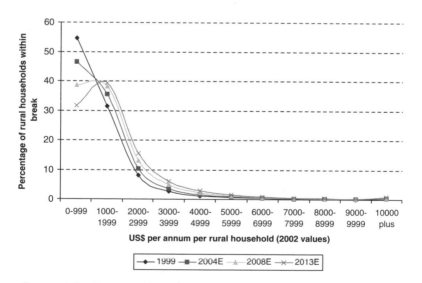

Source: Asian Demographics Income/Expenditure Model and CSFB research.
Reproduced by permission of Asian Demographics Ltd
Figure 4.22   Income distribution of rural households using the worst-case scenario

Even in the event of the worst-case scenario, there is still a thickening of the distribution of income above US$10 000 in urban regions. In the best-case scenario, the distribution is spread over the defined breakpoint to an extent that nearly all households earn over US$10 000 annually. However, as before, the probabilities of these two scenarios are unlikely and we assign 75 % of the probability distribution between the base case and the best case and only 25 % between the base case and the worst case.

As these scenario analyses illustrate, the actual number of households in each defined income break varies considerably with the assumed GDP growth rate.

EXPENDITURE AND PROPENSITY TO SPEND OUT OF INCOME

Analysis of the historical data by province for China indicates that the propensity to spend out of income generally:

- decreases as income increases;
- but increases over time (as consumerism and credit becomes more acceptable).

As household income and wealth increase, so typically does the propensity to spend decrease. This is owing to the ability to save a higher percentage of income as subsistence spending to meet basic needs (food and shelter) becomes less important within total spending. Since China does not have a welfare state, Chinese households have more of an incentive to save for old age and as a precaution against illness than their counterparts in the US, Japan and Europe. However, there is also evidence that over time the propensity to spend out of income is rising on a secular basis owing to urbanisation, increased consumerism, openness to Western values (see the following subsection) as well as easier access to credit.

Taking these two offsetting effects into account, Figure 4.23 shows our projections for average urban household income and expenditure. We project that the proportion of household income spent will fall from the current level of 76 % to 72 % by 2014. Note that this implies a rise in the household savings rate from 24 % of income to 28 % of income.

We therefore project that the total value of urban household expenditure will grow in US$ terms by a CAGR of 17.3 % over the next 10 years. This uses our base case as outlined previously with 7 % GDP growth and revaluation to RMB3/US$1. We also make the conservative assumption that the household leverage ratio remains essentially zero in all our calculations and modelling.

KEY CONCLUSIONS FROM DEMOGRAPHICS ON IMPLICATIONS FOR CONSUMPTION SPENDING PATTERNS

Our first key conclusion is that there is a much larger opportunity in China in products and services geared towards the older segment of the population. An older population consumes different products to a younger population.

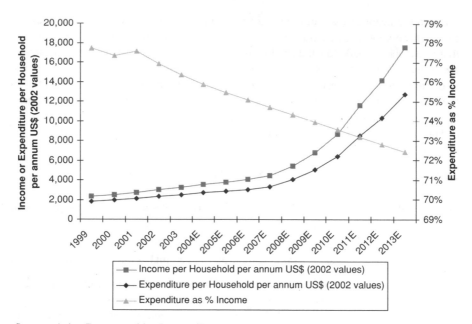

Source: Asian Demographics Income/Expenditure Model and CSFB estimates. Reproduced by permission of Asian Demographics Ltd

Figure 4.23   Income and expenditure as a percentage of income per urban household, 1999–2013E

Product categories that would *a priori* seem to us to benefit from the dramatically ageing population are: health items, restaurant and leisure facilities and tourism destinations that have an orientation to the older consumer (emphasising cultural/quality of experience attributes over speed of service), luxury goods including spirits aimed at the older person, automobiles that emphasise safety and fuel efficiency over speed, household care, and cosmetic and healthcare products that are oriented to the older consumer.

Smaller numbers of people per household probably mean that the density of consumer durables such as TVs/washing machines and other white goods per person is likely to rise over time. Although the proportion of the population in the young singles categories is likely to decline slightly over the next 10 years, gains in income and rising income inequality will probably make nightclubs and bars (aimed at the young single market) and beer and other alcohol products (which are more typically consumed by young urban workers) relatively more attractive segments. Those product categories orientated towards the child are likely to be less attractively positioned: toys, confectionery, packaged food products aimed at the family and child-driven tourism destinations.

The implications of rising educational status for consumption are likely to be profound. At the simplest level the market for books and other educational services orientated particularly at the secondary and tertiary level are likely to gain dramatically. There is also likely to be a rapid rate of expansion in the market for products that allow these higher educational skills to be deployed (in particular these results are consistent with our forecast rapid growth rate in PC ownership). With education also comes sophistication and this implies significant changes in tastes in relation to food (Italian pizza restaurants and nonlocal cuisine), clothing and a desire for foreign travel.

The major implication of our analysis of the change in income distribution is that the affluent segment of the market rises more quickly than the overall market but remains small in absolute size (at least on our base-case scenario). At least for the next 10 years the most exciting part of the market is likely to consist of the large number of new consumer households passing the US$5000 threshold at which smaller ticket discretionary spend items can be purchased. The strategic conclusions for companies are clear: price to meet a particular income level and hold the price point and gear up to meet the volume increase. Distribution systems and scalable business models will be crucial. In our view, companies must realise that with increased affluence and wealth of consumers, production-orientated approaches in marketing may not be adequate.

The major implication of our analysis of savings behaviour is that there is a large potential opportunity for retail banks and financial services providers to offer savings and investment products. The consumer survey in the following chapter contains detailed information on financial products currently owned by Chinese households.

REFERENCE

US Census Bureau (2004) *Income; Poverty, and Health Insurance Coverage in The United States: 2003*, US Government Printing Office, Washington, DC.

5
Social and Cultural Influences on Consumption

In addition to demographic change, the social and cultural background of consumers clearly influences overall consumption spending as well as product and brand preferences. In this report we have chosen to talk to consumers directly by undertaking the survey, the results of which are analysed in detail in Section 2. We want to avoid making sweeping generalisations as they can all too often lead to stereotyping. Nevertheless, in our view it is worth summarising certain enduring key features affecting consumption behaviour that arise from China's unique social and cultural history as well as structural changes underway. These are summarised in Figure 5.1 and have been identified by other authors writing about the Chinese consumer as well as leading practitioners in the advertising industry in China. For readers interested in a comprehensive, although now somewhat out-of-date, study that focuses heavily on the social and cultural dimension of consumer behaviour, we recommend Conghua Li's 1998 publication *China: The Consumer Revolution.*

A first key feature is regional diversity in tastes arising from the sheer geographical size of China, linguistic differences, a historical legacy of strong provincial loyalties and until recently poor communications. Our survey in eight different Chinese cities provides clear evidence of the importance of this feature.

A second key feature is the rural/urban income and wealth divide, the role of migration and the uncertain status of migrant workers in China's large coastal cities. We have already discussed this in some detail earlier. The divergent pace of economic development in China leads to diversity in consumption behaviour. For example, in the tourism sphere consumers in China's southern cities may have already visited Hong Kong/Macau frequently and now aspire to travel to Europe, but many more continue to look forward intensely to their first visit.

A third key feature that is deeply rooted in China's culture is the greater role played by the family, reverence for age and intense focus on the educational development of the child compared with Western societies. Hence there is often a great deal of

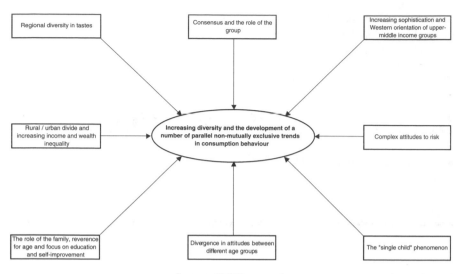

Source: CSFB research

Figure 5.1   Enduring key features and structural change in Chinese consumption spending

disconnection between the purchaser and end user of a product. An example includes the extensive purchase by middle-aged adults of health tonics to help prolong the life of their parents.

Self-improvement is a huge trend in consumption, reflecting traditional values but also the upward mobility of the current young generation, who aspire to work at multinational firms, have their own business (spurred on by the generation of Internet millionaires) and gain educational experience overseas, etc. Two years ago it was reported that the best-selling publication in the busiest bookstore in Shanghai was the English dictionary.

A fourth key feature is the role that China's recent history has played in the shaping of attitudes among consumers of different ages. The country has moved from being essentially closed to outside influence and trade to a high degree of openness on both counts, while income and wealth inequality have risen substantially. An individual who will be aged 55–60 years old in 10 years' time would have grown up in the very difficult times in the 1950–60s. This may limit the kind of leisure expenditure of the same generation in the US, Europe or even Japan, who would have grown up in a more affluent environment with probably very different views on consumption values.

Even as the proportion of younger people shrinks in 10 years' time, as disposable incomes and the consumption environment continue to develop they are likely to be much more consumerism-orientated than someone of the same age today. Indeed, Conghua Li and other authors provide numerous examples of the development of what he termed an 's-generation' of single-child consumers with radically different attitudes to their parents and in particular the expectation of a higher degree of correlation between the work they do and the reward they receive. Conghua Li cites the example of his 16-year-old cousin David who brims with self-confidence and 'looks like a young investment banker at a weekend training retreat at a four star country resort'. He notes the difficulties David's parents have in restraining his desires to purchase smart clothes at prices that are high relative to the modest incomes they make from their jobs at state-owned enterprises.

Moreover, government policy is also driving shifts in consumption patterns. In 1999, the Chinese government launched what has become known as 'Holiday Economics', with policies to promote consumer spending during three golden holiday weeks in the year. These holiday weeks now see significant increases in consumer spending and in particular domestic and international travel has grown significantly at this time. As we noted in our discussion on the short-term risks to consumption, government policy currently seems to be aimed at rebalancing aggregate demand away from the investment spend-sensitive parts of the economy to the consumption sectors.

A fifth key feature is the importance of the group and the role of consensus in shaping attitudes, which is often contrasted with the individualistic ethos of the US consumer. As a result, advertising agencies operating in China report the success of strategies that focus on cluster marketing rather than broad cross-country campaigns. Chinese society has extensive networks of personal relationships often summarised under the term Guanxi. Within a given group, gift giving takes place that reflects the giver's respect towards the recipient's status and his/her ability to promote the giver's role within the group. The cost of such gifts can often be high relative to the giver's income. Advertisers report significant success with strategies that focus on the display of status in the social group (for example, branded mobile phones).

Sixth, there is the role of risk. Despite the importance of the group and the role of consensus, there is evidence of a high level of risk taking in Chinese society. Gambling is prevalent and there is a high degree of willingness to consume new products. Yet advertisers operating in China also report the importance that products project protective qualities. Tom Doctoroff, North East Asia Director and Greater China CEO for J Walter Thompson, argues that Procter and Gamble's success in China has been built around the theme of family protection. He cites the example of Safeguard soap, which has maintained a 20–30 % market share for the past 10 years, by focusing on the risks from germs as part of its advertising strategy.

Finally, national pride remains strong and has a major influence on consumer marketing strategies (although not as much as in Korea). We note that a key component of Mengniu Dairy's successful marketing strategy is its use of an 'astronaut' campaign after China sent its first astronaut into space. Its products are also endorsed by China's equivalent of NASA. Yao Ming, the NBA star, and China's recent Olympic medallists are also hot advertising property at the moment.

Notwithstanding the continued validity of these key features, changes in consumer habits have now rendered some old stereotypes rather dated, especially where it concerns China's rising upper-middle class in the first-tier cities. Sophistication has become more important and taste among the upper-middle class is increasingly converging towards that of the Western consumer, especially as many international magazines are publishing local editions in China (fashion magazines and even *Elle Décor*). International retailers are also bringing in Western lifestyle and aesthetics (IKEA, B&Q, Wal-Mart, Carrefour). International designer brands are now increasingly hosting high-profile promotional events in first-tier cities like Shanghai – recently Jean Paul Gaultier had a fashion show in the city while Louis Vuitton had a big party when it expanded its Shanghai flagship store before the Formula One weekend in late September.

In our view, consumer behaviour is increasingly characterised by value migration. Organised retailing started to take off in the late 1990s and has gathered pace (now representing a low double-digit percentage of the overall retail market). Purchasing decisions are no longer made solely on price. As incomes in first-tier cities reach a certain level, people begin to prefer nicer shopping environments, away from street vendors they suspect of selling counterfeits and low-quality goods. We expect a second wave now as traditional attitudes to risk confront the many scandals relating food and product quality this year (for example, protein-deficient powdered milk for babies, ham containing pesticides, padded jackets filled with industrial wastage cotton emitting toxic chemicals, etc).

We have recently identified the following list of the latest consumer fashions for the upper-middle income group: (a) SUV is a lifestyle statement and so are road trips; (b) commuting in style, in a cab at least if not driving your own car; (c) shopping at the hypermarkets and Western-style specialty retailers; (d) shopping for designer brands overseas or any products not yet available in China; (e) going on trophy holidays; (f) experiencing something new (read: Western) and something different, be it a Starbucks coffee or a Western-style funfair complete with Ferris wheel; (g) visiting the doctor, organising your money management and perhaps buying some stocks while overseas; (h) instant messaging your friends; (i) going for anything health conscious, especially post-SARS; (j) sending children to private schools, overseas education . . . and even weight-loss camps; and (k) 'status' sports like golf.

Our observations in this chapter suggest the development of a number of parallel nonmutually exclusive trends in consumption behaviour in China. As a result, while certain key unique features of the consumer landscape in China remain, it is becoming harder to make any generalised statements on the 'Chinese consumer'. Consumer spending patterns have fragmented significantly over the past 10 years as affluence grows and the consumer becomes more sophisticated (and also increasingly spoilt for choice on how to spend their money). Hence, although our demographic work might point to companies that are geared towards caring for older people to be thriving, so could Disney and others be more naturally geared to servicing the 's-generation'.

REFERENCE

Li, Conghua (1998) *China: The Consumer Revolution*, John Wiley & Sons, Inc., New York.

6
China's Growth Potential for Key Product Categories

In this chapter, we analyse China's historical and likely future demand potential for individual product categories. We also put China into a global context by providing projections for other major countries. The product categories for which comparable data are available are: radios, televisions, fixed-line handsets, mobile phone handsets, personal computers, automobiles and air travel. We list and discuss the product categories, starting with smaller-ticket traditional technology items and finishing with bigger-ticket newer technology or luxury items.

In our projections, we estimate the absolute numbers, market shares and CAGRs of each product for 15 selected countries. The datasets used are the IMF World Economic Outlook and the World Bank World Development Indicators publications. Our projection technique uses the historically observed pattern of product ownership for each category in relation to GDP per capita and the base-case projections for GDP growth and population growth for each country that were introduced earlier in this book. A detailed account of the methodology used can be found in Appendix C.

We conclude that China's current levels of ownership or use of these key consumer products vary widely (from as high as 30 % of the total in the case of radios to as low as 4 % in the case of personal computers). In each product category, China is likely to be in the top three markets in terms of CAGRs of product ownership from 2004 to 2014. However, in terms of additional items purchased, China is likely to be the largest potential market for product sales in each case over the next 10 years given its large population size and the fact that the starting level for each product category was already well above zero in 2004.

We expect the highest CAGRs for Chinese consumers' ownership in these key product categories to be in personal computers (17 %) and automobiles (16 %). By contrast, we expect significantly lower CAGRs in the case of televisions (3 %), radios (4 %), fixed-line telephones (8 %) and mobile phone handsets (8 %), where the markets are already more mature, as well as air travel (8 %).

Finally, we provide estimates of the dates at which China is likely to surpass the US as the largest market for these consumer products. This has already occurred in the case of televisions (1991), mobile phone handsets (2001) and fixed-line telephones (2002). We project a date of 2011 for personal computers but later than 2020 for autos and air passenger numbers per annum.

Appendix C gives a summary of the product category projection, showing the product category density and GDP per capita relationships for the 15 selected countries.

TELEVISIONS

China already has the largest number of televisions of any country in the world, surpassing the US as long ago as 1991 (Figure 6.1). In 2004, China accounted for 34 % of televisions owned in the 15 countries we selected, followed by the US with 20 % (Figure 6.2). The number of televisions currently owned in China is nearly twice the number owned in the US.

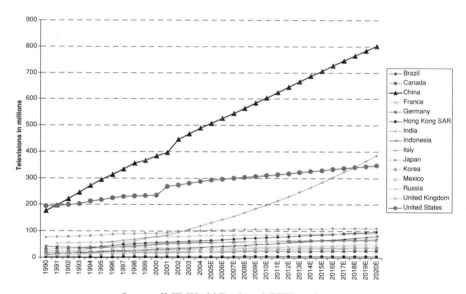

Source: IMF, World Bank and CSFB estimates

Figure 6.1   Number of televisions forecast for the 15 selected countries, 1990–2020E

By 2014, we estimate that China will account for 36 % of total ownership (Figure 6.3). We estimate a CAGR for the number of televisions owned of 3.4 % over the next 10 years, placing China in fourth place in terms of growth rate of ownership among the 15 countries, behind India, Indonesia and Korea (Figure 6.4). However,

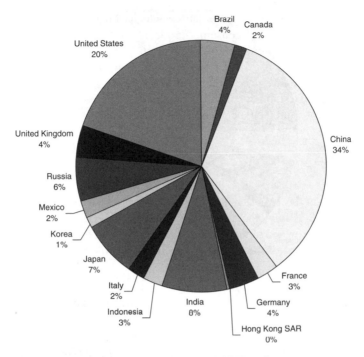

Source: IMF, World Bank and CSFB estimates
Figure 6.2   Percentage shares of televisions in the 15 selected countries in 2004E

in terms of absolute numbers of additional televisions owned, China will add 197 million, representing 41 % of additional product demand over the period.

Television ownership can be taken as a reasonable proxy for the demand for other larger ticket electrical goods items (for example, hi-fis and DVD players) for which comparable data are not readily available. The fact that China is already dominant in the global market for televisions also indicates the scale of the potential market opportunity in bigger ticket product items over time as well as the challenge for global firms to take advantage of that opportunity: the vast majority of televisions sold in China are made by locally owned firms.

MOBILE HANDSETS

Mobile telephony has taken a grip on China's mass population in urban areas at a dramatic rate. China has the largest number of mobile handsets of any country in the world, surpassing the US in 2001 (Figure 6.5). In 2004, we estimate that China accounted for 29 % of mobile handsets owned in the 15 selected countries, followed by the US with 17 % (Figure 6.6). The number of mobile handsets currently owned in China is more than the combined number owned in the US and Japan.

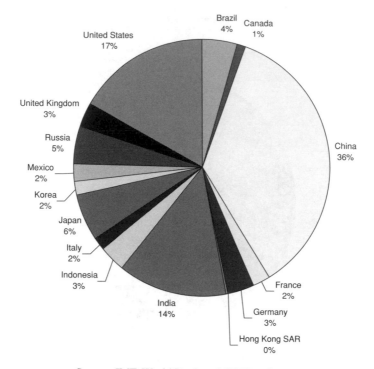

Source: IMF, World Bank and CSFB estimates
Figure 6.3   Percentage shares of televisions in the 15 selected countries in 2014E

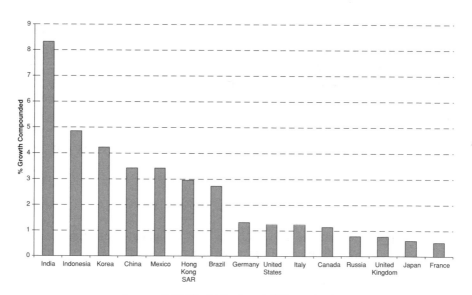

Source: IMF, World Bank and CSFB estimates
Figure 6.4   CAGRs of televisions forecast from 2004 to 2014E for the 15 selected countries

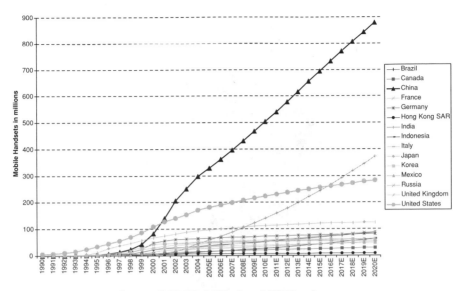

Source: IMF, World Bank and CSFB estimates

Figure 6.5   Number of mobile handsets forecast for the 15 selected countries, 1990–2020E

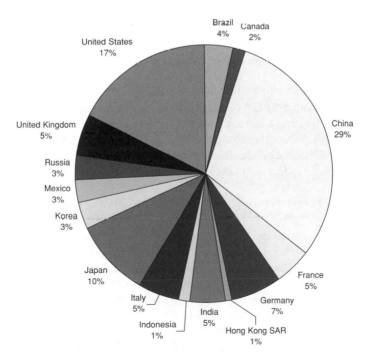

Source: IMF, World Bank and CSFB estimates

Figure 6.6   Percentage shares of mobile handsets in the 15 selected countries in 2004E

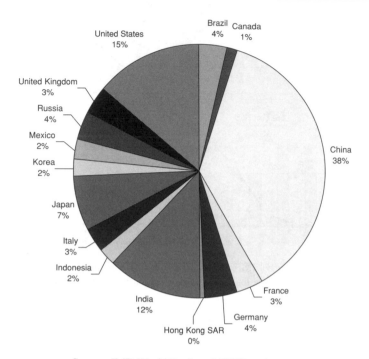

Source: IMF, World Bank and CSFB estimates
Figure 6.7   Percentage shares of mobile handsets in the 15 selected countries in 2014E

By 2014, we estimate that China will account for 38 % of total ownership (Figure 6.7). We estimate a CAGR of 8.2 % for the number of mobile handsets owned, placing China in fourth place in terms of growth rate of ownership among the 15 countries, behind India, Indonesia and Russia (Figure 6.8). However, in terms of absolute numbers of additional mobile handsets owned, China should add 358m, representing 44 % of additional product demand over the period.

FIXED-LINE TELEPHONY

China has the largest number of fixed telephone lines of any country in the world (Figure 6.9). In 2004, we estimate that China accounts for 29 % of fixed telephone lines in the 15 selected countries, with the US trailing with 21 % (Figure 6.10).

By 2014, we estimate China will account for 37 % of total ownership, followed by India with 15 % and the US with 14 % (Figure 6.11). We estimate a CAGR of 7.6 % for the number of fixed-line telephones in China between 2004 and 2014, placing China in third place in terms of the growth rate of ownership among the 15 countries, behind India and Indonesia (Figure 6.12). However, in terms of absolute numbers of additional fixed telephone lines, China should add 302m, representing 50 % of additional product demand over the period.

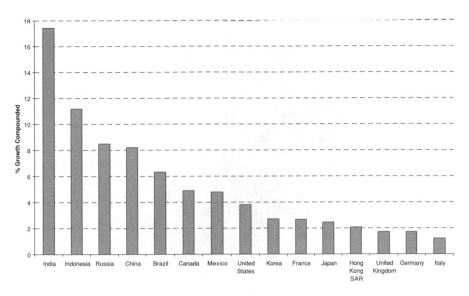

Source: IMF, World Bank and CSFB estimates

Figure 6.8 CAGRs of mobile handsets in the 15 selected countries in 2004E

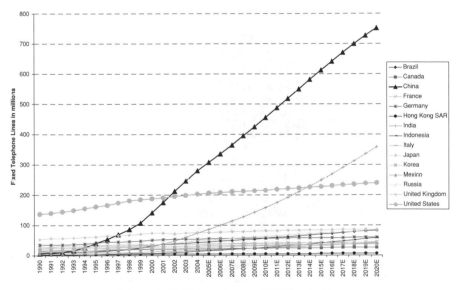

Source: IMF, World Bank and CSFB estimates

Figure 6.9 Number of fixed telephone lines forecast for the 15 selected countries, 1990–2020E

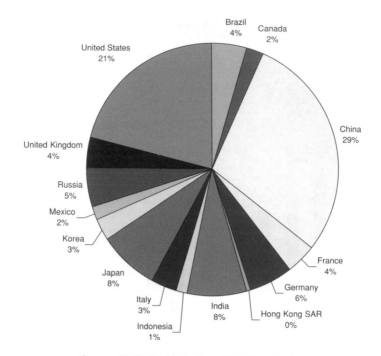

Source: IMF, World Bank and CSFB estimates

Figure 6.10   Percentage shares of fixed telephone lines in the 15 selected countries in 2004E

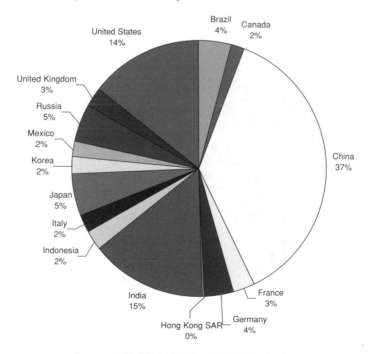

Source: IMF, World Bank and CSFB estimates

Figure 6.11   Percentage shares of fixed telephone lines in the 15 selected countries in 2014E

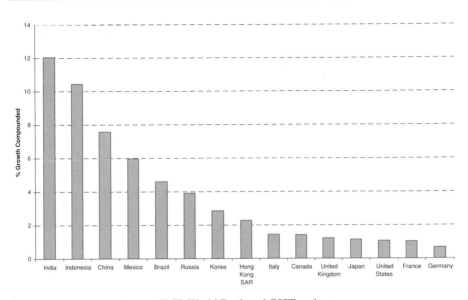

Source: IMF, World Bank and CSFB estimates
Figure 6.12 CAGRs of fixed telephone lines forecast from 2004 to 2014E for the 15 selected countries

PERSONAL COMPUTERS

China has the second-largest number of PCs of any country in the world (Figure 6.13). In 2004, we estimate that China accounts for 14 % of PCs in the 15 selected countries, ahead of Japan and Western European countries including France, Italy and the UK (Figure 6.14). The US accounts for 37 % of total ownership among the selected countries.

By 2014, we estimate that China will account for 32 % of total ownership, displacing the US as the leader (Figure 6.15). We estimate a CAGR of 16.8 % for the number of PCs in China from 2004 to 2014, placing China first in terms of the growth rate of ownership among the 15 countries (Figure 6.16). In terms of absolute numbers of additional PCs, China should add 308m, representing 48 % of additional product demand over the period.

However, this result may well be conservative as the historical data for uptake in ownership dates from a period when unit prices were substantially higher in real terms than they are today or are likely to be in the future. (In other words, the income level needed before one is able to buy a PC is falling constantly.) PC ownership can be taken as a reasonable proxy for the demand for other larger ticket electrical goods items (for example, flat-screen TV) for which comparable data are not readily available.

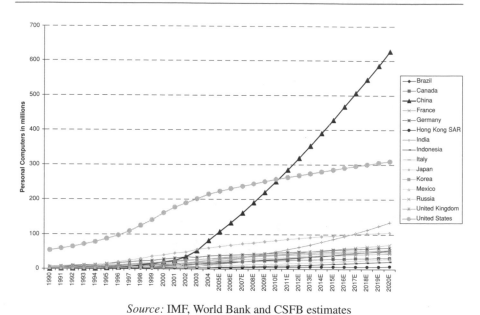

Source: IMF, World Bank and CSFB estimates
Figure 6.13   Number of personal computers forecast for the 15 selected countries, 1990–2020E

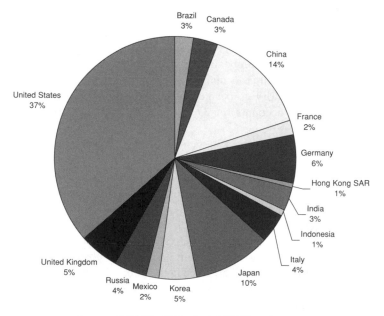

Source: IMF, World Bank and CSFB estimates
Figure 6.14   Percentage shares of personal computers in the 15 selected countries in 2004E

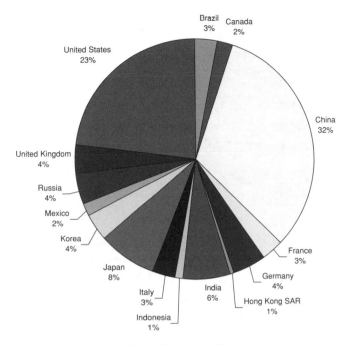

Source: IMF, World Bank and CSFB estimates

Figure 6.15 Percentage shares of personal computers in the 15 selected countries in 2014E

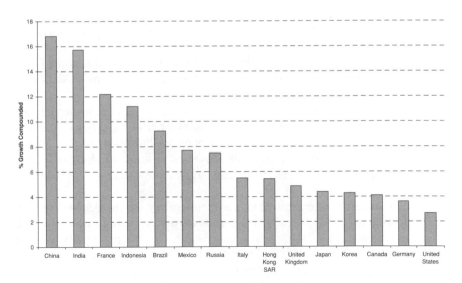

Source: IMF, World Bank and CSFB estimates

Figure 6.16 CAGRs of personal computers forecast from 2004 to 2014E for the 15 selected countries

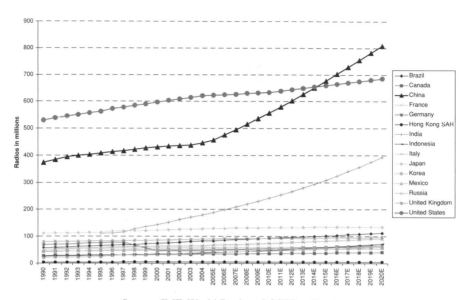

Source: IMF, World Bank and CSFB estimates
Figure 6.17   Number of radios forecast for the 15 selected countries, 1990–2020E

RADIOS

China has the second-largest number of radios of any country in the world (Figure 6.17). In 2004, we estimate that China accounts for 23 % of radios in the 15 selected countries, ahead of Japan and Western European countries including France, Italy and the UK (Figure 6.18). The US accounts for 32 % of total ownership among the selected countries.

By 2014, we estimate that China will account for 28 % of total ownership (Figure 6.19). We estimate a CAGR of 4 % for the number of radios owned, placing China in third place in terms of the growth rate of ownership among the 15 countries, behind India and Indonesia (Figure 6.20). However, in terms of absolute numbers of additional radios owned, China should add 211m, representing 46 % of additional product demand over the period.

Radio ownership can be taken as a reasonable proxy for the demand for other smaller ticket items that are already in widespread use (for example, newspapers and basic personal care products) for which comparable data are not readily available. The fact that China is already dominant in the global market for radios also indicates the scale of the potential market opportunity in bigger ticket product items over time, as well as the challenge for global firms to take advantage of that opportunity: the vast majority of radios sold in China are made by locally owned firms.

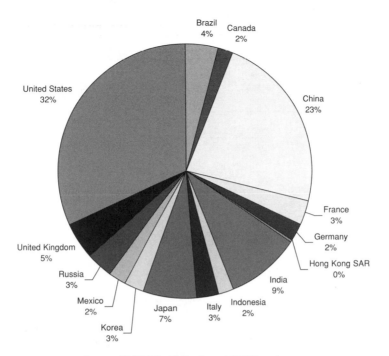

Source: IMF, World Bank and CSFB estimates

Figure 6.18   Percentage shares of radios in the 15 selected countries in 2004E

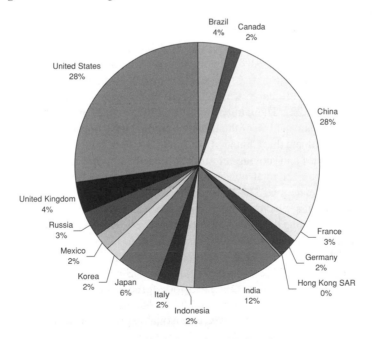

Source: IMF, World Bank and CSFB estimates

Figure 6.19   Percentage shares of radios in the 15 selected countries in 2014E

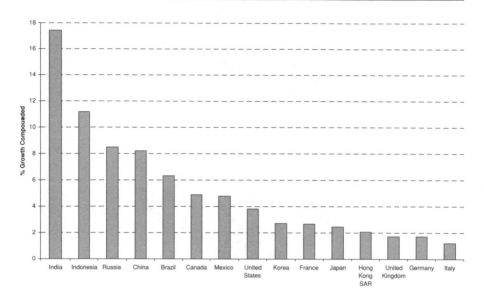

Source: IMF, World Bank and CSFB estimates

Figure 6.20   CAGRs of radios forecast from 2004 to 2014E for the 15 selected countries

AUTOS

Automobile ownership in China has accelerated dramatically in recent years although the market is currently sluggish following this year's credit-tightening measures (Figure 6.21). In 2004, we estimate China accounts for 2 % of automobiles owned in the 15 selected countries, similar to Korea and only just ahead of countries like India and Indonesia (Figure 6.22). The number of automobiles owned in both the US at 42 % of the total and Japan at 11 % of the total are significantly higher.

By 2014, we estimate that China will account for 6 % of total ownership, displacing most other countries and moving into fourth place behind the US (Figure 6.23). We project a 37 % share of total ownership for the US, 10 % for Japan and 8 % for Germany. We estimate a CAGR of 16.4 % for the number of automobiles in China over the next 10 years, placing China in first place ahead of India in terms of growth rate of ownership among the 15 countries (Figure 6.24). However, in terms of absolute numbers of additional automobiles, China is likely to be dominant – adding 29m – representing 27 % of additional product demand over the period.

On our projections, China will not displace the US as the market with the largest automobile numbers until after the end of our forecast horizon in 2020. However, China will have reached 72 % of the numbers of automobiles in the US by this time. Automobile ownership can be taken as a reasonable proxy for the demand for other bigger ticket discretionary spend items (for example, luxury good purchases and housing) for which comparable data are not readily available.

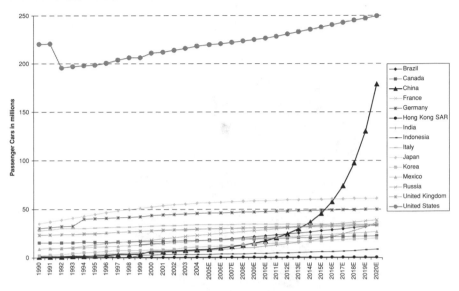

Source: IMF, World Bank and CSFB estimates

Figure 6.21   Number of passenger cars forecast for the 15 selected countries, 1990–2020E

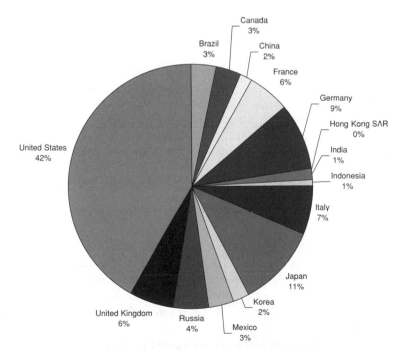

Source: IMF, World Bank and CSFB estimates

Figure 6.22   Percentage shares of passenger cars in the 15 selected countries in 2004E

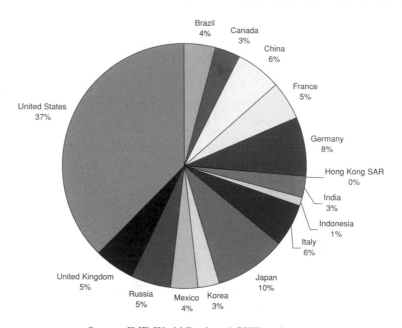

Source: IMF, World Bank and CSFB estimates
Figure 6.23   Percentage shares of passenger cars in the 15 selected countries in 2014E

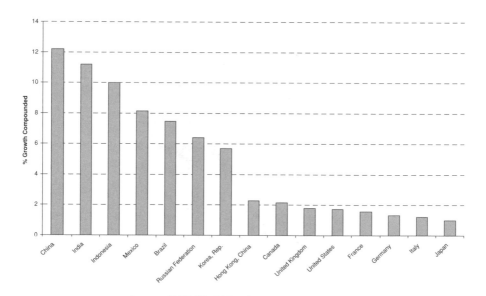

Source: IMF, World Bank and CSFB estimates
Figure 6.24   CAGRs of passenger cars forecast from 2004E to 2014E for the 15 selected countries

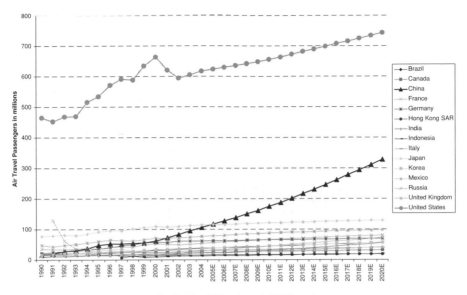

Source: IMF, World Bank and CSFB estimates
Figure 6.25   Number of air passengers forecast for the 15 selected countries, 1990–2020E

AIR TRAVEL

Figure 6.25 shows that historically and currently air travel has been dominated by the US. Despite the relatively high income of their citizens, the growth in air passenger numbers per annum in Western Europe and Japan has been slower than in the US, owing to their smaller land surface areas and smaller distances between major cities.

In 2004, we estimate that China accounts for 8 % of air passenger numbers among the 15 selected countries, slightly behind Japan and ahead of the UK (Figure 6.26). The number of air passenger numbers in the US is 50 % of the total while Japan is in second place at 9 % of the total.

By 2014, we estimate that China will account for 14 % of total air passenger numbers, displacing Japan and moving into second place behind the US with a projected 44 % of total passenger numbers (Figure 6.27). We estimate a CAGR of 8 % for the number of air passengers in China over the period, placing China in first place ahead of Russia and India in terms of growth rate of air travel among the 15 countries (Figure 6.28). However, in terms of absolute numbers of additional air passengers, China should add 124m, representing 36 % of additional product demand over the period.

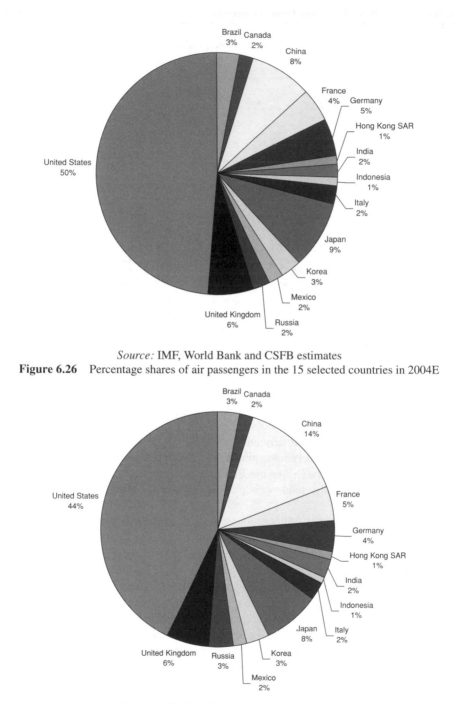

Source: IMF, World Bank and CSFB estimates

Figure 6.26   Percentage shares of air passengers in the 15 selected countries in 2004E

Source: IMF, World Bank and CSFB estimates

Figure 6.27   Percentage shares of air passengers in the 15 selected countries in 2014E

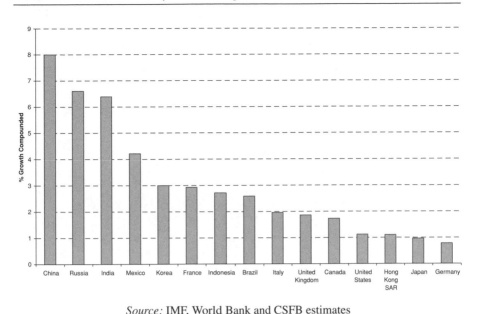

Source: IMF, World Bank and CSFB estimates
Figure 6.28 CAGRs of air passengers forecast from 2004 to 2014E for the 15 selected countries

On our projections, China will not displace the US as the market with the largest air passenger numbers – even by 2020. China will have only reached 44 % of the US in terms of air travel passengers by this time. Air passenger numbers can be taken as a reasonable proxy for the demand for other bigger ticket discretionary spend items. Although we would expect the majority of air travel to be within China's own borders, there is likely to be a rapid associate growth in international travel for leisure purposes.

Section 2
EVIDENCE

7
Introducing the Proprietary China Consumer Survey

Section 2 summarises the conclusions from a proprietary survey of Chinese consumer lifestyle and spending patterns undertaken in September 2004. We organise our discussion of the survey by sector by first presenting in this chapter the main conclusions from the survey for that sector before discussing the implications for the business strategies and performance of the major participants in the sector (both local and foreign).

SURVEY INTRODUCTION

Our survey was designed to capture information regarding the spending pattern and general lifestyle of the Chinese consumer. The survey data are proprietary to CSFB and based on interviews with 2700 people in eight major Chinese cities in the second half of September 2004. The survey collected individual and household level data on a broad range of products and services as well as more general information on income and attitudes. Products and services covered include:

- Autos
- Beverages
- Electronics goods
- Food producers
- Food retail
- Food services
- Household and personal care
- Luxury goods
- Telecom equipment
- Tobacco
- Transport and travel

Integrating the conclusions of Section 1 with the survey results of Section 2 we identify in each industry section those global corporations that, in our view, currently have leadership positions in exposure to the rise of the Chinese consumer. For some of these companies China currently represents a small percentage of revenues only versus their US, European and Japanese businesses. However, relative to their competitors, in our view they are making the strategic moves to benefit if the thesis of our piece is correct.

The interview method used was CATI (computer aided telephone interviewing). This is a special form of telephone interview using a pre-programmed questionnaire on a computer. The questionnaire guides the interviewer through the interview process. The telephone numbers are randomly generated by the computer telephone directory database with a quota control (explained later). This is known as random-digit dialling, which is part of the CATI system. The benefits provided by this method are: greater sample randomness and representation of the population; full automation of questionnaire and data entry; quantitative data analysis can be performed; and better fieldwork management. The latter is achieved through the ability to monitor easily the track records of all calls made via central workstations of the supervisors (Figure 7.1). Serious errors can arise from questionnaire design faults. These were, to our knowledge, corrected during pilot tests in Beijing.

- **Topology of CATI system**

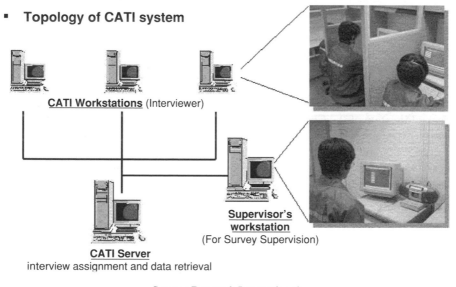

Source: Research International
Figure 7.1   The network of CATI systems used in our survey

The fieldwork was conducted in four Research International offices that have installed CATI stations: Beijing, Guangzhou, Shanghai and Chengdu. This regional dispersion was vital in overcoming the barriers of different dialects within China.

Eight cities are covered in the survey (Table 7.1). Two types of cities were surveyed: Tier 1 and Tier 2. Tier 1 cities were the largest in number and most highly developed. Tier 2 cities were smaller in size and less developed than Tier 1 cities. The sample sizes in each were 400 and 300, respectively.

Table 7.1   Cities surveyed and sample sizes.

	Location in China[a]	Sample size ($N = 2700$ district)
Tier 1 cities		1500
Beijing	North	400[c]
Shanghai	East	400
Guangzhou	South	400
Shenzhen[b]	South	300
Tier 2 cities		1200
Shenyang	Northeast	300[c]
Chengdu	Southeast	300
Xi'an	Northwest	300
Wuhan	Central	300

[a] The selected cities are geographically representative.

[b] Shenzhen is a small-sized but highly developed city.

[c] Maximum sampling error for 300 samples is 5.66 % and 4.90 % for 400 samples at 95 % confidence level.

Source: CSFB research.

Setting quotas of age and gender achieved representative samples of the cities surveyed. The demographic quotas were based on the official census data of the China Statistical Bureau, shown in Table 7.2. The results are weighted back to the total population of each city.

Table 7.2   Demographic quotas set for cities surveyed.

		Gender (%)		Age (%)			
	Total	Male	Female	20–29	30–39	40–49	50–59
Beijing	400	51	49	27	30	27	15
Shanghai	400	50	50	24	24	32	21
Guangzhou	400	51	49	29	34	22	14
Shenzhen	300	53	47	29	34	22	15
Shenyang	300	50	50	22	33	28	17
Chengdu	300	51	49	23	35	21	20
Xi'an	300	52	48	23	34	25	18
Wuhan	300	52	48	20	33	27	20
Total	2700	51	49	25	32	26	17

Source: China Statistical Yearbook and CSFB research.

Target respondents were local city residents aged 20–59. The income threshold for our survey qualification was RMB 1500 or more for Tier 1 cities and RMB 1000 or more for Tier 2 cities. This value is the after-tax monthly income including bonuses for their households. Low-income households were therefore excluded. If not stated otherwise, all percentage data in this report are based on this redefined sample frame instead of on the total population. In particular, our survey does not cover the large migrant worker populations present in these cities.

Respondents who work or have family members/close friends working for marketing/market research/media/ PR (public relations) companies were disqualified. Those who work or have family members/ close friends working for related industries skip the corresponding industry sections. The respondent's qualification for the survey was determined via a set of screening questions.

All interviews were carried out from 16:30 to 22:00 on weekdays and all day on weekends to ensure representative samples. People who stay at home in the daytime tend to be unemployed or self-employed, thus interviewing in the daytime of working days would have generated a biased sample structure. Interviewers dialled telephone numbers generated randomly from CATI programs. No-answer numbers were pursued three times on five-minute intervals before abandonment.

Interviewers introduced themselves to the respondents and briefly explained the objectives of the market research. CSFB's identity was kept confidential.

Screening questions were asked of respondents who were willing to cooperate. Qualified respondents continued to the main questionnaire. Only fully complete interviews were accepted as successful interviews. All respondents who completed the full interview were incentivised by a prize draw organised by Research International. Respondent reliability had an impact on the validity of the results.

Misinterpretation and false communication are potentially major limitations to the analysis. For example, inflated incomes could not be adjusted and taken at face value. However bias, reticence and misinterpretation were removed by screening

Table 7.3 Abbreviations.

Full	Abbreviation
Beijing	BJ
Shanghai	SH
Guangzhou	GZ
Shenzhen	SZ
Shenyang	SY
Wuhan	WH
Chengdu	CD
Xi' an	XA
Next 1 year/next 3 years	N1Y/N3Y
Last 3 years	L3Y

Source: CSFB research.

questions and a trained interviewer. All dial-out attempts, including the successful and unsuccessful interviews, were recorded and categorised in the CATI Disposition Reports.

A total of 24 512 residents were contacted to conduct 2700 successful interviews, with a 13 % success rate. Rejections (immediate and midway) were the largest source of failing interviews (67 %). The average successful interview length was 33 minutes.

The maximum sampling error for cities with 300 interviews was 5.66 % and 4.90 % for cities with 400 interviews (both at 95 % confidence level).

The abbreviations used in the report for the cities and timeframes are listed in Table 7.3.

8
General: Lifestyle, Income and Leverage

We found in our survey that the average permanent resident Chinese urban household in the eight cities surveyed currently has 3.4 members. Of these 2.2 are working (Figure 8.1).

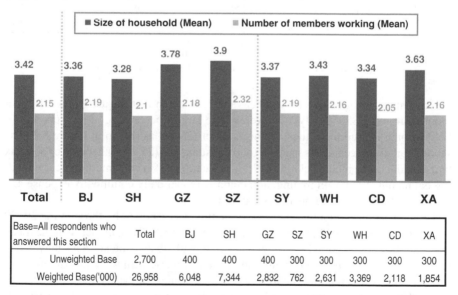

Base=All respondents who answered this section	Total	BJ	SH	GZ	SZ	SY	WH	CD	XA
Unweighted Base	2,700	400	400	400	300	300	300	300	300
Weighted Base('000)	26,958	6,048	7,344	2,832	762	2,631	3,369	2,118	1,854

Source: CSFB research

Figure 8.1   Average size of household and number of working members

Average after-tax household income is RMB 4486 per month (see Figure 8.2). There is significant disparity between household incomes in the different cities. Shenzhen has the highest value of all eight cities at RMB 8727 per month (over US$1000 at

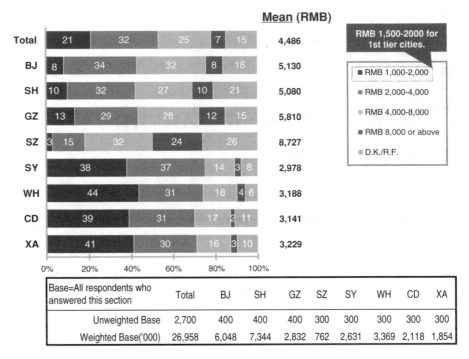

Source: CSFB research
Figure 8.2   Average monthly household after-tax income by city

the current exchange rate) while Shenyang has the lowest at just RMB 2978 per month (around US$350 only). On average the largest percentage of post-tax household income is used in savings and investment (26 %), as shown in Figure 8.3. The second-largest percentage is spent on food consumption (25 %). Other uses of post-tax household income include clothing (9 %), education (8 %) and entertainment including eating out (8 %). Commuting, home and personal daily commodity expense and mortgage debt service are on average all below 4 %.

The highest mean monthly household income was reported by those in the 20–29 age bracket at RMB 5308, as shown in Figure 8.4. This is 37 % higher than the mean household income reported by respondents in the 40–49 age bracket. This may be the result of younger respondents continuing to live at home with working parents.

Interestingly, the reported savings rate is also highest in the 20–29 age bracket at 30 % of household income (see Figure 8.5). It is lowest in the 40–49 age bracket at 22 %. Younger households tend to spend more on entertainment and eating out (between 8 % and 10 % of household income in the 20–29 and 30–39 age brackets) as well as on education. Older households tend to spend more on education (particularly in the 40–49 age bracket with the beneficiary presumably being the child in the household).

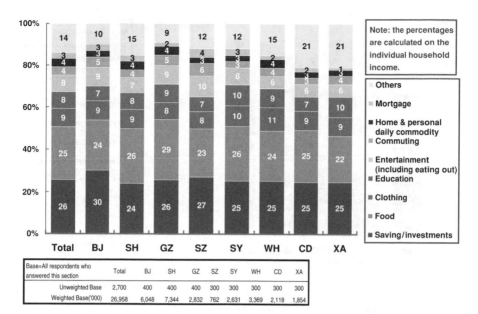

Source: Company data and CSFB estimates
Figure 8.3   Spending of household income by city

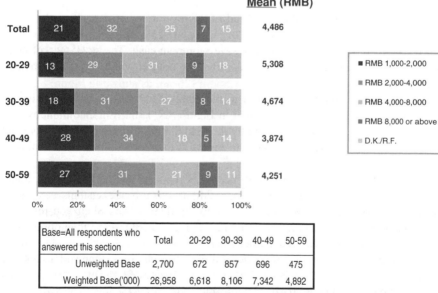

Source: CSFB research
Figure 8.4   Average monthly household after-tax income by age

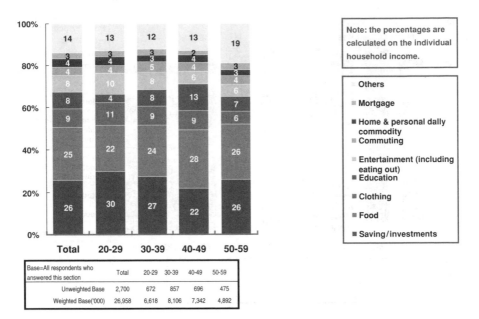

Source: Company data and CSFB estimates

Figure 8.5   Spending of household income by age

We find that the most popular method of saving money is deposits in bank accounts (81 % of all households), shown in Figure 8.6. Life insurance is used by 33 %
of households to save money and 31 % save money in cash. The stock market, trea-
sury bill and mutual fund products in contrast are not yet widely used as a savings
mechanism.

Bank account penetration is highest in the 20–29 age bracket (89 %) and lowest
in the 50–59 age bracket (74 %), shown in Figure 8.7. Life insurance policies tend
to be used more frequently for saving by those in the middle age brackets. Those in
the 40–49 age bracket are most likely to invest in the stock market or own mutual
funds.

Average after-tax monthly personal income is reported at RMB 2013 per month
for all cities (see Figure 8.8) or around US$240 at the current exchange rate. At the
household level there is a significant skew to the distribution. Shenzhen residents
report the highest personal income of RMB 3101 per month, more than double that
reported by residents of Xi'an and Shenyang.

In the four Tier 1 cities 18 % of residents report income of less than RMB 1000 per
month and 46 % less than RMB 2000. By contrast, over 30 % of Tier 2 city residents
have income of less than RMB 1000 per month and over 70 % less than RMB 2000.
At the other end of the income spectrum 11 % of respondents in Shenzhen and 7 % of
those in Shanghai reported personal incomes of over RMB 5000 per month (US$600).

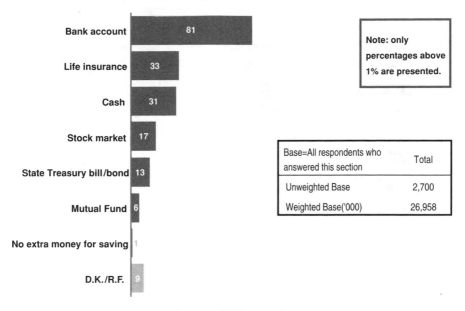

Base=All respondents who answered this section	Total
Unweighted Base	2,700
Weighted Base('000)	26,958

Source: CSFB research

Figure 8.6 Methods of saving money

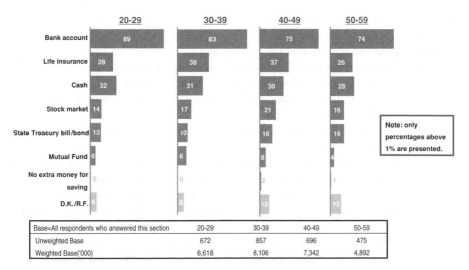

Base=All respondents who answered this section	20-29	30-39	40-49	50-59
Unweighted Base	672	857	696	475
Weighted Base('000)	6,618	8,106	7,342	4,892

Source: CSFB research

Figure 8.7 Methods for saving money by age

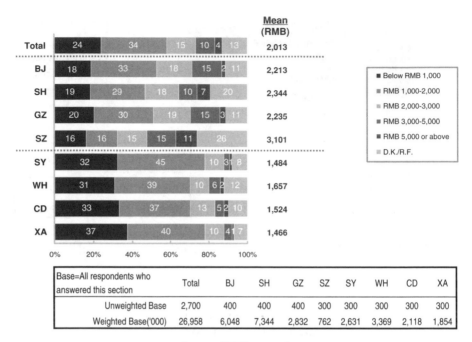

Source: CSFB research
Figure 8.8   Average monthly personal after-tax income by city

By contrast fewer than 2 % of all respondents reported incomes above this level in the four Tier 2 cities and – surprisingly – in the capital city Beijing.

Crucially our survey finds that younger respondents reported higher incomes, probably due to their greater participation in the globally integrated manufacturing and services industries. At the personal level mean income was reported as highest in the 30–39 age bracket at RMB 2348, some 46 % above the income reported in the 50–59 age bracket, as shown in Figure 8.9.

We find that personal income has increased on average by 23.8 % in the last three years (see Figure 8.10). In real terms this represents a gain of 18 %. This is direct empirical evidence for the theoretical conclusion – as discussed in Section 1 above – that global factor price equalisation is tending to push up real wages in China. On average over the sample, respondents expect their personal incomes to rise by 19 % over the next three years (see Figure 8.11), with the highest gain expected in Shenzhen (25 %).

Younger survey respondents report a more rapid growth rate of income in the last three years than older respondents. Those in the 20–29 age bracket report a mean income growth of 33 % over the last three years versus just 9 % growth for those in

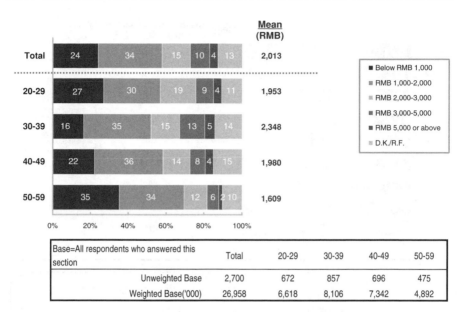

Source: CSFB research

Figure 8.9   Average monthly personal after-tax income by age

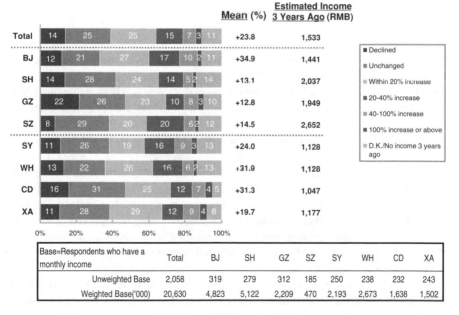

Source: CSFB research

Figure 8.10   Average monthly personal income change in the last three years by city

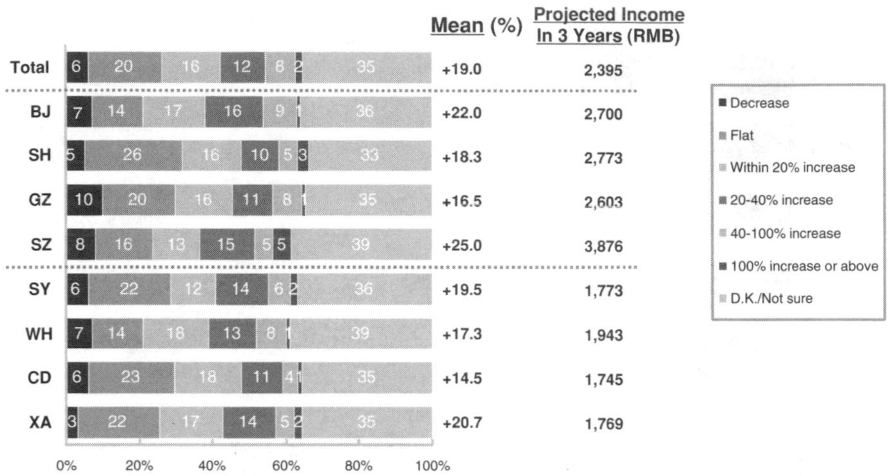

Base=Respondents who have a monthly income	Total	BJ	SH	GZ	SZ	SY	WH	CD	XA
Unweighted Base	2,058	319	279	312	185	250	238	232	243
Weighted Base('000)	20,630	4,823	5,122	2,209	470	2,193	2,673	1,638	1,502

Source: CSFB research

Figure 8.11 Expected average monthly personal income change in the next three years by city

the 50–59 age bracket (see Figure 8.12). Younger respondents are also more confident about their future income growth potential. Those in the 20–29 age bracket expect their monthly personal income on average to rise by 37 % in the next three years versus an expectation of just 5 % for those in the 50–59 age bracket (see Figure 8.13).

Our survey also finds evidence that labour is beginning to be priced by market forces and in particular in accordance with educational attainment. Figure 8.14 shows that those of our respondents who have a university-level qualification have experienced on average a 30 % increase in personal income over the last 3 years. This compares with just 9 % for those with an attainment of junior high school or below. Meanwhile, those individuals who identify themselves as self-employed or company owners have experienced on average a 58 % increase in personal income versus just 15 % for those without a job (either unemployed or student). Meanwhile, Figure 8.15 shows that expectations for future income growth over the next 3 years are also positively correlated with educational attainment. It seems that the market is starting to price labour within the Chinese economy with rewards accruing for education and entrepreneurship. This is a hugely positive development towards greater economic efficiency.

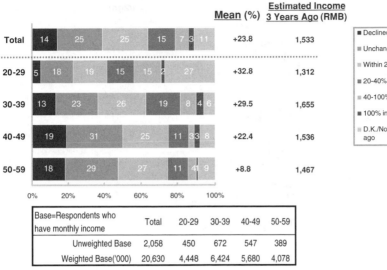

Source: CSFB research

Figure 8.12   Average monthly personal income change in the last three years by age

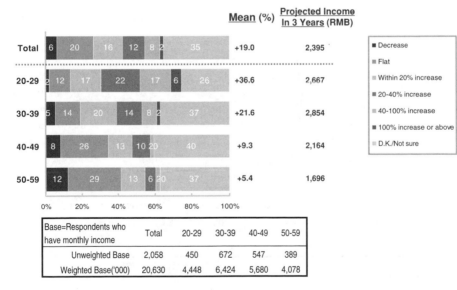

Source: CSFB research

Figure 8.13   Expected average monthly personal income change in the next three years by age

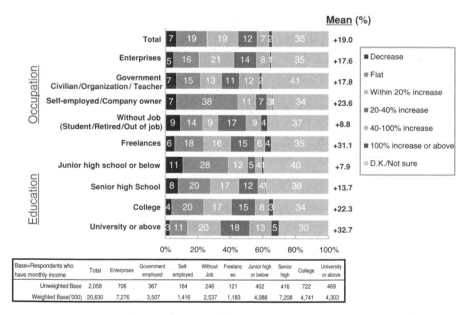

Mean (%)

Total	14 25 25 15 7 3 11	+23.8
Enterprises	13 27 27 14 6 2 10	+19.3
Government Civilian/Organization/ Teacher	7 19 30 19 12 2 11	+29.8
Self-employed/Company owner	16 19 18 18 12 5 13	+57.7
Without Job (Student/Retired/Out of job)	26 32 19 7 4 2 11	+14.5
Freelances	23 25 19 12 8 6 6	+21.1
Junior high school or below	20 33 23 9 5 1 10	+9.2
Senior high School	17 26 26 13 5 3 11	+28.4
College	9 24 27 15 11 2 13	+23.9
University or above	7 18 22 23 12 5 15	+30.3

Legend: ■ Declined ■ Unchanged ■ Within 20% increase ■ 20-40% increase ■ 40-100% increase ■ 100% increase or above ■ D.K./No income 3years ago

0% 20% 40% 60% 80% 100%

Base=Respondents who have monthly income	Total	Enterprises	Government employed	Self-employed	Without Job	Freelances	Junior high or below	Senior high	College	University or above
Unweighted Base	2,058	706	367	164	246	121	402	416	722	469
Weighted Base('000)	20,630	7,276	3,507	1,416	2,537	1,183	4,088	7,208	4,741	4,303

Source: Company data and CSFB estimates

Figure 8.14   Estimated personal income increase over the L3Y by occupation and education

Mean (%)

Total	7 19 19 12 7 2 35	+19.0
Enterprises	5 16 21 14 8 1 35	+17.6
Government Civilian/Organization/ Teacher	7 15 13 11 12 2 41	+17.8
Self-employed/Company owner	7 38 11 7 3 34	+23.6
Without Job (Student/Retired/Out of job)	9 14 9 17 9 4 37	+8.8
Freelances	6 18 16 15 6 4 35	+31.1
Junior high school or below	11 28 12 5 4 40	+7.9
Senior high School	8 20 17 12 4 38	+13.7
College	4 20 17 15 8 3 34	+22.3
University or above	3 11 20 18 13 5 30	+32.7

Legend: ■ Decrease ■ Flat ■ Within 20% increase ■ 20-40% increase ■ 40-100% increase ■ 100% increase or above ■ D.K./Not sure

0% 20% 40% 60% 80% 100%

Base=Respondents who have monthly income	Total	Enterprises	Government employed	Self-employed	Without Job	Freelances	Junior high or below	Senior high	College	University or above
Unweighted Base	2,058	706	367	164	246	121	402	416	722	469
Weighted Base('000)	20,630	7,276	3,507	1,416	2,537	1,183	4,088	7,208	4,741	4,303

Source: Company data and CSFB estimates

Figure 8.15   Expected personal income increase over N3Y by occupation and education

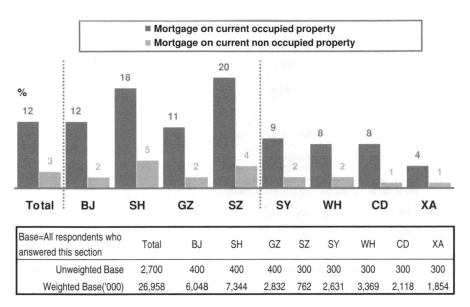

Base=All respondents who answered this section	Total	BJ	SH	GZ	SZ	SY	WH	CD	XA
Unweighted Base	2,700	400	400	400	300	300	300	300	300
Weighted Base('000)	26,958	6,048	7,344	2,832	762	2,631	3,369	2,118	1,854

Source: CSFB research

Figure 8.16   Proportion of respondents with mortgages on currently occupied/nonoccupied property

Our survey finds that 12 % of households have a mortgage on currently occupied properties (see Figure 8.16). While 3 % have mortgages on nonoccupied properties. For those who have a mortgage, servicing payments account for 22.7 % of the average monthly household income (see Figure 8.17). The highest mortgage density is found in Shenzhen (20 %) and Shanghai (18 %). Mortgage density is relatively low compared with countries such as the US and UK due to the nature of the mass privatisation of housing in the late 1990s. Much of the housing stock was transferred on an un-leveraged basis to citizens who had previously rented from the state or state-owned enterprises. Hence, it appears that mortgage debt has only been taken on by those households trading up to larger-sized accommodation in the more expensive cities.

Of all the households owning private cars, 7 % have auto loans (see Figure 8.18). For those who have them, auto loan service payments account for 22.4 % of their average monthly household income (see Figure 8.19).

Our survey finds that mean ownership of debit cards is 1.1 per person. On average the first debit card was acquired 4.4 years ago, as shown in Figures 8.20 and 8.21. However, 55 % of respondents have yet to acquire a debit card. Ownership of credit cards is 0.4 per person with, on average, the first card acquired 3.3 years ago, as shown in Figures 8.22 and 8.23. Of respondents 73 % have yet to acquire a credit card, rising to as high as 85 % in Chengdu and Shenyang.

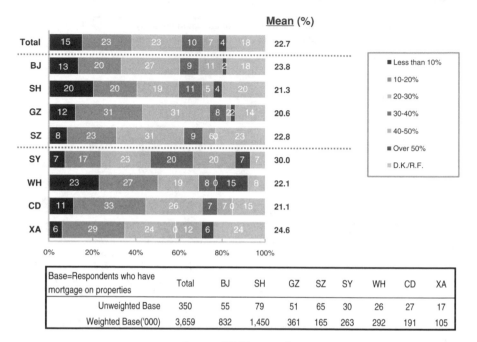

Source: CSFB research

Figure 8.17 Percentage of average monthly household income spent on mortgage payments

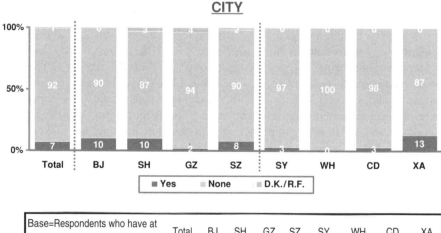

Source: CSFB research

Figure 8.18 Proportion of respondents with auto loans

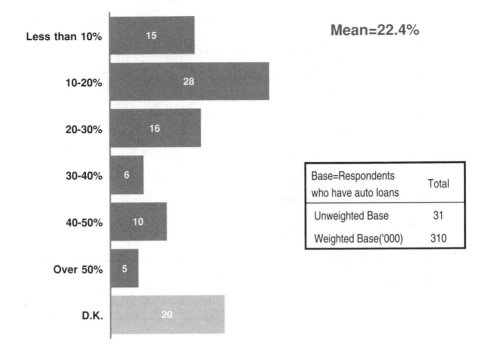

Mean=22.4%

Base=Respondents who have auto loans	Total
Unweighted Base	31
Weighted Base('000)	310

Source: CSFB research

Figure 8.19   Percentage of average monthly household income spent on auto loan payments

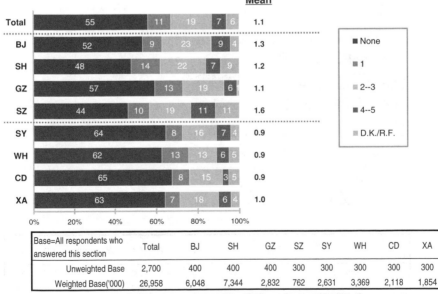

Base=All respondents who answered this section	Total	BJ	SH	GZ	SZ	SY	WH	CD	XA
Unweighted Base	2,700	400	400	400	300	300	300	300	300
Weighted Base('000)	26,958	6,048	7,344	2,832	762	2,631	3,369	2,118	1,854

Source: CSFB research

Figure 8.20   Number of debit cards owned by city

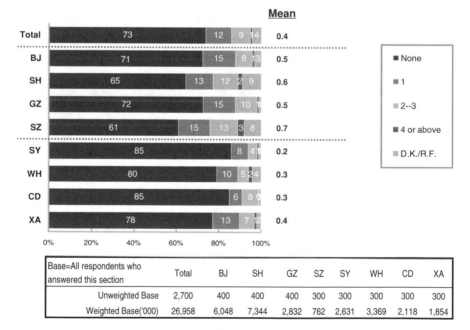

Mean
(years)

	Less than 1 year ago	1-3 years ago	3-5 years ago	5-8 years ago	8 years ago or longer	D.K./R.F.	Mean (years)
Total	6	20	18	19	11	26	4.4
BJ	5	21	22	23	10	19	4.4
SH	5	17	19	17	7	35	4.2
GZ	7	15	11	16	28	22	5.3
SZ	4	16	17	17	12	33	4.7
SY	6	22	14	20	13	26	4.5
WH	9	22	19	17	5	26	3.7
CD	5	26	18	17	10	25	4.1
XA	5	29	26	15	10	15	4.0

Base=Respondents who have at least 1 debit card	Total	BJ	SH	GZ	SZ	SY	WH	CD	XA
Unweighted Base	1,181	191	210	170	169	109	115	105	112
Weighted Base('000)	12,057	2,888	3,856	1,204	429	956	1,291	741	692

Source: CSFB research
Figure 8.21   Acquisition of first debit card by city

Mean

	None	1	2--3	4 or above	D.K./R.F.	Mean
Total	73	12	9		14	0.4
BJ	71	15	8		13	0.5
SH	65	13	12	2	9	0.6
GZ	72	15	10		1	0.5
SZ	61	15	13	3	8	0.7
SY	85	8	4	1		0.2
WH	80	10	5	2	4	0.3
CD	85	6	8			0.3
XA	78	13	7		2	0.4

Base=All respondents who answered this section	Total	BJ	SH	GZ	SZ	SY	WH	CD	XA
Unweighted Base	2,700	400	400	400	300	300	300	300	300
Weighted Base('000)	26,958	6,048	7,344	2,832	762	2,631	3,369	2,118	1,854

Source: CSFB research
Figure 8.22   Number of credit cards owned by city

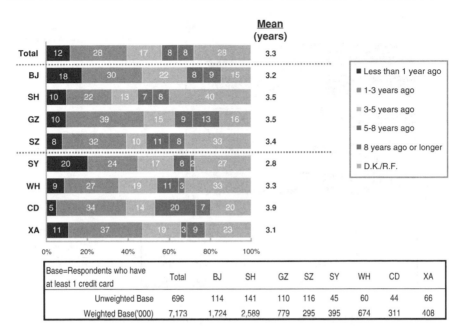

Source: CSFB research
Figure 8.23 Acquisition of first credit card by city

Debit card ownership is inversely correlated with age. Of those in the 50–59 age bracket 74 % reported nonownership versus only 43 % of those in the 20–29 age bracket (see Figure 8.24). Credit card ownership is also inversely correlated with age. Of those in the 50–59 age bracket 83 % reported nonownership versus only 69 % in the 20–29 age bracket (see Figure 8.25). Multiple-card ownership is also largely a younger person's phenomenon, with 15 % of those in the 20–29 age bracket reporting having two or more credit cards versus just 5 % of those in the 50–59 age bracket.

Perhaps surprisingly we find there is relatively little variation by city in the timing of acquisition of a first debit card (Figure 8.21) or credit card (Figure 8.23) although the debit card product does appear to have become prevalent somewhat earlier in Guangzhou and Shenzhen. However, we do find that on average over the sample the first debit card was acquired somewhat earlier than the credit card (4.4 years versus 3.3 years). Meanwhile, those in the 40–49 age group have on average owned both debit and credit cards for longest (4.9 years and 4.1 years, respectively – see Figures 8.26 and 8.27) while those in the 20–29 age group have acquired them more recently (3.8 years and 2.5 years).

For those who have debit cards or credit cards, out of every 100 payments, our survey finds that 82.7 are by cash, 10.0 by debit cards and 7.4 by credit cards (see Figure 8.28). We found that hypermarkets (35 %) and department stores (35 %) are the most common locations to pay with either debit or credit cards, as shown in Figure 8.29.

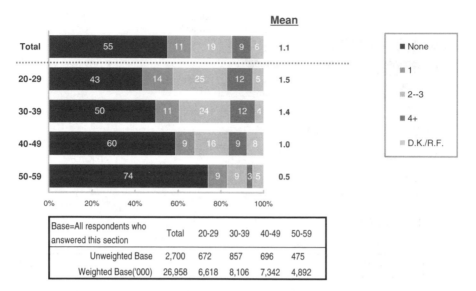

Source: CSFB research

Figure 8.24   Number of debit cards owned by age

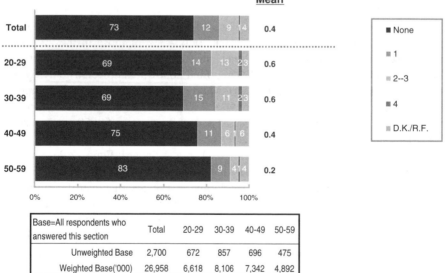

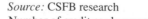

Source: CSFB research

Figure 8.25   Number of credit cards owned by age

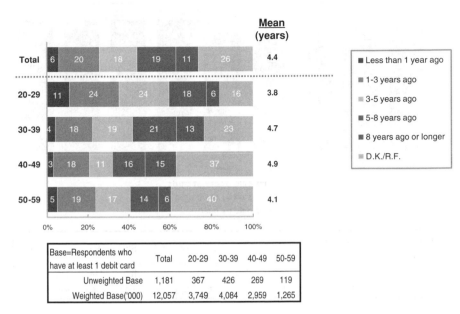

Source: CSFB research

Figure 8.26   Acquisition of first debit card by age

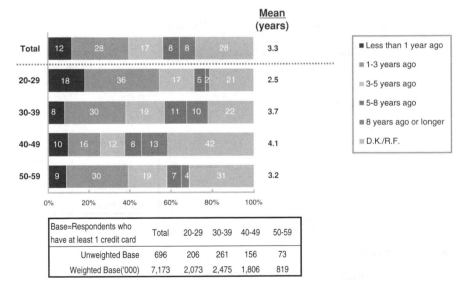

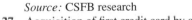

Source: CSFB research

Figure 8.27   Acquisition of first credit card by age

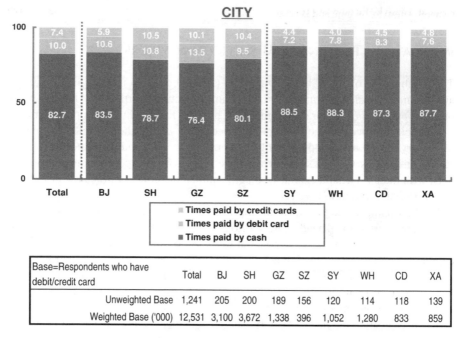

Source: CSFB research

Figure 8.28 Percentages of financial transactions made with different types of payment

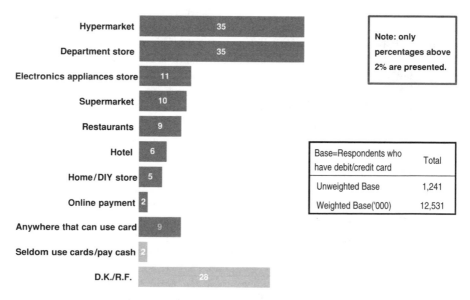

Source: CSFB research

Figure 8.29 Locations where debit/credit cards are used most often

IMPLICATIONS FOR FINANCIAL SERVICES PROVIDERS[1]

The combination of a very high saving ratio (26 % of post-tax income on our survey) and an underdeveloped financial services infrastructure (particularly for fee-based products) suggests a major opportunity in China for financial services providers.

Financial services for consumers have been long constrained, limited to being a repository for the tremendous savings power of the people and facilitator of (largely cash) transactions. China's state-owned banks were to finance production, not individuals, with their very names, industrial and commercial, construction and agriculture, signifying their function.

Not surprisingly, the first wave of improved consumer financial services has been focused on transactional needs. The development of efficient nationwide money transfers and debit cards (with 45 % penetration based on our survey and 1.1 cards per capita on average) meet this immediate and practical need. A transactional bank account is at the core of the financial services relationship and 81 % of households see a bank account as their most likely saving vehicle. This is a relatively high bank account penetration for an emerging market.

These basic banking needs are dominated by the local banks and should be among the highest potential sources of profitability. They are likely to remain profitable and local as the market opens.

While the bank account dominates saving needs, life insurers (China Life and Ping An are among the most prominent) seem to have built strong awareness as a savings option, with 33 % of households seeing this as a likely savings vehicle. However, in our view, they need to do a better job of selling protection products. The insurers remain well ahead of mutual funds (6 %) as a likely home for savings. It is perhaps surprising that direct stock market equity ownership is reported at 17 % given its volatile performance.

We conclude that there is a wide-open field for banks to offer more in the way of wealth management products, insurers to build on current awareness and specialists in areas such as mutual funds to create a franchise.

Conservatism and awareness of risk seems to be a feature of current behaviour but new savings and investment options have a strong base from which to grow. That caution points to a huge investment required for new entrants and foreign players to build a brand and image of reliability in the mind of the Chinese financial consumer. Only a small number of international firms (Citigroup, HSBC and AIG have a strong lead) have any depth of recognition.

The large cities of China have reached levels of income where consumer finance typically starts to grow significantly. Our survey looked at auto loans and credit cards, likely to be the two largest segments.

Only 7 % of car owners have financed their car but of those that do it takes on average 22.4 % of monthly household income. Car ownership is a spreading luxury.

[1] Bill Stacey contributed to this section.

Financing of autos has a long way to develop, with auto dealers' captive finance operations well placed, but banks and specialist providers are also likely to be options. We would expect that difficulty in managing security and uncertain residual values, as the second-hand car market is immature, will constrain foreign involvement in auto financing.

In contrast the credit card market has been a favoured entry point. HSBC and Citigroup have targeted this market with their partners in their first attempts to build their consumer operations in the country. GE Money, AIG and Standard Chartered are likely to follow based on our assessment of their strategic priorities.

These new entrants front into a market where our survey indicates credit card penetration is 27 %, there are 0.4 cards per customer and credit or debit cards are used for 17 in every 100 payments. The fairly wide use of debit cards points to potential for explosive growth in the credit card market, driven by convenience, reward schemes and access to a credit facility. We see a relatively liberal attitude to foreign involvement in the card market from authorities that are keen to ensure that the best skills globally are accessed to avoid excess growth, credit problems and further pressure on domestic banks.

Our survey results are broadly in line with an ACNielsen study in August 2004 which reported that the credit card penetration rate in the three cities it surveyed (Beijing, Shanghai and Guangzhou) rose to 22 % from 18 % a year ago. (The ACNielsen survey was conducted via telephone interviews with 2700 respondents from the three cities between the ages of 18 and 54.) The highest penetration was found in Guangzhou at 25 %, with Beijing at 23 % and Shanghai at the lowest with 21 %. ACNielson found that ownership of credit cards was highest among the 25–34 age bracket, with 35 % of respondents owning one or more than one credit card. Among this age group in the three cities, those in Beijing had the highest ownership level at 39 %.

One of the most extraordinary feats of China's economic reform has been the privatisation of the housing stock. This has created an asset base for consumers, the possibility of trading up to a more modern home and a pool of potential co-lateral growth of a mortgage market. In practice, it is likely to be new housing stock that is mortgaged – and our survey suggesting that just 12 % of households have a mortgage on their residence is consistent with this, as is the much higher 20 % figure in Shenzhen, which has a higher proportion of more recently constructed property.

Mortgages look to offer banks a stable, lower credit risk opportunity to lend in a market with potential for substantial long-term growth. Average repayments representing 22.7 % of income do not look overly stretched in international terms, but added to car repayments for some households this may be a more demanding burden. With the average household (of 3.4 people) having over two people working, the mortgage burden is likely to be shared. Unemployment, as much as property values, is the source of credit risk in the emerging mortgage market.

We see domestic players having an edge in the mortgage business. Local titles to property, wide distribution, the advantage of integrating transactional and mortgage repayments all suggest that this will for some time be more a local than a national business. Foreign involvement is likely to be more through joint venture and strategic partners. However, entry of domestic insurers, with wide agent networks, and growth of the city commercial banks into consumer areas are likely to see plenty of competition for the bank incumbents.

Our survey points to the size of the China financial services opportunity. Modern transactional products, a saving culture and wide banking penetration provide a strong foundation for rapid growth into wealth management, consumer finance and mortgage businesses. However, local banks have significant advantages in the core transactional and mortgage businesses – domestic competition will set the scene in these markets, possibly aided by advice from international strategic partners.

This leaves a wide array of international and local firms seeking to create national businesses in credit cards and wealth management niches. We will look to future surveys to show which brands make it in markets that elsewhere have supported a few very large players.

9
Autos

The majority of people in the surveyed cities use buses (43 %) or bicycles (28 %) as means of daily transportation. While only 7 % use private cars, this figure can be expected to grow significantly given respondents' indicated intentions (see Figure 9.1). The highest rate of actual and intended usage of private cars for transportation is found in the 30–39 age bracket and the lowest in the 50–59 age bracket (see Figure 9.2). Actual and intended bicycle usage is highest in the 40–49 and 50–59 age brackets and significantly lower in the 20–29 age bracket.

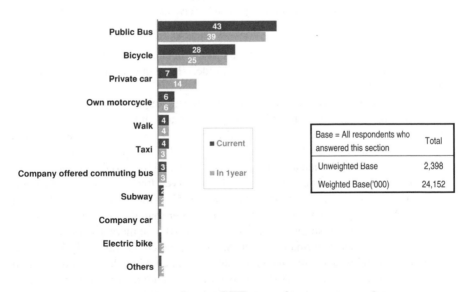

Source: CSFB research

Figure 9.1   Current daily means of transport and likely changes within next year by city

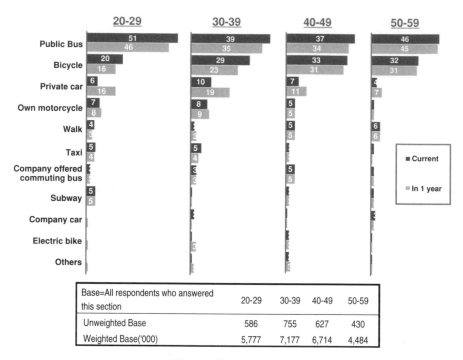

Source: CSFB research

Figure 9.2   Current daily means of transport and likely changes within next year by age

Of the surveyed population 35 % have a driving licence (see Figure 9.3). Beijing
has the largest percentage: 48 %. Of all nonholders 18 % intend to apply for driving
licences within the next year.

The average household penetration rate for ownership of private cars is estimated at
12 % (assuming negligible ownership among low-income households not addressed
in this survey). On this basis the lower half of Figure 9.4 shows that Shenzhen and
Beijing have the highest penetration rates of 30 % and 25 %, respectively. By contrast,
the penetration rate in Wuhan and surprisingly also Shanghai is only around 7 %.

In terms of major brands currently owned, our survey finds that foreign car companies and their joint venture brands have seized 65 % of the private car market (see
Table 9.1). Volkswagen (VW) has a 32 % share, larger than the sum of all domestic
Chinese brands. No other single brand has more than 10 % of market share. However,
Volkswagen is strongest in Shanghai and Shenyang which are relatively low penetration markets and weakest in Guangzhou and Shenzhen which have relatively high
penetration rates. General Motors (GM), its number two competitor, has it strongest
showing in Shanghai where it has a major plant. In terms of the age breakdown, Table
9.2 shows that VW's market penetration is highest for those in the 40–49 age group
(43 % for this group versus 32 % for the overall sample) while Chinese brands appear

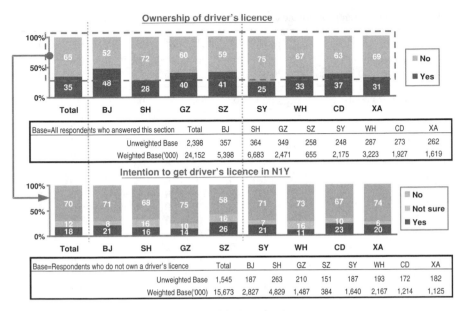

Source: CSFB research

Figure 9.3   Ownership of driving licence and intentions to apply for driving licence in N1Y

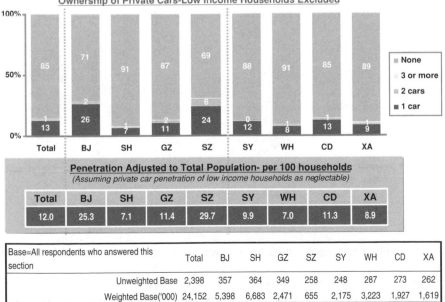

Source: CSFB research

Figure 9.4   Ownership of private cars by households excluding and including low-income households

Table 9.1   Major brands of private cars currently owned (%).

	Total	BJ	SH	GZ	SZ	SY	WH	CD	XA
Unweighted base	382	103	30	47	77	30	25	40	30
Weighted base('000 households)	2040	923	325	205	133	151	164	164	104
Foreign brands/model	65	62	83	57	64	77	80	43	53
Volkswagen	32	36	50	15	13	47	24	15	17
Santana	12	10	33	0	3	17	12	8	7
Jetta	12	20	0	4	4	27	4	8	3
Passat	3	3	7	2	4	0	4	0	3
Polo	2	2	3	2	0	3	4	0	0
Bora	2	1	7	6	1	0	0	0	0
GM	7	4	17	0	9	3	12	5	17
Buick	4	2	13	0	5	3	0	3	13
Sail	2	2	0	0	1	0	8	0	3
Citroen	6	8	0	4	3	0	20	8	3
Fukang	5	7	0	2	3	0	16	8	3
Honda	4	2	0	11	8	3	16	0	0
Accord	2	1	0	6	5	0	4	0	0
Fiat	3	6	0	2	1	0	4	0	3
Palio	2	3	0	0	0	0	4	0	0
Kia	2	1	3	4	1	0	0	3	3
Qianlima	2	1	3	2	1	0	0	3	3
Audi	2	1	3	2	5	0	0	0	3
Toyota	2	1	0	4	9	3	0	0	0
Chinese brands/model	26	32	7	30	13	13	16	50	33
Changan-Suzuki	6	8	3	2	0	0	0	20	17
Alto	4	6	0	0	0	0	0	13	7
Geely	3	6	0	0	0	3	0	3	0
Tianjin-faw	2	4	0	4	0	0	4	0	0
Xiali	2	4	0	4	0	0	4	0	0
Chery	2	2	0	4	0	7	0	8	0
Other Chinese brands	2	2	0	4	3	0	0	3	0
D.K.	5	5	3	2	14	7	4	3	7
R.F.	3	1	7	4	6	0	0	3	7
Total	100	100	100	100	100	100	100	100	100

Base = respondents who have at least 1 car in their household.

Note: only percentages above 2 % are presented.

Source: CSFB research.

to be slightly more popular with the younger consumer (29 % versus 20 % for the overall sample).

We find that between 15 % and 41 % of private car owners are likely to re-place their cars or buy another for the household within the next three years (see Figure 9.5). The lower-bound percentages are for those who are definite about their purchase intentions, whereas the upper-bound percentages are made up of those who are definite and probable. For nonowning households, 3–10 % intend to purchase a

Table 9.2   Major brands of private cars currently owned by age (%).

	Total	20–29	30–39	40–49	50–59
Unweighted base	382	108	130	88	56
Weighted base('000 people)	3648	903	1307	881	557
Foreign brands/model	65	55	67	77	60
Volkswagen	32	26	35	43	19
Santana	12	6	17	17	6
Jetta	12	11	11	19	8
Passat	3	4	3	2	3
Polo	2	3	1	3	2
Bora	2	2	3	2	0
GM	7	7	7	8	6
Buick	4	5	3	5	4
Sail	2	1	3	1	1
Citroen	6	4	5	8	9
Fukang	5	3	4	6	9
Honda	4	4	5	3	—
Accord	2	2	3	0	—
Fiat	3	3	1	2	10
Palio	2	0	1	0	7
Kia	2	2	—	2	5
Qianlima	2	1	—	2	5
Audi	2	1	3	2	0
Toyota	2	2	2	1	—
Chinese brands/model	26	29	27	20	27
Changan-Suzuki	6	7	6	6	6
Alto	4	4	4	2	5
Geely	3	3	2	3	5
Tianjin-faw	2	3	2	3	1
Xiali	2	3	2	3	1
Chery	2	3	3	0	3
Other Chinese brands	2	2	1	0	4
D.K.	5	9	1	2	13
R.F.	3	5	4	1	0
Total	100	100	100	100	100

Base = respondents who have at least 1 car in the household.

Note: only percentages above 2% are presented.

Source: CSFB research.

private car for the household within the next year and 8–27% within the next three years, as shown in Figure 9.6.

Using these data we calculate that the penetration rate of private cars is likely to grow by between 18 and 61% within the next year and by between 49 and 172% within the next three years. Again the ranges arise from the certainty of responses. The total number of new purchased cars in the next three years would, on this basis, be between 1.3m and 4.3m for the eight cities, as shown in Tables 9.3 and 9.4. This

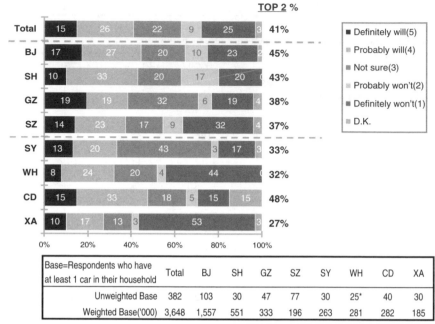

Source: CSFB research

Figure 9.5 Purchase or replacement intentions of households currently owning one or more private cars

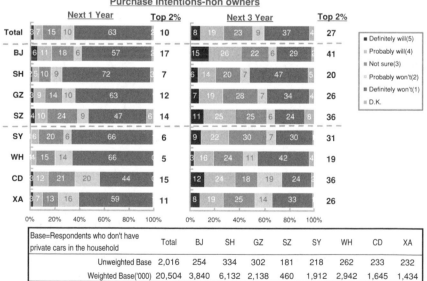

Source: CSFB research

Figure 9.6 Purchase intentions in next year and next three years of households currently not owning a private car

Table 9.3 Estimated private car market within the next year.

	Total	BJ	SH	GZ	SZ	SY	WH	CD	XA
Total number of households ('000) (a)	16 906	3647	4569	1796	447	1604	2246	1453	1144
Low income excluded (%) (b)	14	10	11	12	1	22	19	19	17
Number of involved households ('000) (c = a × b)	14 570	3297	4062	1577	443	1254	1817	1173	947
Household owning at least 1 private car (%) (d)	14	28	8	13	30	12	9	14	11
Number of households owning at least 1 private car ('000) (e = c × d)	2040	923	325	205	133	151	164	164	104
Household owning no private car (%) (f)	86	72	92	87	70	88	91	86	89
Number of households owning no private car ('000) (g = c × f)	12 530	2374	3737	1372	310	1104	1653	1009	843
Nonowning households definitely will purchase N1Y(%) (h_1)	3	6	2	3	4	1	1	3	3
Nonowning households definitely will + probably will purchase N1Y(%) (h_2)	10	17	7	12	14	6	5	15	11
Projected growth N1Y from nonowning households – definitely will purchase ('000) ($j_1 = g \times h_1$)	376	142	75	41	12	11	17	30	25
Projected growth N1Y from nonowning households – definitely + probably will purchase ('000) ($j_2 = g \times h_2$)	1253	404	262	165	43	66	83	151	93
Projected penetration growth rate N1Y–definitely will purchase (%) ($j_1/e \times 100\%$)	18	15	23	20	9	7	10	18	24
Projected penetration growth rate N1Y–definitely + probably will purchase (%) ($j_2/e \times 100\%$)	61	44	81	80	33	44	51	92	89

Source: CSFB research.

Table 9.4 Estimated private car market within the next three years.

	Total	BJ	SH	GZ	SZ	SY	WH	CD	XA
Total number of households ('000) (a)	16906	3647	4569	1796	447	1604	2246	1453	1144
Low income excluded(%) (b)	14	10	11	12	1	22	19	19	17
Number of involved households ('000) (c = a × b)	14570	3297	4062	1577	443	1254	1817	1173	947
Household owning at least 1 private car (%) (d)	14	28	8	13	30	12	9	14	11
Number of households owning at least 1 private car ('000) (e = c × d)	2040	923	325	205	133	151	164	164	104
Household owning no private car (%) (f)	86	72	92	87	70	88	91	86	89
Number of households owning no private car ('000) (g = c × f)	12530	2374	3737	1372	310	1104	1653	1009	843
Nonowning households definitely will purchase in N3Y (%) (h_1)	8	15	6	7	11	9	3	12	8
Nonowning households definitely + probably will purchase in N3Y (%) (h_2)	28	40	20	26	36	31	19	36	26
Projected growth N3Y from nonowning households – definitely will purchase ('000) ($j_1 = g \times h_1$)	1002	356	224	96	34	99	50	121	67
Projected growth N3Y from nonowning households – definitely + probably will purchase ('000) ($j_2 = g \times h_2$)	3508	950	747	357	112	342	314	363	219
Projected penetration growth rate N3Y – definitely will purchase (%) ($k_1 = j_1/e \times 100\%$)	49	39	69	47	26	66	30	74	64
Projected penetration growth rate N3Y – definitely + probably will purchase (%) ($k_2 = j_2/e \times 100\%$)	172	103	230	174	84	226	191	221	211
Current owners definitely will purchase in N3Y (m_1)	15	17	10	19	14	13	8	15	10
Current owners definitely + probably will purchase in N3Y (m_2)	41	45	43	38	38	33	32	48	27
Projected growth N3Y from current owners – definitely will purchase ('000) ($n_1 = e \times m_1$)	306	157	32	39	19	20	13	25	10
Projected growth N3Y from current owners – definitely + probably will purchase ('000) ($n_2 = e \times m_2$)	836	415	140	78	50	50	52	79	28
Total projected market N3Y in number of cars – definitely will purchase ('000) ($j_1 + n_1$)	1308	513	257	135	53	119	63	146	78
Total projected market N3Y from current owners in number of cars – definitely + probably will purchase ('000) ($j_2 + n_2$)	4345	1365	887	435	162	392	366	442	247

Market size in the next 3 years is calculated by summing repeat purchasers and noncurrent car owners.
Source: CSFB research.

Table 9.5 Brand preferences of private cars from the base of households currently not owning a private car (%).

	Total	BJ	SH	GZ	SZ	SY	WH	CD	XA
Unweighted base	577	102	68	79	65	68	50	84	61
Weighted base('000)	5643	1542	1248	559	165	596	562	593	377
Foreign brands/model	41	42	53	48	37	26	40	23	34
Volkswagen	17	25	22	4	12	15	10	10	13
Jetta	4	7	3	1	2	7	4	1	2
Santana	3	4	4	0	0	3	2	0	5
Polo	2	4	1	0	5	0	0	0	2
Bora	2	4	0	0	2	1	0	1	3
VW (unspecified)	5	4	10	3	5	3	2	5	2
GM	6	2	19	4	0	1	4	0	7
Buick	3	1	9	3	0	0	4	0	5
Excelle	2	0	6	1	0	1	0	0	2
Honda	4	2	0	20	6	4	2	2	3
Honda (unspecified)	3	1	0	13	1	3	0	1	2
Citroen	3	3	0	3	3	0	16	0	5
Fukang	2	1	0	0	3	0	14	0	3
Toyota	2	2	3	4	3	1	0	0	2
Chinese brands/model	8	10	1	5	5	10	6	17	8
Changan-Suzuki	2	4	0	0	2	1	0	6	2
Chery	2	0	0	3	2	3	0	8	2
D.K.	51	48	46	47	58	63	54	58	54
Total	100	100	100	100	100	100	100	100	100

Base = respondents who currently own no private cars but intend to buy in N3Y.

Note: only percentages above 2 % are presented.

Source: CSFB research.

suggests that notwithstanding the current slowdown in car sales growth the market remains far from fully developed.

We identify brand preferences from the base of those who indicate they will either definitely or probably purchase private cars. Table 9.5 shows that Volkswagen has the highest share of stated brand preferences of noncar owners at 17 %. However, this is well below the current ownership share of 32 %. Meanwhile, General Motors' share of stated preferences is 6 % versus a current ownership share of 7 %. This may indicate that VW is in danger of losing market share to other foreign brands such as GM, Honda, Citroen and Toyota. However, the main implication of the survey result is that the market is likely to remain highly competitive. Fully 51 % of noncar owners are not able to state a brand preference. This suggests that margins may be difficult to capture in this sector for the auto manufacturers.

The perception of auto brands by consumers in China is, at first sight, somewhat surprising. Figure 9.7 shows that most of the owners of private cars think that their foreign branded cars, such as VW or GM, are in fact local brands (see Figure 9.8

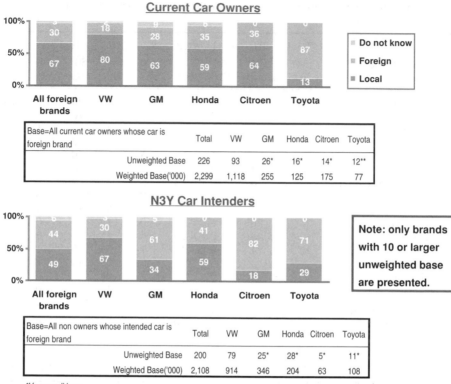

*Very small base

Source: CSFB research

Figure 9.7 Brand perception on whether foreign auto brands are viewed as local

for a photograph of a VW Santana). Hence, 80 % of current car owners perceive Volkswagen as a local brand versus just 13 % for Toyota. This is because historically most foreign cars sold in China are manufactured by joint ventures between global and local producers.

We find that 30 % of people intending to purchase private cars for the first time are willing to pay a premium for foreign branded cars while 53 % are not willing to do so (see Figure 9.9). The former group believes that foreign branded cars have better quality (82 %), hence the premium. The latter group has three major reasons for choosing not to pay a premium: local cars are of equal good quality (36 %), better after-sales service (31 %) and patriotism to support domestic goods (29 %).

For first time buyers of private cars, the average budget is RMB 131 300 (around US$16 000 at the current exchange rate). Beijing and Shenzhen have the largest number of people intending to spend in the highest spend brackets on autos (see Figure 9.10).

Figure 9.8   Volkswagen Santana automobile

IMPLICATIONS FOR AUTOMOTIVE PRODUCERS[1]

China remains a huge opportunity for all global automotive OEMs in the foreseeable future. From our analysis of the mature markets of North America and Western Europe, we know that disposable personal income growth is the single biggest driver of consumer spending and automotive demand. Chinese personal incomes continue to grow at 8–10 % annually in nominal terms (as confirmed in our survey). As the Chinese economy continues to develop, as we expect it will, we believe the current annual level of car sales of around three sales per 1000 of the population should start to grow towards other developing country levels of 10–12 unit sales in Eastern Europe and Latin America. This suggests that the Chinese car market should quadruple in size in the medium term, underpinning trend demand growth forecasts of 15–20 % pa.

The slowdown in 2004 in our view has had much to do with the reduced availability of automotive financing, as the Chinese financial system develops a more sophisticated credit analysis system, and as a result of the government's austerity programme. However, with financing accounting for just 10 % of China car sales in 2004, down

[1] Chris Ceraso, Harald Hendrikse, Koji Endo and Jeannie Cheung contributed to this section.

Reasons for Paying a Premium For Foreign Car Brands	
	%
Better in quality	82
More reliable/trustworthy	17
Better after-sale service	14
Have better manufacturing technology	13
Have better designs	10
Give me prestige	7

Yes 30%   No 53%   D.K. 17%

Reasons for Not Paying a Premium For Foreign Car Brands	
	%
Chinese brands are equally good in quality	36
Chinese brands have better after-sale service	31
Chinese should use Chinese goods	29
Restricted by own wealth/foreign brands are expensive for me	8
Whether the brand is foreign or Chinese is not important to me	8
I don't trust foreign goods because they may be counterfeits	3

Base=Respondents who currently own no private cars but intend to buy in N3Y	Total	Willing to pay a premium	Unwilling to pay a premium
Unweighted Base	577	177	309
Weighted Base('000)	5,643	1,705	2,996

Source: CSFB research

Figure 9.9   Willingness to pay a premium for foreign brands of autos and reasons

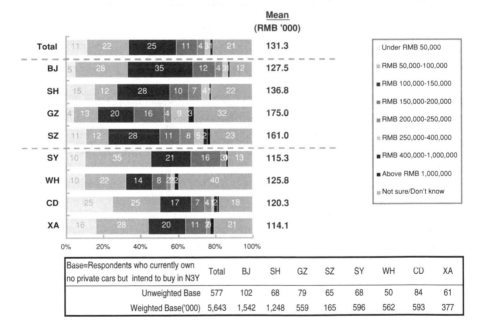

	Mean (RMB '000)
Total	131.3
BJ	127.5
SH	136.8
GZ	175.0
SZ	161.0
SY	115.3
WH	125.8
CD	120.3
XA	114.1

Under RMB 50,000
RMB 50,000-100,000
RMB 100,000-150,000
RMB 150,000-200,000
RMB 200,000-250,000
RMB 250,000-400,000
RMB 400,000-1,000,000
Above RMB 1,000,000
Not sure/Don't know

Base=Respondents who currently own no private cars but intend to buy in N3Y	Total	BJ	SH	GZ	SZ	SY	WH	CD	XA
Unweighted Base	577	102	68	79	65	68	50	84	61
Weighted Base('000)	5,643	1,542	1,248	559	165	596	562	593	377

Source: CSFB research

Figure 9.10   Planned budget for spending on a private car from the base of households currently not owning private cars

from 30 % in 2003, the future risk is limited. Furthermore, the cash market must have continued to grow strongly in 2004 for the market not to have slowed further. As a result, we expect the 2004 slowdown in China automotive sales growth to be a temporary issue. Growth should start to re-accelerate in the second half (H2) of 2005 and 2006, as comparatives get easier and as credit availability returns. Indeed, the results from our survey suggest that the underlying demographic and income trends will serve to further strengthen the Chinese consumer's desire and ability to own a new vehicle.

What is more worrying for the automotive investor is the enormous and continued growth in capacity. Supply already exceeds demand in the Chinese market and this is set to get worse in coming years if current capacity plans are completed. With the slowdown in demand, pricing has become significantly more negative, with major price reductions announced by GM and VW in the summer of 2004. As Chinese car prices in 2004 were some 15–20 % above international prices, we foresee further price deflation in the medium term. This should continue to depress earnings before interest and taxation (EBIT) margins in the Chinese auto market from current exceptional levels closer to international levels. Much of this margin depression already seems to have taken place in 2004 and some of the capacity growth plans are already being delayed.

In addition, our survey finds that only 30 % of first-time car buyers in China are willing to pay a premium for foreign brand cars while 53 % are not. Interestingly, many Chinese car drivers regard VW, GM and Honda as local brands but not Toyota. This reflects the sale of foreign brand vehicles under Chinese names through joint venture (JV) agreements. It suggests that an aggressive pricing strategy remains the most effective means to grab market share and that brand recognition in China is somewhat distorted for many of the global majors. The implication is negative for automakers, which will continue to see margin pressure.

Of the European original equipment manufacturers, only VW has a very significant position in the Chinese market. In the short term, this has been a drag on earnings, as the € 550m contribution in 2003 has been cut in half by 2004 margin compression. VW's market share has fallen from over 50 % five years ago to under 30 %, but VW remains a comfortable market leader. We believe this position will prove to be extremely valuable in the longer term, as China resumes its growth path towards becoming the second-largest automotive market globally. VW is also securing its position in the market by increasingly concentrating on majority-owned JVs in manufacturing of local major components such as engines and transmissions, rather than just focusing on assembly.

Other European OEMs with some exposure to the Chinese market are Peugeot SA and BMW, both of which have established assembly JVs and have local production in place. However, both businesses are of minimal size compared with the size of each group. Mercedes and Renault remain somewhat behind, having been late in getting to market in Mercedes' case and with Renault relying more on its minority-owned subsidiary, Nissan.

For the US producers, when China's car sales were booming in 2002 and 2003, it was the best of times for GM, who saw the contribution from Asia Pacific jump to a US$1.0bn per annum pace from next to nothing in only two years (just in time to make up for an ailing North American business). After the Chinese government applied the brakes, tightening credit standards, the contribution from China was cut in half (and then some) and GM's earnings expectations were revised sharply lower, as the company said it anticipates that the slowdown will last through the middle of 2005. For the next 18 months, therefore, it looks like China will be a drag on the results at GM – so much for the best of times.

Ford Motor, who had completely missed the party in China during the 2002–3 boom period for auto demand, now looks to be in a better position as it relates to China – at least for the next 18 months or so, as the slowdown will not pose any meaningful drag on earnings. While Ford expects to boost production capacity in China over the next few years, we think that GM, with its near 10 % market share and the strong brand perception identified in the survey, will have a distinct advantage and be better positioned to benefit from any pent-up demand that may develop in H2 2004 and 2005.

The major Japanese automakers still have a relatively low market share in China. Honda is the top Japanese brand, with a 4 % share. Compared with VW and GM, the Japanese are well behind in terms of marketing. Yet the speed of capacity buildup by the Japanese has been surprisingly fast. It will be interesting to see if the Japanese, and in particular Toyota, ever catch up VW and GM in China and, if so, how soon.

10
Beverages

Our survey finds that carbonated soft drinks are the most frequently consumed beverages during meals (see Table 10.1). This includes normal restaurant meals (32 %) and restaurant banquets (29 %), as well as meals at home (18 %).

Beer is the most frequently consumed beverage at entertainment locations (bar/karaoke/night club/disco). Of these, 12 % drink Chinese beer and 7 % foreign beer.

While at home but not during meals, people mostly drink water (25 % tap water and 11 % bottled water – see the food producers section following for more survey information on this product category) or self-brewed tea (25 %).

Western spirits are rarely consumed. The most likely places are at entertainment locations and the percentage is still only 1 %. Meanwhile, wine features strongly only in banquet meals at restaurants for special occasions.

Coca-Cola is the most frequently consumed nonalcoholic beverage (see Table 10.2). On our survey it has 27 % of the market. It is the strongest brand in every one of

Table 10.1 Occasions and locations for different types of beverage consumption (%).

Unweighted base: 2533 Weighted base ('000): 25 398	Normal meal in restaurants	Banquet meal in restaurants	Normal meal at home	At home without meal	Bar/KTV /night club/disco
Carbonated soft drinks	32	29	18	11	9
Chinese beer	17	18	13	2	12
Fruit drink/juice	12	12	7	6	5
Tea(self-brewed)	10	4	6	25	3
Yogurts	4	2	1	1	0
Coconut drink/almond drink/walnut drink	3	3	1	0	1
Boiled tap water	2	1	8	25	1
Bottled water	2	0	3	11	1
Chinese high alcohol content spirits (Baijiu)	2	8	3	0	0
Packaged/bottled tea drink	2	0	1	2	1

continued

Table 10.1 *Continued*

Unweighted base: 2533 Weighted base ('000): 25 398	Normal meal in restaurants	Banquet meal in restaurants	Normal meal at home	At home without meal	Bar/KTV /night club/disco
Foreign brand beer	1	2	1	0	7
Functional drinks	1	1	1	1	0
Milk	1	0	1	2	0
Western wine	1	10	2	0	3
Chinese wine (yellow wine)	0	1	0	0	0
Coffee	0	0	0	1	2
Soup	0	0	7	0	0
Soybean milk/soybean syrup	0	0	0	0	0
Western spirits (whiskey, cognac, etc.)	0	0	0	0	1
None	4	2	26	10	3
Don't know/never go to such places	5	6	1	1	52
Total	100	100	100	100	100

Base = all respondents who answered this section.

Note: only percentages 1 % or above are presented.

Source: CSFB research.

Table 10.2 Most consumed brands of nonalcoholic beverage by city (%).

	Total	BJ	SH	GZ	SZ	SY	WH	CD	XA
Unweighted base	2533	366	386	365	280	281	294	283	278
Weighted base('000)	25 398	5534	7087	2584	711	2464	3302	1998	1718
Coca-Cola	27	25	28	23	18	34	28	18	29
Coca-Cola	18	20	17	18	14	19	19	13	18
Sprite	7	4	11	3	3	9	7	5	7
Pepsi	10	6	15	10	14	3	12	15	4
Pepsi Cola	9	5	14	9	12	3	11	14	4
President	10	13	7	7	6	5	17	16	6
President	10	13	7	6	6	4	17	16	6
Mr Kon	8	11	4	7	8	14	2	7	14
Mr Kon	7	11	3	7	8	13	2	6	13
Wahaha	4	7	0	—	1	15	5	2	7
Wahaha	4	7	0	—	1	12	4	2	7
Nongfu Spring	3	5	4	1	1	2	3	1	2
Nongfu Spring	3	5	4	1	1	2	3	1	1
Robust	2	3	—	2	2	4	5	5	3
Huiyuan	2	4	2	0	1	1		—	4
Huiyuan	2	4	2	0	1	1	—	—	4
None	8	8	6	11	7	7	7	8	10
D.K.	14	10	16	12	19	10	17	16	16
Total	100	100	100	100	100	100	100	100	100

Base = all respondents who answered this section.

Note: only percentages above 2 % are presented.

Source: CSFB research.

Table 10.3 Most consumed brands of nonalcoholic beverage by age (%).

	Total	20–29	30–39	40–49	50–59
Unweighted base	2533	626	777	674	456
Weighted base('000)	25 398	6243	7365	7125	4666
Coca-Cola	27	25	24	30	27
Coca-Cola	18	19	17	20	15
Sprite	7	4	6	10	9
Pepsi	10	15	11	7	8
Pepsi Cola	9	14	10	7	7
President	10	15	10	9	5
President	10	15	10	8	5
Mr Kon	8	13	8	5	4
Mr Kon	7	12	7	4	3
Wahaha	4	3	5	4	5
Wahaha	4	3	5	4	4
Nongfu Spring	3	3	4	2	2
Nongfu Spring	3	3	4	2	2
Robust	2	3	3	2	2
Huiyuan	2	1	2	1	4
Huiyuan	2	1	2	1	3
None	8	2	7	10	13
D.K.	14	8	12	17	20
Total	100	100	100	100	100

Base = all respondents who answered this section.

Note: only percentages above 2 % are presented.

Source: CSFB research.

the eight cities surveyed, a rare feat for any consumer product in our survey. Its main competitors are: Pepsi (10 %), President (10 %) and Mr Kon (8 %). Coca-Cola is strongest relative to Pepsi in Shenyang, while Pepsi is strongest in Shanghai and Chengdu. Coca-Cola is most dominant in the 40–49 age bracket while the gap between Coca-Cola and Pepsi is lowest in the 20–29 age bracket (see Table 10.3).

Frequency of alcohol consumption differs greatly between males (8.5 times per month) and females (1.8 times per month). This averages to 5.2 times per month per person, as shown in Figure 10.1. Alcoholic beverage consumption is least frequent in the 20–29 age bracket with a reported mean of 3.3 times per month (see Figure 10.2). Only 3 % of respondents in this bracket report consuming alcoholic beverages every day. Reported consumption is highest in the 40–49 age bracket with a reported mean of 6.3 times per month. Of respondents in this age bracket 13 % report consuming alcohol on a daily basis.

The beer market is heavily regionalised with each city led by its own local brands (see Table 10.4), some of which are now foreign owned (see below). Foreign brands have an overall 10 % market share; Shanghai (19 %) and Guangzhou (26 %) have the largest foreign brand penetration. Budweiser and Heineken are the top two foreign

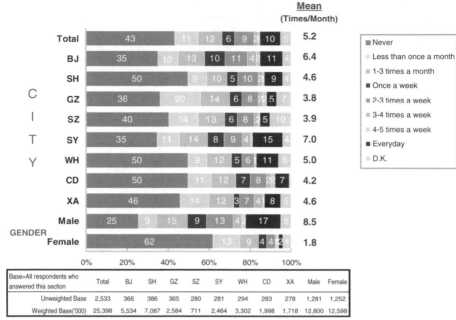

Source: CSFB research

Figure 10.1   Frequency of alcohol consumption by city and gender

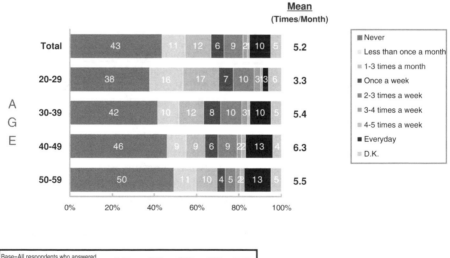

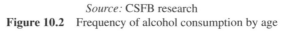

Source: CSFB research

Figure 10.2   Frequency of alcohol consumption by age

Table 10.4   Most consumed brands of beer by city (%).

	Total	BJ	SH	GZ	SZ	SY	WH	CD	XA
Unweighted base	1011	185	140	133	100	142	103	109	99
Weighted base('000)	10 347	2797	2570	942	254	1245	1157	770	612
Chinese brand	78	94	67	59	41	80	80	77	88
Yanjing	24	86	0	1	1	4	0	1	1
Suntory	12	0	50	0	2	0	0	0	0
Tsingdao	9	5	9	5	32	19	9	2	3
Xuehua	8	1	0	0	0	49	8	9	0
Xingyinge	5	0	0	0	1	0	48	0	0
Zhujiang	5	0	0	54	4	0	0	0	0
Hansi	5	0	0	0	1	0	1	0	81
Lanjian	3	0	0	0	0	0	0	40	0
Reeb	2	0	8	0	0	0	0	0	0
Luye	2	0	0	0	0	0	0	25	1
Jinlongquan	2	0	0	0	0	0	15	0	0
Foreign brand	10	3	19	26	6	2	4	15	3
Budweiser	5	1	13	10	2	1	2	10	2
Heineken	2	0	4	5	2	0	0	0	0
Don't drink beer	4	2	9	4	3	1	7	6	1
Don't know	3	1	4	6	2	2	4	0	4
Total	100	100	100	100	100	100	100	100	100

Base = respondents who drink alcohol at least once a month.

Note: only percentages above 2 % are presented.

Source: CSFB research.

beer brands. Younger consumers appear to be more willing to experiment with foreign brands of beer. Of those in the 20–29 age bracket 16 % consume foreign beers most often versus just 5 % of those in the 50–59 age bracket (see Table 10.5).

The market for Chinese spirit (baijiu) is not as large as that of beer. Of those who drink alcohol once a month, 46 % do not drink this type of alcohol versus only 4 % who do not drink beer. This market is also led by local brands in each area (see Table 10.6).

We find that the number of people who drink foreign spirits is very small compared with the number who consume beer and Chinese spirits. Only 22 % of those who drink alcohol at least once a month drink products in this category (see Table 10.7). Only in one city, Guangzhou, did we find somewhat higher consumption – only 47 % of our sample in Guangzhou indicate that they do not drink foreign spirits (highlighted in Table 10.7). Across the eight cities Chivas Regal is the most consumed brand, followed by Remy Martin.

The average monthly spend on alcoholic beverages is RMB 164 or around US$20 at the current exchange rate (see Figure 10.3). Guangzhou and Shenzhen are the two cities with the highest monthly spends, RMB 303, and RMB 300, respectively.

Table 10.5   Most consumed brands of beer by age (%).

	Total	20–29	30–39	40–49	50–59
Unweighted base	1011	248	335	266	162
Weighted base('000)	10 347	2530	3204	2971	1641
Chinese brand	78	71	78	82	79
Yanjing	24	23	21	26	28
Suntory	12	12	8	17	13
Tsingdao	9	8	10	9	6
Xuehua	8	8	9	7	6
Xingyinge	5	3	7	6	5
Zhujiang	5	5	6	5	4
Hansi	5	4	6	4	5
Lanjian	3	3	5	1	3
Reeb	2	0	3	3	1
Luye	2	2	2	2	2
Jinlongquan	2	2	1	2	3
Foreign brand	10	16	11	7	5
Budweiser	5	7	6	4	4
Heineken	2	3	1	2	—
Don't drink beer	4	6	2	4	9
Don't know	3	1	4	4	1
Total	100	100	100	100	100

Base = respondents who drink alcohol at least once a month.

Note: only percentages above 2 % are presented.

Source: CSFB research.

Therefore the total market is estimated to be RMB 20bn (or US$2.4bn) per year for the eight cities in all.

IMPLICATIONS FOR ALCOHOLIC BEVERAGE PRODUCERS[1]

China is becoming increasingly important to the alcoholic beverage industry given its potential on a three- to five-year basis. However, the market is very different for beer and spirits players. The beer market is the largest in the world at 256m hectolitres. Although volume growth in the market is strong (+5–6 % per annum) profitability is poor because of overcapacity. Prices are low versus international standards and operating margins are therefore suppressed by comparison. By contrast, the international imported spirits market is very small (less than 1 % of the total market) but with a very high margin because demand is primarily high-end bar restaurant business. High personal income growth is fuelling a rapid growth in the bar/ restaurant trade where

---

[1] Andrew Conway, Michael Bleakley, Guillaume Dalibot, Shuichi Shibanuma, Michelle Yan and Nathalie Wan contributed to this section.

Table 10.6 Most consumed brands of Chinese spirits (%).

	Total	BJ	SH	GZ	SZ	SY	WH	CD	XA
Unweighted base	1011	185	140	133	100	142	103	109	99
Weighted base('000)	10 347	2797	2570	942	254	1245	1157	770	612
Er Guo Tou	10	34	0	2	5	1	1	3	2
Wu Liang Ye	4	1	6	7	11	0	6	5	5
Bei Jing Chun	3	10	0	0	0	0	0	0	0
Lu Zhou Lao Jiao	2	1	3	1	0	1	0	16	3
Zhi Jiang	2	0	0	0	1	0	16	0	0
Jinliufu	2	4	1	0	0	1	1	0	2
Lao Long Kou	2	0	0	0	0	13	0	0	0
Tai Bai	1	0	0	0	0	0	0	0	21
Xi Feng	1	0	0	0	0	0	1	0	14
Others	2	1	1	4	3	4	5	3	6
None	3	3	1	5	4	6	0	4	0
Don't drink Chinese baijiu	46	37	66	42	47	56	34	35	31
Don't know	10	5	11	10	11	13	19	8	8
Total	100	100	100	100	100	100	100	100	100

Base = respondents who drink alcohol at least once a month.

Note: only percentages above 2 % are presented with the exception of Tai Bai and Xi Feng which are heavily consumed in Xi'an.

Source: CSFB research.

Table 10.7 Most consumed brands of foreign spirits (%).

	Total	BJ	SH	GZ	SZ	SY	WH	CD	XA
Unweighted base	1011	185	140	133	100	142	103	109	99
Weighted base('000)	10 347	2797	2570	942	254	1245	1157	770	612
Chivas Regal	3	3	2	6	1	0	2	10	0
Remy Martin	2	2	1	10	8	0	4	1	0
XO (brand unspecified)	2	2	1	5	8	1	5	1	1
Hennessey	2	1	1	11	4	1	0	0	0
Johnnie Walker	1	1	1	2	0	1	0	0	2
Martell	1	1	1	4	4	0	1	0	0
Others	1	0	0	3	1	1	0	0	1
None	2	1	3	2	2	1	1	2	0
I don't drink foreign spirit	78	82	79	47	64	89	80	76	92
Don't know	7	6	9	13	7	4	7	7	4
Total	100	100	100	100	100	100	100	100	100

Base = respondents who drink alcohol at least once a month.

Note: percentages above 1 % are presented due to the large size of nonconsumption for this category.

Source: CSFB research.

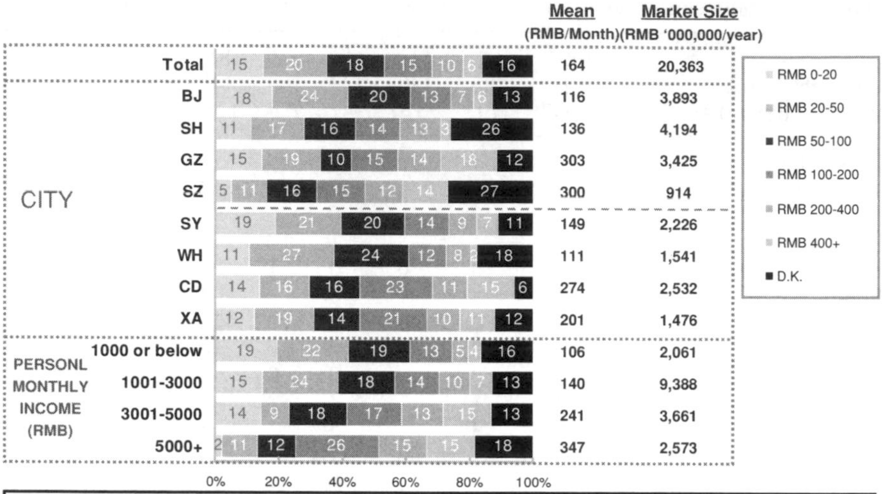
Mean
Market Size
(RMB/Month)(RMB '000,000/year)
Total 15 20 18 15 10 6 16 164 20,363
CITY
BJ 18 24 20 13 7 6 13 116 3,893
SH 11 17 16 14 13 3 26 136 4,194
GZ 15 19 10 15 14 18 12 303 3,425
SZ 5 11 16 15 12 14 27 300 914
SY 19 21 20 14 9 7 11 149 2,226
WH 11 27 24 12 8 2 18 111 1,541
CD 14 16 16 23 11 15 6 274 2,532
XA 12 19 14 21 10 11 12 201 1,476
PERSONL MONTHLY INCOME (RMB)
1000 or below 19 22 19 13 5 4 16 106 2,061
1001-3000 15 24 18 14 10 7 13 140 9,388
3001-5000 14 9 18 17 13 15 13 241 3,661
5000+ 2 11 12 26 15 15 18 347 2,573
0% 20% 40% 60% 80% 100%
RMB 0-20
RMB 20-50
RMB 50-100
RMB 100-200
RMB 200-400
RMB 400+
D.K.

Base=Respondents who drink alcohol at least once a month	Total	BJ	SH	GZ	SZ	SY	WH	CD	XA	1000 or below	1001-3000	3001-5000	5000+
Unweighted Base	1,011	185	140	133	100	142	103	109	99	165	544	123	63
Weighted Base('000)	10,347	2,797	2,570	942	254	1,245	1,157	770	612	1,620	5,588	1,266	618

Source: CSFB research

Figure 10.3 Average monthly spend on alcohol consumption

Scotch whisky sells for US$150–350 per bottle versus c.US$60 as the international average.

Anheuser-Busch, SAB Miller and Inbev (through the acquisition of Lion Group's beer operation in China and a number of regional brands) are the most exposed of the international brewers to emerging markets including China and offer the highest levels of volume growth in the beer sector. China is likely to deliver volume growth in the short term for these groups through market expansion and industry consolidation. Profit growth will be limited, in our view, by low margins for another three to five years but in the long term the market will become a major driver for these companies' global profitability.

Consolidation in the beer industry should ultimately ease pricing pressure. Anheuser-Busch is number one in the market (18 % market share) given a 27 % stake (9.9 % now and to rise to 27 % in a few years) in Tsingtao and 100 % ownership of recently acquired and privatised Harbin Brewery. SAB Miller is the number two in China (10 % market share) through its China Resources Enterprise partnership. Inbev has the number five position. The only major local brand that is without a foreign partner is Beijing Yanjing Brewery.

The Chinese beer market is highly regional despite years of consolidation. This also explains the weak pricing power and low profitability of local brewers. The large geographical differences in income, eating habits and consumption preferences imply that a brand strategy may have its limitations in China.

We believe industry consolidation will continue and China's beer industry clearly does not need its current brand proliferation – the largest player, Tsingtao, following its acquisitive strategy over the past few years, now has as many as 100 brands in its portfolio (it wishes to consolidate to four eventually). However, a multibrand strategy that caters to both consumers' price point requirements as well as attachment to local brands seems a more practical strategy for local brewers at this point in order to tackle the diversified Chinese market while maintaining the brand equity of its dominant brand.

Our survey clearly indicates that foreign brands are seeing increasing market shares in Tier 1 cities. For instance, foreign brands account for 10 % of the national market but 26 % share in Guangzhou and 19 % in Shanghai according to our survey (although other data points indicated that Suntory has a 40 % market share in Shanghai). Heavy investment in advertising and packaging by global brands will continue to gain market shares from dominant regional brands which is an increasing challenge for the traditional local market leaders – for example, Tsingtao and Yanjing.

Anheuser-Busch has targeted China as its most important growth market over the next decade. Over the past two years, it has purchased an ownership stake in Tsing Tao, China's biggest brewery, and bought 100 % of Harbin, the biggest player in the Northeastern part of the country. However, as our survey clearly shows, the Chinese beer market remains very unconsolidated. We believe it will take several years before Anheuser-Busch's Chinese operations have a material impact on the overall financial performance of the company. However, with much of the global beer market largely consolidated in Western Europe, North America and Latin America, China is a critical long-term growth initiative for the company.

Other international brewers like Carlsberg and Heineken have also made some inroads into China. After its initial failure in major developed cities, Carlsberg has now turned to the less-competitive inland markets such as Tibet and Yunan through acquisitive growth. Meanwhile, Heineken, through its partnership with Asia Pacific Brewer (its JV partner in Singapore), stepped up its China ambitions by acquiring 21 % of the regional brand Guangdong Brewery. Finally, Scottish & Newcastle extended its long cooperation with local brewer, Chongqing Brewery, to acquire a 19.5 % stake. Meanwhile, Suntory of Japan, categorised by survey respondents as a local brand, is enjoying considerable success in Shanghai. With the exception of Suntory, Japanese brewers with business concerns in China operate on a small scale in specific regions of the country.

The imported spirits market should see a continuation of the strong growth in scotch and cognac as import duties are reduced from 60 % to 15 % of landed value in 2006. At this time Pernod Ricard has the leading position in the premium scotch market through Chivas Regal and the greatest profit exposure to the country. We estimate that China should account for c.4 % of the company's EBIT in FY 2004E. Volume growth has been triple digit in recent years for Chivas Regal and high double digit for Martell. Line extensions on both brands are delivering exceptional growth at very high margins.

With China becoming more Westernised and the average selling price (ASP) of wine dropping to affordable levels, we expect wine consumption revenue growth to exceed that of overall alcoholic consumption in the remaining years of this decade. The fast growth is driven by: (a) increased penetration of Western culture into China and (b) the government's intention to use wine as a substitute for grain-consuming liquor. Three domestic wineries control more than half of the wine market and we believe import tariff cuts should not affect domestic wineries much, as it will take time for local consumers to understand Western wine culture and for foreign brewers to tap into local distribution networks. Among the three domestic wineries Yantai Changyu is the largest. The company's dominant market position, firm control on raw materials and a motivated management expected after the forthcoming management buy-out should allow it to post a 19 % earnings CAGR over the next three years.

In the autumn of 2004 Suntory started marketing wine in China with the launch of two types of red wine in Shanghai. Suntory will initially sell the wines, produced by French wine maker Groupe Castel and sold under the Suntory label, at restaurants with an eye to expanding sales channels to supermarkets and other retailers later.

China's output of domestic liquor spirits by 2003 had dropped by almost half from its peak in 1996. However, after this long and painful consolidation, pricing power is returning to the surviving leaders. In China, more than 99 % of liquor is made of domestic grain. We can categorise domestic grain liquors according to their fragrances, determined by the processing techniques and especially the cellars required for storing (see Table 10.8).

The soy-fragrance liquor sector is not as crowded as other liquor sectors due to its high entry barriers – years of fermentation, blending and storage are required. The leader in the sector, Kweichow Moutai, has no competitors as its 'Moutai' liquor can be distilled only in the Huairen area where it is located and, due to the unique geographical features there, cannot be replicated elsewhere. Kweichow Moutai is China's most prestigious liquor maker. Its Moutai liquor has long been regarded as China's number one premium liquor and is always in short supply. The company went public as a matter of industrial pride for local government only, rather than for any capital need, yet we believe its asset value is underestimated by the market. This is a typical natural monopoly, which does not necessarily need superior management. In our view current valuations are attractive compared with its global peers.

Unlike the soy-fragrance sector, China's strong-fragrance liquor sector has lower entry barriers due to its short fermentation cycle. Yibin Wuliangye leads this sector and faces competition in each segment within the strong-fragrance sector and therefore has had to gain market share by pursuing strong sales volumes. Therefore, we believe Yibin Wuliangye enjoys less room for an ASP rise than Kweichow Moutai, which has tended not to release sufficient volume on to the market.

Table 10.8 Categorising domestic liquor by fragrance.

Fragrance type	Cellar required	Fermentation and storage required	Feature	Representatives
Strong fragrance	Made of soil and earth	No more than a year	Low-to-mid-end (except market leaders), with the lowest margins	Wuliangye, Gujing Tribute, Luzhou Lao Jiao, Jian Nan Chun, Quan Xing Da Qu, Tuopai Qu Jiu
Soy fragrance	Made of stone and soil	3–5 years or even longer for high-end products	The most high-end with the highest margin	Moutai
Mellow fragrance	Made of soil and earth	Even shorter than strong fragrance liquor	Mid-end, margin higher than strong fragrance due to short fermentations	Shanxi Fen Jiu, Xing Hua Cun, Zhu Ye Qing

Source: CSFB research.

IMPLICATIONS FOR NONALCOHOLIC BEVERAGE PRODUCERS

With its two Chinese businesses, Wahaha and Robust, Danone is by far the largest beverage company in China. The survey indicates that Wahaha and Robust combined have the largest market share in the surveyed cities. Furthermore, Wahaha has the largest brand awareness in the overall food sector (see Chapter 12, for example, Table 12.1), a rather impressive feat for a company only created in 1988 in Hangzhou, Zhejiang.

China is a key market for Danone as it represents 9% of the group's total revenues – the largest exposure to China among European food companies. Wahaha and Robust generate most of these revenues as Danone biscuits are a much smaller business and dairy revenues are very modest. Overall 85% of Danone's sales in China are realised in beverages.

The most interesting aspect of Danone's strategy in China is that it has always relied on investing in local companies selling their own brands rather than just introducing the group's brands from scratch and growing them organically. Generally, active consumption of soft drinks, mainly of the carbonated variety, closely resembles the pattern of beverage consumption prevalent in Japan in the 1970s.

Today Wahaha has leading and often dominant positions in bottled water (number one), LAB (lactic acid beverages), carbonated soft-drinks (number three), ready-to-drink tea (number three) and functional beverages, etc. Major competitors include Tingyi and Unipresident in ready-to-drink teas and juice drinks, Coca-Cola and Pepsi in carbonated soft drinks and Nongfu Spring and Shanghai-based Meilin Aquarius in water. The relative shift towards noncarbonated drinks in recent years has seen traditional carbonated players like Coca-Cola going into noncarbonated products, such as bottled water. Coca-Cola successfully built up the Qoo brand of juice drinks built around a proprietary cartoon character 'Qoo'.

In our view one of Wahaha's and Robust's key strengths is their distribution networks which allow them to cover 60% of the stores in rural areas and 78% in urban areas – representing a staggering total of 2.7m points of sales. What is more, the advance payment system implemented by Wahaha shields the company from any bad debt risk, with the business effectively operating with negative working capital.

With this infrastructure, we expect Danone to carry on growing its beverage revenues in China well into the double-digit range, at least in volumes. One should bear in mind that the bottled water category should continue to face price deflation as production capacity continues to increase. However, we expect Danone to mitigate this impact through new product launches, notably in the functional drink area, with higher price points creating a positive mix impact. Meanwhile, Danone's stake in Bright Dairy gives it an exposure in the dairy market where Bright currently is ranked the third largest dairy company in China.

China also represents a major growth market for The Coca-Cola Company (Coke) and a critical one given the slowing growth rate for many of Coke's more mature markets. Coke has a dual-track strategy in China: (a) to increase availability in rural China with a focus on affordability (returnable glass bottle packaging) and (b) to continue to innovate in the overall beverage portfolio in urban centres and drive brand value.

Developing markets in Asia have lower penetration rates than developed markets for carbonated soft drinks. Recently, Coke announced that it would be increasing significantly marketing investment in several high-growth developing markets, including China. For Coke to meet its targeted range of 6–8 % operating income growth over the long term, the continued evolution and growth of the Chinese consumer remains critical. We believe significant opportunity exists to drive growth for the category. Coke management is targeting 10 % annual volume growth in China over the next several years.

Coke currently holds four of the top five carbonated beverage brands in China and has an approximate 48 % volume share. We believe that, over time, the major urban centres in China will evolve to look like the Japanese market, where the share for noncarbonated beverages such as sports drinks and tea-based drinks is significantly higher than for carbonated beverages. Currently, noncarbonated brands account for less than 5 % of Coke's China portfolio. We regard Kirin Beverage as beneficiary of this trend. It operates in Shanghai and recently commenced operations in Beijing.

It is interesting to see Mr Kon (the primary brand of Tingyi) come in at number four in our survey of nonalcoholic beverage producers and ranked after President by two percentage points. This contradicts ACNielsen's data provided by Tingyi where Mr Kon is ranked well above President in both ready-to-drink tea and fruit juice. The divergence could be due to sample size (ACNielsen's survey covered a much wider geographical region while our survey mainly focuses on key cities).

The milk market, which is seeing 30 % growth per annum, is currently one of the fastest growing beverage sectors in China. This is driven by an increased income level and government support: for example, the launch of the student milk programme in 2001 to allow local students to drink one glass of milk every day. The dominant milk brands in China remain the local names with Yili as the largest milk company, followed by Mengniu, Bright Dairy and Beijing Sanyuan. Foreign brands tried green field investments but failed (including Danone, Kraft) although some of them are now returning to the market through mergers and acquisitions (M&A). For instance, Danone acquired a stake in the number three player, Bright Dairy, and has increased its stake to the current 9.7 %. With an attractive industry growth prospect (+30 % per annum), we believe the milk market will continue to attract interest from international companies.

Mengniu Dairy is, in our view, the most interesting locally controlled player in the food and beverage sector in China. Being the second-largest player in UHT milk, with a strong marketing strategy and experienced management, Mengniu is the fastest growing dairy company in China. National pride remains strong and has a major influence on consumer marketing strategies in China. A key component of the successful marketing strategy of Mengniu Dairy was its use of an 'astronaut' campaign after China sent its first astronaut into space. Its products are also endorsed by China's equivalent of NASA. Yao Ming, the NBA star and also the new badge of Olympic medallists are also relevant promotional properties at the moment.

11
Electronic Goods

Our survey respondents indicate that digital cameras have the largest potential to be purchased in the next year (see Figure 11.1). Of respondents 18 % intend to purchase this product. MP3 players and broadband Internet services also have a relatively high likelihood of being purchased. Meanwhile, dial-up Internet services appear to offer the least potential, with only 4 % of respondents indicating that they would make such a purchase. Televisions of all types are also less prioritised according to our survey.

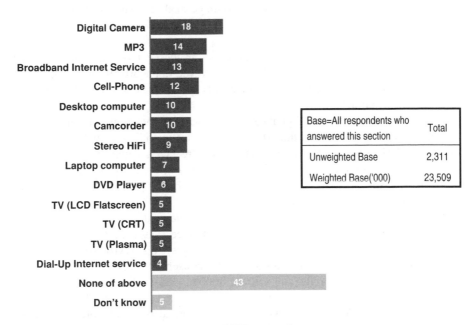

Base=All respondents who answered this section	Total
Unweighted Base	2,311
Weighted Base('000)	23,509

Source: CSFB research

Figure 11.1 Purchase intentions for electronic goods in the next year

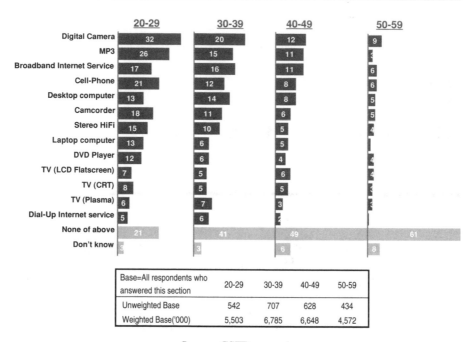

Base=All respondents who answered this section

Base=All respondents who answered this section	20-29	30-39	40-49	50-59
Unweighted Base	542	707	628	434
Weighted Base('000)	5,503	6,785	6,648	4,572

Source: CSFB research

Figure 11.2   Purchase intentions for electronic goods in the next year by age

Those intending to purchase electronic goods in the next year are mainly in the younger age bracket (Figure 11.2). Of those surveyed in the 50–59 age bracket 61 % do not intend to buy any of the electronic goods specified, versus just 21 % of those in the 20–29 age bracket.

The preference for buying digital cameras is particularly strong for younger consumers with 32 % of those in the 20–29 age bracket intending to make a purchase versus just 9 % of the 50–59 age bracket (see Figure 11.2). Younger consumers also exhibit a strong preference for MP3 players (26 %) in comparison with older age brackets. Age appears to be much less important in terms of purchasing intentions for desktop computers and broadband Internet services.

The average budget for electronics products for the next year is RMB 8444 or a little over US$1000 at the current exchange rate (see Figure 11.3), which appears high relative to monthly incomes. This value ranges from RMB 5162 for lower-income households (RMB 1000–2000 monthly household income) to RMB 17 075 for higher-income households (above RMB 8000 monthly household income).

For those who intend to purchase personal computers, Lenovo is the brand they are most likely to buy (16 %), shown in Figure 11.4. Unbranded (compatible) PCs are the next most preferred option (10 %). The Lenovo brand appears to be strongest in the 40–49 age bracket (see Figure 11.5).

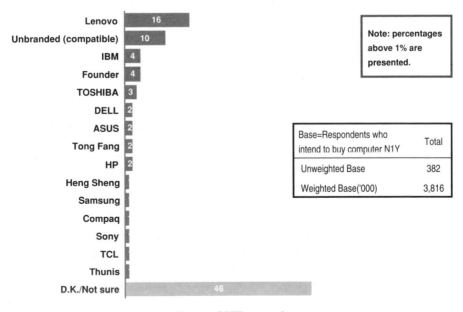

Figure 11.3 Planned budget for spending on electronic goods for the next year

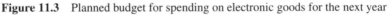

Figure 11.4 Brands of personal computers most likely to be purchased

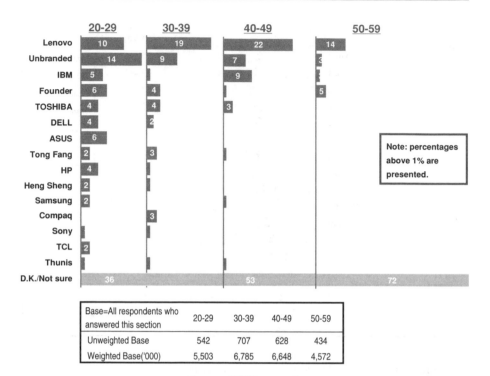

Source: CSFB research
Figure 11.5   Brands of personal computers most likely to be purchased by age

Of those who intend to buy a PC 42 % would consider buying a locally produced unbranded PC. Younger (aged 20–29, 55 %) and better educated (college or above, 47 %) consumers are the biggest potential consumers for unbranded PCs, shown in Figure 11.6.

It was found that 35 % of respondents are willing to pay a premium for foreign brands of electronics products and 47 % are not (see Figure 11.7). For those who would pay a premium the rationale given is – as in the case of automobiles – overwhelmingly perceived quality. Many respondents (47 %) are not willing to pay a premium owing to the perception that Chinese and foreign goods are equal in quality (46 %), better after-sale service of Chinese products (24 %) and patriotism in support of domestic goods (24 %).

More than half of the respondents (52 %) have access to the Internet (see Figure 11.8). Beijing has the highest percentage (65 %) and Chengdu and Wuhan the lowest (both 44 %). Internet access increases with education status, ranging from 13 % or below for junior high school to as high as 80 % for consumers with college or above education. Figures 11.9 to 11.11 illustrate a Lenovo distribution centre and the general environment for computer retailing in Shanghai.

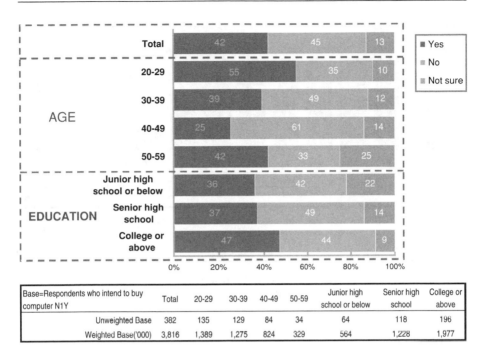

Base=Respondents who intend to buy computer N1Y	Total	20-29	30-39	40-49	50-59	Junior high school or below	Senior high school	College or above
Unweighted Base	382	135	129	84	34	64	118	196
Weighted Base('000)	3,816	1,389	1,275	824	329	564	1,228	1,977

Source: CSFB research

Figure 11.6 Purchase intentions with regards to considering unbranded, locally produced personal computers

Reasons for Paying a Premium For Foreign Electronics Brands	%
Must be better in quality /performance	82
Are more reliable/trustworthy	13
Have better after-sale service	8
Have better manufacturing technology	8
Give me prestige	7
Have better designs	5

Yes 35%
No 47%
D.K. 18%

Reasons for Not Paying a Premium For Foreign Electronics Brands	%
Chinese brands are equally good in quality	46
Chinese brands have better after-sale service	24
Chinese should use local Chinese goods	24
Restricted by personal wealth /foreign brands are too expensive	9
Whether foreign or Chinese brand is not important to me	9
I don't trust foreign goods because they may be counterfeits	3

Base=All respondents who answered this section	Total	Willing to pay a premium	Unwilling to pay a premium
Unweighted Base	2,311	776	1,119
Weighted Base('000)	23,509	8,131	10,987

Source: CSFB research

Figure 11.7 Willingness to pay a premium for foreign brands of electronics and reasons

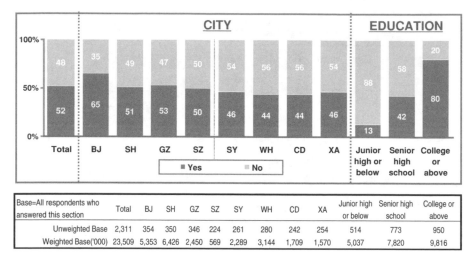

Base=All respondents who answered this section	Total	BJ	SH	GZ	SZ	SY	WH	CD	XA	Junior high or below	Senior high school	College or above
Unweighted Base	2,311	354	350	346	224	261	280	242	254	514	773	950
Weighted Base('000)	23,509	5,353	6,426	2,450	569	2,289	3,144	1,709	1,570	5,037	7,820	9,816

Source: CSFB research

Figure 11.8   Access to the Internet

Source: CSFB research

Figure 11.9   Lenovo distribution centre

Source: CSFB research
Figure 11.10   Computer shopping mall

Source: CSFB research
Figure 11.11   Hewlett Packard stall in a computer shopping mall

IMPLICATIONS FOR SEMICONDUCTORS
AND CONSUMER ELECTRONICS[1]

Our survey includes key semiconductor end markets (in other words, consumer electronics, PCs, handsets and autos). In the digital consumer arena, consumers ranked (in order) digital cameras, MP3 players, broadband Internet, cell-phones and PCs as top priorities. Surveyed consumers prefer local and unbranded PCs, where our respondents tended to believe that quality is similar or better than foreign brands. However, recent trends towards comparable-priced branded PCs could change that dynamic. By contrast, consumers of handsets – discussed in detail in Chapter 17 – show a strong preference for foreign brands, feature/functionality and quality.

Our China semiconductor consumption forecast model projects that China will grow from the current 8.6 % of global semiconductor consumption to roughly 17.5 % within a decade. China already represents the largest embedded base and/or growth opportunity for some key semiconductor end markets (e.g. ~30 % of global handset subscribers, 15 % forecast PC semiconductor compound annual growth rate (CAGR) over the medium term). With the shift to increasing Chinese semiconductor consumption, we expect: (a) another leg to the handsets and PC penetration cycle, (b) deflationary pricing pressure from a volume adoption drive in China and (c) further 'consumerisation' of broader semiconductor demand.

Today, while China's semiconductor revenue (by shipping destination) represents 12 % of global demand, aggregate household consumption in China of US$704bn represents just 3 % of the global total (see Figure 11.12). Looking at the profile of semiconductor devices shipped to China versus globally, we see a limited distinction (relative ASICs, MCUs and discrete strength are likely to be slightly skewed towards the consumer). This profile supports our belief that China is still predominantly the factory for global electronics production today rather than a significant end market.

However, underlying this export-driven semiconductor industry in China are some compelling data points about the emergence of the Chinese consumer:

- China today already represents the largest base of mobile handset owners (29 % of global handsets versus the US with 17 %).
- China has long been the largest base of televisions in the world and purchases of advanced televisions today.
- PC penetration in China remains at just 4 %.

As outlined in Chapter 1 in Section 1, the burgeoning urban Chinese consumer population is expected to drive 18 % consumption CAGR in the next 10 years versus just 2.1 % in the US. It is, therefore, important to consider the potential impact of the increasing Chinese consumer share on the global semiconductor industry. As China increasingly

---

[1] Michael Masdea, Robert Semple, Koya Tabata, Kunihiko Kanno and Jeannie Cheung contributed to this section.

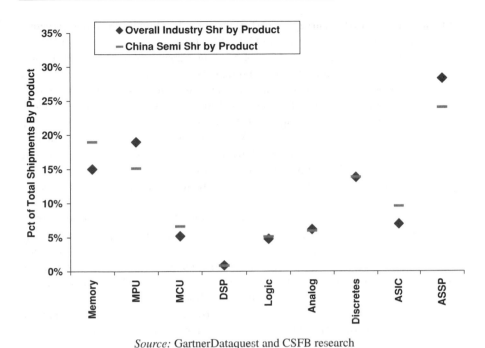

Source: GartnerDataquest and CSFB research
Figure 11.12 Relative China versus global shipments by product (Pet, per cent; Shr, share; MPU, microprocessor unit; MCU, microcontroller unit; DSP, digital signal processing; ASIC, application-specific integrated circuit; ASSP, application-specific standard product)

orders semiconductors for *domestic* consumption, we expect (a) further 'consumerisation' of broader semiconductor demand; (b) deflationary pricing pressure from a volume adoption drive in China; (c) handsets as a possible product-cycle-driven exception to our secular concerns; (d) digital consumer strength continuing to benefit Japanese semiconductor vendors near term; and (e) auto semiconductor adoption far more dependent on non-China growth, where the bulk of high-end automobiles are sold.

Lower absolute income among Chinese consumers (median household US$2000 versus US$43 300 in the US) has not prevented strong electronics demand. More impressive, these purchases have occurred despite electronics prices in China that are roughly comparable in US$ terms to goods sold in the US (as opposed to basic products such as food which are far cheaper on a relative basis). Our survey confirms this point, showing a relatively high intended spend relative to income. While we expect continued unit strength, particularly as wealth increases significantly in China over the next 10 years, we believe the persistent wealth disparity (versus developed countries) will drive increasing commoditisation and pricing pressure as semiconductor and electronics companies attempt to grow sales in China.

Included in our CSFB survey as part of the broader digital consumer category, Chinese consumers gave the desktop PC the fifth highest purchase intention rating, behind (in order) digital cameras, MP3 players, broadband Internet and cell-phone. Lower scores were given for TV/DVD and laptops. One of our secular concerns for semiconductor pricing is the increased consumerisation of semiconductor demand.

The relative ranking indicates that emerging Chinese consumers see greater value in more cost-effective electronic equipment (in other words, cameras, MP3 players, cell-phones) than traditional, high-cost PCs. We expect significant adoption of low-cost digital consumer electronics given the relatively fewer discretionary dollars available to Chinese consumers. The primary beneficiaries of digital consumer strength are the Japanese consumer ASIC manufacturers (Sony, Toshiba, Matsushita, Fujitsu, NEC, Renesas and Sharp).

Already the largest community of mobile handset (29 % of global handsets versus the US with 17 %) and television owners, our economics team expects less growth in China from these relatively mature markets (we project 8 % handset CAGR and 3 % TV CAGR – see Section 1 projections in Chapter 6). Instead, growth will come disproportionately from less-penetrated products such as personal computers (project 17 % CAGR) and automobiles (project 16 % CAGR – again see Section 1 projections in Chapter 6), from lower bases. We expect auto ownership to come on more slowly, with advanced semiconductor intensive auto functionality consumed largely outside China in the next decade.

According to TCL International, the market for televisions in China has grown to a scale of 32.67m units in 2004. At the high end, cathode-ray tube (CRT) televisions account for an estimated 14.16m units, plasma televisions for 120 000 units, liquid crystal display (LCD) televisions for 200 000 units and rear-projection televisions for 1.23m units, illustrating the overwhelming strength of the CRT. TCL estimates that, even in 2007, LCD TV sales will total 300 000 units and plasma television sales will total 270 000 units, with CRT televisions and rear-projection televisions still likely to account for the lion's share of the market. The volume zone in the CRT segment is 29-inch sets. TCL also predicts that high-definition televisions are unlikely to gain swift market penetration until analogue broadcasts end in 2015.

Among the Japanese manufacturers of consumer electronics products, Sony and Matsushita Electric Industrial stand out as the two major beneficiaries as the television market expands in China. Casio Computer is a related stock to watch in the China space, with a 40 % share of the market for TFT (thin-film transistor)-LCD materials.

Sony (China) is investing US$200m (¥22bn) in FY 3/2005 to strengthen its branding, design and production functions. To strengthen its brand image, the company has opened a 'Sony Gallery' in China. To boost its R&D and design function in the region, the company established the Shanghai Technology Center in East China as an engineering and production platform for AV and IT equipment. To further strengthen its product development capabilities, the subsidiary established the engineering and production platform firm EMCS (China).

Sales of digital still cameras (DSCs) in China will total an estimated 5.0m units in 2004, almost doubling from 2003 levels, to account for an estimated 7–8 % of global sales. The main buyers will tend to be high-income earners residing in coastal regions, with high-end cameras (4–5m pixels) accounting for almost half of all sales. Japanese manufacturers are major players by market share. Sony, we estimate, accounted for little less than 30 % of DSC shipments in China during the period January–August, Canon for a little less than 20 % and Olympus for a little less than 15 %. Other big names by market share, behind those mentioned above, are Kodak and Nikon.

The DSC market in China is set to draw attention as a growth area going forward. To be sure, it will be necessary to stimulate demand among prospective consumers in low- and medium-income brackets if the market is to become a truly major one. However, in such a case, low-end products offered at low prices are likely to become the biggest product grouping; therefore, it would not necessarily be desirable for Japanese DSC manufacturers to channel their energies into such a market. With this in mind, we would regard manufacturers of core components and components for which there are generally few supplier manufacturers as major beneficiaries when the DSC market in China does start to balloon. Specifically, we would point to Hoya, which holds more than 70 % of the aspheric lens market and Sanyo Electric which holds an 80 % share of the market for lithium-ion rechargeable batteries for use in DSCs.

China already represents 14 % of global PCs versus 37 % accounted for by the US. As discussed above we expect China to account for 32 % of ownership by 2014, adding 308m units and overtaking the US in 2011. One key driver of PC growth from the low 4 % ownership level today will be the rising educational status of the broader population. From a supply perspective, a growing number of US companies are outsourcing production of PCs to China owing to the growing skillset of the working class along with the favourable cost environment. Within the Asia Pacific region, China and Taiwan are now most popular countries for the manufacturing of PCs, a trend that is likely to favour China going forward.

China, in our view, represents a great opportunity for the PC industry from a supply and demand perspective. While we estimate the long-term growth of the PC industry to be 7–8 %, we believe emerging markets, and China in particular, will be one of the largest drivers of industry growth for years to come. The numbers are very compelling when one considers that the household PC penetration in China sits at less than 5 % today but China already is the second-largest consumer of PCs in the world. If penetration rates were to double to just 10 % the PC industry's long-term unit growth of 7–8 % would easily move into double-digit territory. However, for this to happen we believe that the Chinese government needs to release some of its control over IT spending, which would enable businesses, and eventually consumers, to become larger adopters of technology. Furthermore, we believe PC points need to be further reduced as the consumers in the region tend to be very price sensitive.

However, we believe the relatively low ranking of PCs as a purchase priority in our survey hints at a different paradigm for the PC sector than that seen in the 1990s in the US. With more than half the respondents in China already having Internet access, a plethora of digital consumer gadget complements and a preference for non-branded PCs, we believe that the Chinese consumer will view the PC as just another high-end digital product that they can use for their households. In other words, the PC represents more of a place to store/view digital pictures, access the Internet or play games.

From a vendor perspective, local companies such as Lenovo and Founder have historically dominated the Chinese market and we expect this trend to continue as the Chinese government is likely to favour domestic vendors as it awards contracts. In the survey, Chinese consumers indicated that local Chinese PC brands and unbranded products are perceived as of equal quality to foreign PCs, hinting at the challenge ahead for PC OEMs and PC semiconductor companies. The local brand Lenovo (Legend) and unbranded PCs were preferred by 25 % of respondents.

However, many US branded companies have begun making progress in the region, the most notable being Dell Computer, which has worked diligently to establish a presence in the region. Dell, in particular, views China as a key component of its international growth strategy, evidenced by its 35 % year-on-year revenue growth in the first quarter of this year. In addition, Dell has continued to roll out new growth initiatives in China, such as printers and services. In the third quarter, Dell opened an Enterprise Command Centre to support its enhanced services in China, even before it opened its first centre in Western Europe. Over the long term, we continue to believe Dell's efficient operating model and component purchasing power will enable it to compete effectively with local white box vendors and gain market share.

Lenovo, which recently acquired IBM's PC business, is a key local producer player on China's future consumption growth. Our survey indicates that it is by far the most widely recognised brand in the PC segment. This bodes well for further expansion in its market share (currently 27 %). Strong brand image, good product and service quality, and provision of a wide product range will continue to support Lenovo's leading position. This is particularly important for Lenovo's strategy to penetrate into the Tier 4–6 cities. Confidence in the brand is very important for low-cost PC buyers.

We discuss the handset market in more detail in Chapter 17. China today already represents the largest community of mobile handset owners (29 % of global handsets versus the US with 17 %). Among the surveyed cities, handset penetration has already reached 81 %. Surveyed consumers indicated that functionality/features (55 %) and quality (42 %) are the two most important reasons for purchasing a given handset brand. These rated higher than price (25 %). Unlike PCs, brand ownership leaned more towards foreign brands Nokia (25 %), MOT (22 %) and Samsung (15 %). TCL was the largest local brand with just 3 %. Handset owners intend to replace their current handsets in 1.4 years on average, further supporting the feature elasticity of the market. Handsets are a market where desire for increased functionality may trump broader price-driven unit growth. If this pans out, handsets would represent a relatively unique opportunity among electronics and semiconductors.

12
Food Producers

Our survey respondents indicate that, compared with three years ago, they on average eat processed meat somewhat less often (see Figure 12.1); 24 % indicate that they consume a little or much more than previously versus 29 % who indicate a little or much less. However, packaged/processed food consumption appears to have increased (see Figure 12.2); 28 % indicate that they consume a little or much more than previously versus 23 % who consumer a little or much less.

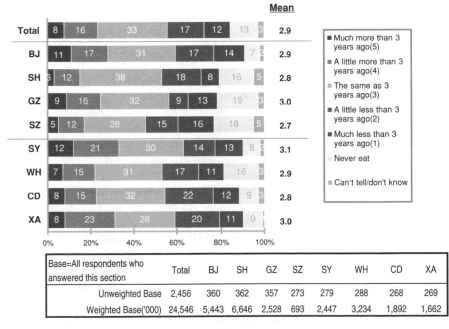

Base=All respondents who answered this section	Total	BJ	SH	GZ	SZ	SY	WH	CD	XA
Unweighted Base	2,456	360	362	357	273	279	288	268	269
Weighted Base('000)	24,546	5,443	6,646	2,528	693	2,447	3,234	1,892	1,662

Source: CSFB research

Figure 12.1 Change in frequency of eating processed meat

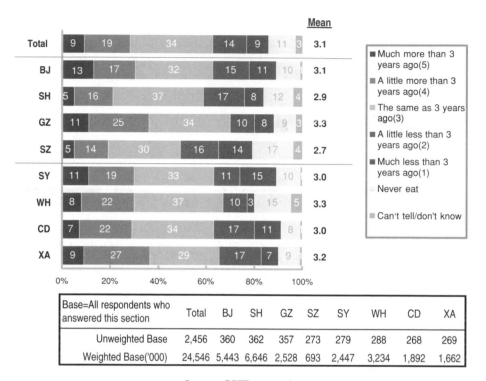

Base=All respondents who answered this section	Total	BJ	SH	GZ	SZ	SY	WH	CD	XA
Unweighted Base	2,456	360	362	357	273	279	288	268	269
Weighted Base('000)	24,546	5,443	6,646	2,528	693	2,447	3,234	1,892	1,662

Source: CSFB research

Figure 12.2   Change in frequency of eating processed/packaged food

In the case of cheese there is much more clear-cut evidence from our survey for a change in consumption patterns. It was found that 18 % of respondents indicate that they consume much or a little more versus just 6 % who consume much or a little less. The frequency increase is especially high in Guangzhou, as shown in Figure 12.3. However, overall the market remains substantially underpenetrated, with 57 % of respondents indicating that they never eat cheese.

Around half of all respondents (49 %) drink bottled water at home, almost equal to the number that drink tap water (51 %) as shown in Figure 12.4. Consumption of bottled water at home increases as household income increases, reaching 69 % of households with a monthly income of over RMB 8000.

Similarly to alcoholic beverages, brands of bottled water drunk at home are highly localised. Nationally, Nongfu Spring (8 %), Wahaha (8 %), Zhengguanghe (7 %) and Robust (7 %) are the most cited by those of our respondents who drink bottled water (see Table 12.1).

Among the food producers surveyed, Wahaha (94 %) and Nestle (91 %) have the highest brand awareness (see Figure 12.5). Both brands also have high purchase intention scores, 40 % and 52 %, respectively, of respondents reporting either a 4 or

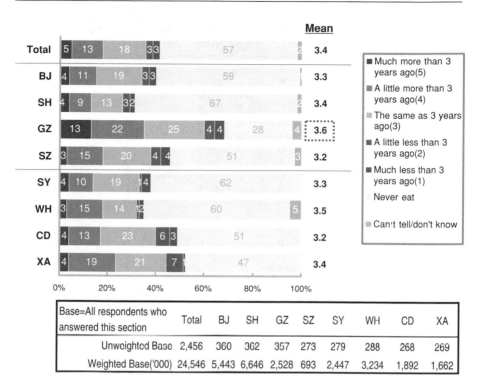

Source: CSFB research
Figure 12.3   Change in frequency of eating cheese

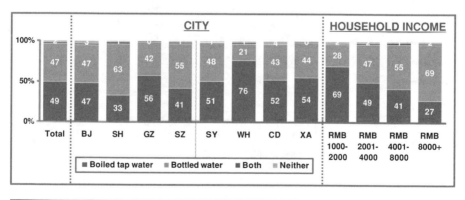

Source: CSFB research
Figure 12.4   Regular consumption of bottled water compared to boiled tap water at home

Table 12.1 Brand of bottled water drunk most often at home (%).

	Total	BJ	SH	GZ	SZ	SY	WH	CD	XA
Unweighted base	1163	178	239	153	154	135	66	116	122
Weighted base('000)	12 052	2691	4388	1083	391	1184	741	819	754
Nongfu Spring	8	7	16	3	3	3	5	1	1
Wahaha	8	23	1	1	2	10	14	0	7
Zhengguanghe	7	0	19	0	1	0	6	0	0
Robust	7	9	2	7	3	7	20	21	7
Da Qing Bao Quan	3	0	0	0	0	36	0	0	0
Yanjing	3	14	0	0	1	0	0	0	0
Yibao	3	0	0	27	9	0	0	3	0
Waterman	3	1	7	0	1	0	0	0	0
Yanzhong	2	0	7	0	1	0	0	0	0
Nestle	2	5	2	1	1	2	0	1	0
Sparkling	2	0	5	0	0	0	0	1	0
Quanxing	2	0	0	0	0	0	0	22	0
Hao Kuai Huo	1	0	0	0	0	0	0	0	16
Lian Yi	1	0	0	0	0	0	0	0	15
None	4	4	6	3	5	2	0	5	3
Don't know	14	13	15	8	14	6	33	8	16
Total	100	100	100	100	100	100	100	100	100

Base = respondents who normally drink bottled water at home.

Note: Only percentages above 2 % are presented with the exception of Hao Kuai Huo and Lian Yi, which are heavily consumed in Xi'an.

Source: CSFB research.

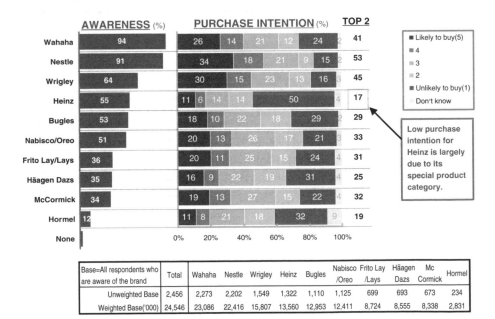

Source: CSFB research

Figure 12.5 Brand awareness of the food producers and intentions of purchasing their products

Reasons for Paying a Premium For Foreign Food Brands	%
Good quality	48
Good taste	39
More trustworthy/reliable	19
More healthy	7
Lots of variety/novelty	7
Good packaging	6
Give me prestige	2
Origin of the products /brand names	2
Fancy a try on foreign brands	2

Yes 22%
No 55%
D.K. 22%

Reasons for Not Paying a Premium For Foreign Food Brands	%
Chinese brands are better in quality	41
Chinese should use local Chinese goods	27
Chinese brands suits my taste more	20
Chinese brands are healthier	10
Restriction of personal wealth /foreign brands are too expensive	10
Chinese brands use fresh raw material	5
Know little about foreign brands	3
Don't care whether foreign or Chinese brands	2

Base=All respondents who answered this section	Total	Willing to pay a premium	Unwilling to pay a premium
Unweighted Base	2,456	556	1,398
Weighted Base('000)	24,546	5,502	13,571

Source: CSFB research

Figure 12.6   Willingness to pay a premium for foreign brands of food and reasons

5 score on an ordinal ranking from 1 to 5 in terms of likelihood of purchase. Wrigley and Heinz also have high brand recognition while Hormel (19 %) has the lowest brand recognition.

Importantly, Figure 12.6 shows that only 22 % of consumers are willing to pay extra for foreign brands while the majority (55 %) are not willing to do so. This is one of the least favourable ratios (from a foreign company perspective) that we found when asking this question in each sector.

For those who are willing to pay a premium, the extra price is perceived to be worth paying for good quality (48 %) and good taste (39 %). For those who are not willing to pay a premium, Chinese brands are perceived as better in quality (41 %), to suit personal needs more (20 %) or are bought because of a perceived duty to use domestic products (27 %). The use of celebrities for advertising snacks is a frequent marketing strategy. Figures 12.7 and 12.8 illustrate the marketing and distribution of branded food products.

IMPLICATIONS FOR FOOD PRODUCERS[1]

Throughout the world, dietary patterns tend to evolve along an almost identical path as incomes grow. This starts with a shift towards Western-style food from traditional fare and is followed by an emphasis on convenience and then health. More specifically, there is a shift from carbohydrates to meat and dairy products. The market then goes

[1] David Nelson, Shuichi Shibanuma, Michelle Yan and Marisa Ho contributed to this section.

Source: CSFB research
Figure 12.7 Frito Lays snacks

through a maturation phase with the development of frozen foods and restaurant chains. This is followed by a heavier focus on health. We see the urban areas of China covered in our survey as being in the final phase of the shift towards Western-style foods.

At the same time, traditional foods (including Chinese cuisine) are alive and well, as is true in Japan. Our impression is that the era of rapid growth in the overall market for Western-style foods, including meat and dairy, may now be passing in the big cities. This probably explains the current sluggish level of demand for ham and sausages in China.

In contrast to cigarettes – dealt with in Chapter 18 – where product choice is heavily influenced by taste factors, Chinese consumers are very price sensitive when it comes to food. As a result, overseas brands very frequently find themselves embroiled in price wars and it is difficult to communicate messages concerning high-quality ingredients or other attributes that contribute to a premium image. Furthermore, local food makers often launch copycat products.

Consumers are increasing consumption of packaged food according to our survey, driven by growth in disposable income and the trend towards convenience. Western companies have a strong presence in rapidly growing hypermarkets, but competition from low-cost local competition continues to be strong. The marketing skills of

Source: CSFB research
Figure 12.8   Häagen Dazs ice cream parlour

domestic competitors are also improving. The theory and attraction is that now is a critical time for brand establishment in the mind of the Chinese consumer.

The critical question is whether the market can ever be profitable. According to our survey, over half (55 %) of respondents are unwilling to pay a premium for foreign brands. Among them, 48 % cite the reason that quality of local brands is equally as good as foreign brands. This result should set off alarm bells for foreign brands that are priced at a premium. That said, food is a wide category and such a trend may only be representative for certain products. A few possible explanations for such perceptions would include (a) the preference for fresh food; (b) long-rooted eating and drinking habits; and (c) poor distribution controls affecting the quality of both local and foreign brands – for example, crushed biscuits, melted and re-frozen ice-cream in supermarkets are as common an issue for local brands as foreign brands due to poor distribution. The insufficient cold food distribution chain is one issue that has daunted packaged food companies and distributors for years. Even today operators comment that the supply chain in China is 'very primitive', especially when compared with the multinational companies' home markets.

Consumer sophistication at this point may not be enough to allow better-quality products to translate into strong returns. One example is chocolates; even the more expensive indigenous chocolate brands are priced 50 % cheaper than foreign brands, as local grinders mainly buy low-quality beans from Indonesia, which they process into butter and powder. Domestic makers also use cocoa butter substitutes heavily, which are much cheaper. While foreign players currently command more than half of China's chocolate market (and the top 12 home-grown players together control a 40 % share), Cadbury's China operations, which started in Beijing in the mid-1990s, are believed to be still in the red. In the processed-food category, the ability to compete on price is of paramount importance.

China's food processing and packaged food industry remains a very fragmented, ill-regulated industry resulting often in a fair number of rogue players who put their own profit motives well ahead of consumer interests. This has resulted in a number of food scandals – protein-deficient baby's milk powder, pesticide-treated processed meat – that have increasingly been uncovered in recent years thanks to a CCTV weekly programme exposing them. These are typically low-priced local products aimed at the low-income and rural consumers who make their purchase decisions on price alone. As a response to the significant ensuing public outcry, China's quality inspection authorities pledged last year to stop any food products that fail to pass the 'strict scrutiny of a new market access system'. Already, a nationwide examination of producers of five major staple food categories – wheat flour, vinegar, sauce, cooking oil and rice – has resulted in a banning of products from more than 30 000 food companies. Only 36 % of the products examined of the five food categories were awarded production permits to produce foods labelled with the 'Quality Safe' mark. Next to be examined will be meats, dairy, drinks, condiments, snack noodles, biscuits and puffed food products. However, this new system is to be fully implemented by the end of 2005. With these scandals involving low-quality processed and packaged foods, we do expect the more discerning consumers to opt for trusted brands, just as consumer concerns about counterfeit products sold on the streets had resulted in fast adoption of organised retail by the late 1990s. While the foreign names will probably never be able to compete with the local companies on price, the higher-income consumers' value migration towards better quality products could avail opportunities to them.

Compared with three years ago, consumers eat processed meat slightly less often according to our survey. This is quite different from what we hear from the few foreign multinational meat companies operating in China. The discrepancy could possibly be explained by an overall market decline, but foreign-based companies with higher quality/food safety standards are taking share rapidly. Such companies include Hormel and Smithfield.

There are enormous interregional differences in eating habits within China. Inhabitants of large cities view instant noodles as a handy product and are major consumers of the category, but many people living in the provinces still have to make their own noodles. What this means is that markets for low-priced processed foods, such as beverages and instant noodles, have strong growth potential outside major urban areas. Existing home-grown brands – for example, Mr Kon of Tingyi and Uni-President – have also entered the lower-end noodle business. Nissin Food Products stands out among Japanese companies as one that could benefit. However, while the low-end market provides new growth areas for the incumbents, it inevitably has diluted the profitability of its existing margin given that the margin for low-end noodles is typically 10–20 pp lower in gross margin than their existing brands.

The high brand awareness of Nestle and Wrigley in our survey does not come as a surprise based on our recent field visits. Wrigley has little domestic or multinational competition for its chewing gum products. Heinz's high awareness is a surprise given that most of its sales in China are with locally branded products. Heinz's awareness may come from international media such as television and film. General Mills' products, Bugles and Häagen Dazs, are posting strong gains according to the company (over 20 % per annum sales growth). Kraft's major presence in China is through Nabisco/Oreo which appears to be doing well. The business models of McCormick and Hormel in China are similar in that they are establishing a base of sales through foodservice (McCormick with McDonald's, Hormel with Pizza Hut) to create critical mass and then build brand awareness at the retail level – the strategies for both seem to be working.

That only 22 % of consumers are willing to pay a premium for foreign brands is not surprising and highlights the challenge of multinational penetration and profitability. We therefore tend to believe that the bigger opportunities within the food sector relative to the foreign multinationals are with agribusiness companies such as Archer Daniels Midland and Bunge, or with foodservice-based business models such as McCormick and Hormel, rather than most packaged food companies.

13
Food Retail

Our survey indicates that, compared with three years ago, hypermarkets and super-markets have increased their frequency of patronage from consumers (see Figure 13.1). Many respondents (85 %) say they now buy food in hypermarkets whereas 58 % say they bought in hypermarkets three years ago. The respective figures for supermarkets are 53 % and 46 %. Traditional food retailers (such as wet market and food stalls) appear to be visited somewhat less often than before.

Hypermarkets have developed most in Shanghai and Shenzhen, as shown in Table 13.1. Medium-sized supermarkets have developed most in Beijing and Chengdu.

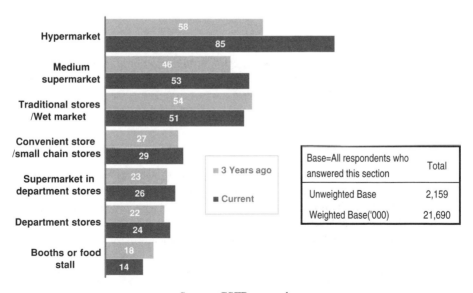

Source: CSFB research

Figure 13.1 Current locations for purchasing food compared with three years ago

Table 13.1 Regional breakdown of locations for purchasing food: current compared with three years ago (%).

	Total	BJ	SH	GZ	SZ	SY	WH	CD	XA	
Unweighted base	2159	307	334	316	241	225	265	234	237	
Weighted base('000)	21 690	4642	6132	2237	612	1973	2976	1652	1465	
Hypermarket	58	58	68	59	69	44	47	53	48	← 3 years ago
	85	78	91	87	92	80	86	81	85	← Current
Medium	46	69	31	53	34	43	34	61	35	
supermarket	53	74	37	55	39	67	39	70	45	
Traditional	54	45	41	77	48	71	56	67	60	
stores/wet market	51	45	41	73	39	63	50	63	57	
Convenient	27	26	21	33	15	40	15	45	38	
store/small chain stores	29	28	32	34	14	33	20	39	25	
Supermarket	23	36	9	40	19	32	13	27	21	
in department stores	26	37	10	46	27	40	15	33	23	
Department	22	29	10	35	21	33	16	28	19	
stores	24	31	11	39	20	31	20	35	23	
Booths or	18	16	10	21	14	26	18	27	28	
food stall	14	14	9	19	10	16	11	24	18	
Total	100	100	100	100	100	100	100	100	100	

Base = all respondents who answered this section.
Source: CSFB research

When choosing hyper/supermarkets for purchasing food as opposed to other types of retailers, our respondents indicate that price is the most important factor (42 %), as shown in Figure 13.2. This is followed by the freshness of food (32 %), variety of food (31 %), convenience of location (29 %) and quality of service (25 %). The importance attached to price is in contrast to its relative unimportance for consumers in the food service sector discussed in Chapter 14. Our respondents indicate that the product types bought most at hypermarkets or supermarkets are food and personal/household care items (see Figure 13.3).

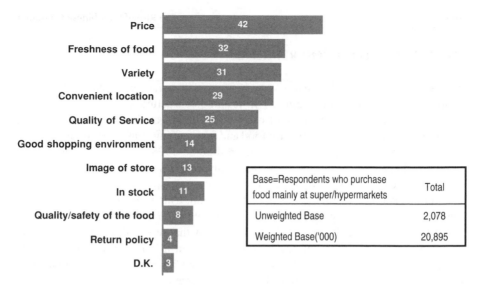

Price	42
Freshness of food	32
Variety	31
Convenient location	29
Quality of Service	25
Good shopping environment	14
Image of store	13
In stock	11
Quality/safety of the food	8
Return policy	4
D.K.	3

Base=Respondents who purchase food mainly at super/hypermarkets	Total
Unweighted Base	2,078
Weighted Base('000)	20,895

Source: CSFB research

Figure 13.2 Reasons for choosing super/hypermarkets for purchasing food

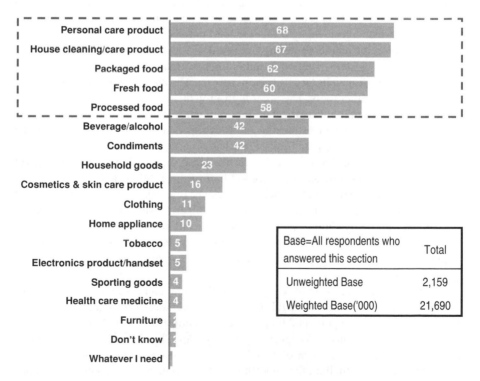

Personal care product	68
House cleaning/care product	67
Packaged food	62
Fresh food	60
Processed food	58
Beverage/alcohol	42
Condiments	42
Household goods	23
Cosmetics & skin care product	16
Clothing	11
Home appliance	10
Tobacco	5
Electronics product/handset	5
Sporting goods	4
Health care medicine	4
Furniture	2
Don't know	2
Whatever I need	

Base=All respondents who answered this section	Total
Unweighted Base	2,159
Weighted Base('000)	21,690

Source: CSFB research

Figure 13.3 Products generally purchased at super/hypermarkets

IMPLICATIONS FOR FOOD RETAILERS[1]

The survey indicates the reality of changing consumer preferences for more formalised formats of food retailing. This is a major structural change in the Chinese retail marketplace. From the time of early-bird foreign retailers complaining about consumers' resistance to shopping for food and fast-moving consumer goods in a nice, climate-controlled shopping environment in the mid-1990s, organised retail took a rapid growth path by the late 1990s, which if anything has only accelerated in the last two years. We think this trend could very well have been spurred by the prevalence of counterfeits and low-quality goods in distribution in China. As consumers' incomes reach a certain level, they start to appreciate the better shopping environment and the better assurance of quality and product authenticity that reputable organised retailers are able to provide (although not a guarantee, given a long and primitive supply chain in China). From a low of 6 % of retail sales in China in 2001, we estimate that organised retail now makes up a low double-digit percentage of China's retail market.

Global retailers, as well as a number of indigenous retailers, are increasingly positioning themselves to further capture this structural change. Hypermarkets are at the forefront of this change. Our survey of purchase decisions concludes that hypermarkets have not only experienced the highest growth rate in the last three years but also now represent the largest single format for food purchases.

Almost all foreign retailers entering China did so with the hypermarket format. The thrust of expansion for the Beijing-based indigenous retailer Wumart (ranking in the top ten nationally despite its largely regional presence to date) is also in hypermarkets, despite its supermarket roots. The other high-growth area is convenience stores and, given its lower capital and real estate requirement at the front-end level, this too has attracted significant investments – although to date mainly on the part of the indigenous retailers rather than foreign retailers.

This 'bar-bell' shape development has resulted in a compression of the supermarket segment – not unlike Taiwan in the second half of the 1990s when consumers' excitement over the hypermarket shopping experience together with aggressive roll-out of convenience stores posed a huge challenge to supermarkets there. The experience of Lianhua – currently China's largest organised retail group – underlines this trend, as its supermarket business has been facing pressures and is in a restructuring mode in the past year, while its hypermarket and convenience store businesses continue to grow strongly.

In spite of the rapid growth of organised retail, China remains a difficult market for foreign retailers to make successful. Competitive pressures are huge, coming from fellow global heavyweights, budding indigenous competition (the likes of Lianhua, Wumart, China Resources Vanguard (parent group China Resources Enterprises listed)) to independents, some of which only jumped on to the retail bandwagon in recent years after smelling the opportunities there. Same-store productivity trends

---

[1] Andrew Kasoulis, Marisa Ho and Michelle Yan contributed to this section.

need to be monitored carefully: in some Tier 1 cities where competition has been most intense, we have already started to see new stores cannibalising the sales of existing stores. The sheer competition for real estate, amid more strict government zoning restrictions, also poses pressure on what is structurally a thin-margin business (a local retailer noted that rising rental costs could, in some cases, have taken away 200 basis points of margins – significant considering even the most proficient operators may make just about 2 % pre-tax margin).

Gross margins – typically at 15–20 % excluding vendor rebates – are much lower than the 20–30 % level often seen internationally and an operator generating a 2 % EBIT margin is already considered to be doing very well. With the huge pressure to expand and define one's turf before it gets carved away by a competitor (and at the same time invest in the backroom infrastructure that is the crux of organised retail), the biggest challenge is perhaps the preservation of overall returns while expanding store presence at a sometimes break-neck pace. In addition, even though we earlier highlighted an emerging trend for the Chinese consumer to migrate to higher-value/ better-quality products, having balked at some of the earlier food and fast-moving consumer goods (FMCG) product quality scandals, this does not mean that the Chinese consumers have become less value conscious (except that value now is seen to be a function of both price and quality, rather than price alone). In this regard, we see continuing discounting activities and pricing pressures. Obviously in many cases the manufacturers will be asked to share the burden and there could well be positive demand elasticities. Still, in the face of a trend of upward pressures on costs, retailers will need to push through significantly higher volume sales to maintain store profitability.

There are a number of structural issues that continue to make profitably penetrating China a challenge. These include various levels of government regulation, the difficulty of adopting the centralised distribution model/practice to a still relatively unsophisticated supplier base and real estate development challenges. In addition, sometimes the low policy transparency – not to mention the corruption index – implies challenges that are not usually evident in more developed marketplaces in the world.

A classic example is the confusion back in 2000–1 on whether foreign retailers need a licence from the state council level, or just local government approvals, to start a business in China, and whether retailers can skirt the legal requirement to have a local partner. Retailers like Carrefour or the 7-Eleven local franchisee suffered a setback when Beijing in 2001 decided to clamp down on these 'regulatory irregularities' – although they were also accepted market practice – and ordered these retailers to divest stakes from their businesses and suspend their expansion in the meantime. In both these cases, the situation appeared to have been amicably resolved but it did mean some opportunity costs to both retailers when for a while they were not allowed to add any new stores.

In 2003, there were also talks of whether Beijing would go ahead with a star-rating system that approves foreign retailers' future expansion plans on the number of policy irregularities they have committed in the past. The policy did not go ahead but this does highlight some of the policy fluidity foreign retailers may see, especially amid what could be an increased protectionist policy environment. This occurred after some local governments were criticised for having overly favoured foreign retailers in the pursuit of foreign direct investment (FDI) and after many local industry watchers became vocally concerned about foreign retailers destroying China's indigenous retail industry.

To date, Carrefour seems to have made the most inroads among the foreign players, with the largest store base (slated to reach 59 hypermarkets by the end of 2004). At least for now, it has also been the fastest growing foreign retailer, expanding at a pace averaging one new hypermarket a month starting in 2004 (a pace set to continue into 2005). It was the only retailer to have made it into the domestically compiled top-ten organised retailer league table in 2003 (which included foreign retailers for the first time). It has also started to develop the hard discount format aggressively as well as its own supermarket banner. However, with the final foreign ownership restriction lifted on 11 December 2004 (in other words, foreign retailers are now allowed to wholly own their business) and all remaining restrictions on foreign retailers (for example, geographical) lifted also by 2007, foreign operators are gearing up for accelerated expansion. Wal-Mart recently said it may open as many as 12–15 stores in China in 2005 (versus 10 in 2004); Metro also said it is planning up to 12 new stores in China in 2005 to expand its store base by 50 %. The list goes on.

All the major multinational retailers acknowledge the potential for China. To date Wal-Mart, Carrefour, Metro, Tesco, 7-Eleven, to name some of the key names, have invested in China. However, interestingly, none have overweighted their investment programmes in favour of China. This is a sign, in our opinion, of the cautious stance they have taken to doing business in the country and also the political issues that continue to surround retailing. This cautious stance seems to have originated from the Asia financial crisis of the late 1990s as well as the SARS crisis of 2002. China represents a major opportunity for retailers with the investment horizon and resources to invest over a long cycle, not one to generate dramatic short-term results.

The last few years have seen some break-neck development from various operators in the organised retail segment. To some degree, consolidation is happening now, especially as some inexperienced smaller operators or independents fail, although probably not to an extent required to allow healthier levels of industry profitability yet. Our view is that the competitive landscape remains significantly in flux still and it is way too early to predict what the competitive league table will look like, say, in three years' time. In July 2004, Tesco, which had a zero presence in China, announced the acquisition of a 50 % stake in a local hypermarket chain, Hymall. This is an entry ticket, so to speak, which probably heralds Tesco entering China aggressively soon if its other Asian experience (Thailand, South Korea) is anything to go by. On 2003 price/earnings ratio (P/E), Hymall was valued at a rather rich 50.9 times (and a more reasonable 0.85 times enterprise value/sales, compared with the one-times sale Tesco paid for Lotus in Thailand back during the Asian crisis). Obviously, Tesco would be looking at forward earnings – if we were to make a bold assumption that Hymall's margins are sustained into 2004, based on the forecast 2004 sales figure talked about in the press, our very rudimentary estimate is that Tesco may be paying ~37 times 2004E P/E. We think it is clearly a seller's market when it comes to M&A in the China consumer sector and there has been no shortage of multinational corporations willing to pay high valuations for an entry ticket into what could one day be the world's biggest consumer market.

It would seem hard to see any consumer company with global aspirations ignoring China. While we think China's organised retail market could well see oversupply and hence an industry consolidation could be in the works at some point in the medium term (which itself may avail acquisition opportunities), we suspect that, like in Korea, China's organised retail competitive landscape may become defined in just a few short years, with established winners locking in market shares and consumer loyalty.

14
Food Services

Our survey indicates that, on average, consumers go to restaurants 4.6 times per month (see Figure 14.1). Their average spend per meal at restaurants is RMB 49.9 or around US$6 at the current exchange rate (see Figure 14.2). Using these data, our estimation of the market size per year is RMB 74bn (US$9bn) for the eight cities, shown in Table 14.1.

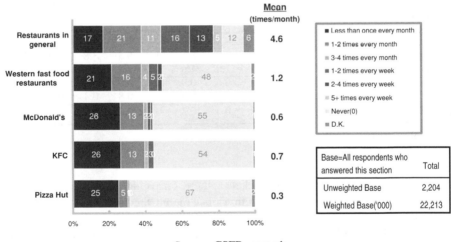

Source: CSFB research

Figure 14.1   Frequency of dining out

Western fast food restaurants were visited by 50 % of respondents. The average frequency is 1.2 times per month and average spending is RMB 39.1 (US$4.70) per meal. We estimated the market size per year of this segment to be RMB 15bn (US$1.8bn) for the eight cities. Eating out in Western fast food restaurants is heavily skewed towards the younger age brackets where income growth is fastest, as shown

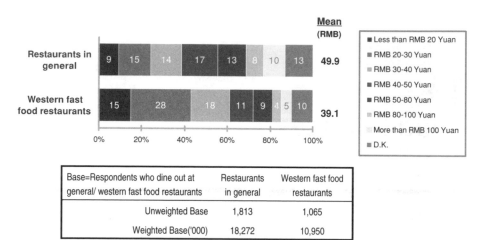

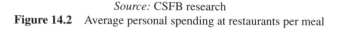

Source: CSFB research

Figure 14.2   Average personal spending at restaurants per meal

Table 14.1   Estimated market size per year of the food services sector.

Average times/month	Total	BJ	SH	GZ	SZ	SY	WH	CD	XA
Unweighted base	2204	315	345	315	254	247	271	235	222
Weighted base('000)	22 213	4763	6334	2230	645	2166	3043	1659	1372
Restaurants in general	4.6	5.6	3.4	5.5	5.0	5.5	3.8	4.6	4.6
Western fast food restaurants	1.2	1.6	1.0	1.6	1.2	1.2	0.8	0.8	0.6
McDonald's	0.6	1.0	0.6	0.9	0.6	0.7	0.4	0.4	0.3
KFC	0.7	1.1	0.6	0.6	0.4	0.8	0.4	0.4	0.4
Pizza Hut	0.3	0.4	0.3	0.3	0.2	0.3	0.2	0.1	0.1

Base = all respondents who answered this section.
Source: CSFB research

in Figure 14.3. Those in the 20–29 bracket eat there, on average, 2.4 times per month, which is six times as often as the 0.4 times per month for those in the 50–59 age bracket.

McDonald's and KFC are similar in terms of average visiting frequency (0.6 compared with 0.7 per month), shown in Figure 14.1. The average visiting frequency for Pizza Hut is 0.3 times per month. We find that McDonald's has a better performance in Southern cities such as Guangzhou and Shenzhen (see Table 14.2), while KFC is stronger in Northern cities such as Beijing, Shenyang and Xi'an. Unsurprisingly, average spend is highest in Shenzhen, which we noted previously has the highest average personal income of the eight cities.

Taste (34 %) is the most important factor for differentiating between Western fast food restaurants (see Figure 14.4). Children requests (28 %), good environment

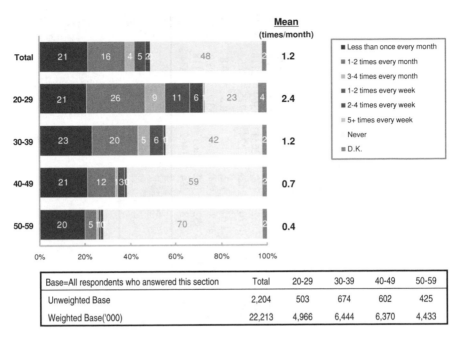

Source: CSFB research
Figure 14.3   Frequency of dining out in Western fast food restaurants by age

(26 %), convenient location (21 %) and speed of service (21 %) are also important factors. By contrast price is identified by only 10 % as a reason for choosing between different brands, a strong contrast with the result discussed in Chapter 13 for food retailing.

Dinner (48 %) and lunch (43 %) are the meals most eaten at Western fast food restaurants, as shown in Figure 14.5. Meanwhile Figure 14.6 shows that younger people aged 20–29 are slightly more likely to eat dinner at a Western fast food restaurant than the older age groups. Figure 14.7 illustrates a KFC outlet in Shanghai.

IMPLICATIONS FOR FOOD SERVICE COMPANIES[1]

China appears to be a solid but still relatively undeveloped market for fast food. According to our survey, looking at the key population demographic of consumers aged 20–59 and focusing on eight major cities only, Western fast food is 21 % of total restaurant sales. Although we do not have this specific data for other parts of the world, in general the fast food market is 25 % of total restaurant sales in Germany, 30 % in the UK and 50 % in the US. We suspect those numbers would be much higher

[1] Janice Meyer contributed to this section.

Table 14.2 Frequency of dining out by cities.

		Total	BJ	SH	GZ	SZ	SY	WH	CD	XA
Restaurants in general	Average frequency (per month)	4.6	5.6	3.4	5.5	5.0	5.5	3.8	4.6	4.6
	Average spending (per meal)	49.9	45.5	66.0	50.4	55.3	41.6	44.1	39.8	37.9
	Population aged 20–59 ('000)	26 958	6048	7344	2832	762	2631	3369	2118	1854
	Market size per year (RMB '000 000)	74 255	18 492	19 776	9420	2528	7224	6775	4653	3879
Western fast food restaurants	Average frequency (per month)	1.2	1.6	1.0	1.6	1.2	1.2	0.8	0.8	0.6
	Average spending (per meal)	39.1	42.2	37.7	40.8	35.0	38.6	33.2	43.0	39.5
	Population aged 20–59 ('000)	26 958	6048	7344	2832	762	2631	3369	2118	1854
	Market size per year (RMB '000 000)	15 178	4900	3322	2218	384	1462	1074	874	527

Base = all respondents who answered this section.

Note: market size is calculated only with a population aged 20–59 and low-income households excluded.

Source: CSFB research

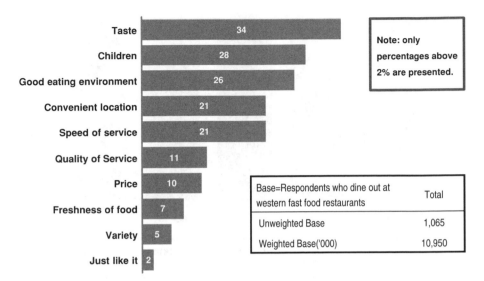

Source: CSFB research

Figure 14.4 Reasons for choosing certain brands of Western fast food restaurants

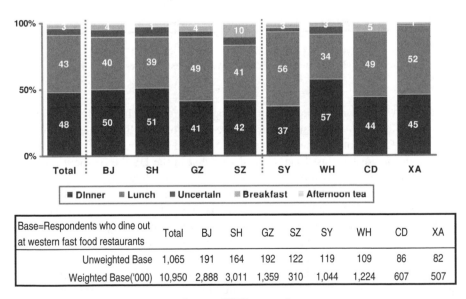

Source: CSFB research

Figure 14.5 Meal eaten most often at Western fast food restaurants by city

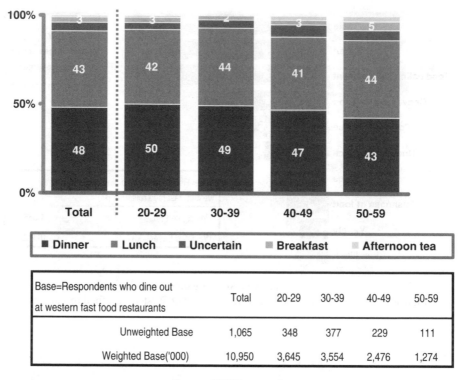

Figure 14.6   Meal eaten most often at Western fast food restaurants by age

if we narrowed down the population and looked at major cities only. In terms of frequency, fast food visits also appear to have room to grow. In the selected markets surveyed in China, total restaurant frequency is 4.6 times per month but only 1.2 times per month for Western fast food. Considering that in the US the frequent fast food customer can visit up to four times per week, that is a huge gap. Encouragingly from the perspective of the companies operating in this sector, our survey shows clear evidence that Western fast food eating is skewed to the younger generation, who we also find tend to have higher income growth. Moreover, price sensitivity is low, ranking seventh in our survey behind other features that allow the margin to be extracted.

Two companies in particular are well positioned to benefit from growth in China in our view: YUM Brands and McDonald's. YUM's business is far bigger than McDonald's, comprising more than 1250 KFC units and 140 Pizza Hut stores. The company is adding stores at a rate of about 300 per year, with the bulk of those being KFCs. Expansion is expected to come in new and existing markets. YUM already operates in almost 300 cities, with 48 new markets coming on stream in 2004. YUM's business in China is profitable, with the company deriving about US$200m of operating profit

Source: CSFB research
Figure 14.7   Kentucky Fried Chicken restaurant

there in 2004. Although chain-specific numbers are not available, the average unit volumes at KFC are higher than international and US KFC averages, the costs to build are lower and the margins are higher. The chain is positioned as an everyday fast feeder, with lunch and dinner evenly split, and taste at a good price as the selling proposition. That seems to mesh nicely with our consumer survey results.

McDonald's business is much smaller than YUM's, with about 600 stores in China. In 2004 it added around 60 stores and plans to ramp that up to 100 in future years. Although China is profitable, we do not believe returns are where the company wants them to be, so a slower approach to growth makes sense. The bad news is that it causes it to fall further behind YUM each year. The menu at McDonald's includes the basic burger line-up but does offer more chicken products, including bone-in chicken and spicy chicken thigh burgers. The chain focuses on affordability, kids and variety, of which affordability and variety were not high rated factors in our survey. However, since our survey covered eight major cities only, these may be more important as McDonald's expands. According to our survey, the frequency for McDonald's is similar to KFC, which is interesting given a preference for chicken in Asian markets. However, as we noted above, McDonald's does offer more chicken on its menu to broaden its appeal. Although McDonald's sits well behind YUM in the race to penetrate China, that is not lost on the management team and we expect this to be a priority over the coming years.

15
Household and Personal Care

Our survey indicates that consumers regard perceived quality as the most important factor for choosing between household and personal care brands (51%), as shown in Figure 15.1. Brand (41%), price (40%) and stated benefits (32%) are also important factors.

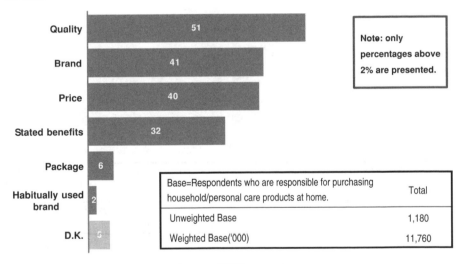

Source: CSFB research

Figure 15.1 Reasons for choosing certain brands of household/personal care products

The seven foreign household/personal care brands surveyed are largely perceived as local Chinese brands (Tide, Ariel, Rejoice, Pantene, Softlan, Crest and Colgate). They range from the lowest of 53% for Colgate to the highest of 72% for Tide (see Figure 15.2).

Our survey finds that 7% of respondents have a child aged below three, shown in Figure 15.3. The highest percentages are in Shenzhen (19%) and Guangzhou (15%),

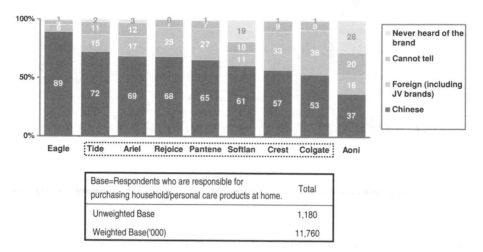

Base=Respondents who are responsible for purchasing household/personal care products at home.	Total
Unweighted Base	1,180
Weighted Base('000)	11,760

Source: CSFB research

Figure 15.2   Brand perception on whether foreign brands are viewed as local

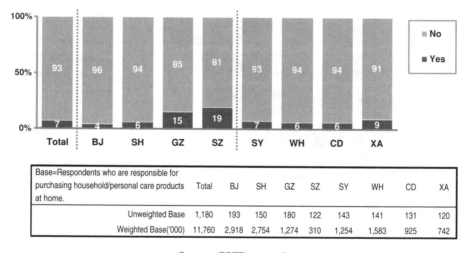

Base=Respondents who are responsible for purchasing household/personal care products at home.	Total	BJ	SH	GZ	SZ	SY	WH	CD	XA
Unweighted Base	1,180	193	150	180	122	143	141	131	120
Weighted Base('000)	11,760	2,918	2,754	1,274	310	1,254	1,583	925	742

Source: CSFB research

Figure 15.3   Has a child below the age of three

which have the highest per capita incomes in our survey. This may provide evidence that the one-child policy is breaking down in the more affluent middle classes. The diaper brand used most is Pampers from P&G (48 %), shown in Figure 15.4. Anerle (18 %) and Mamy Poko (14 %) were also frequently used brands. Of all parents 9 % do not use diapers for their babies.

Skin care/cosmetic products were used by 49 % of respondents, as shown in Figure 15.5. This breaks down to 76 % of all females and 22 % of all males. The tendency

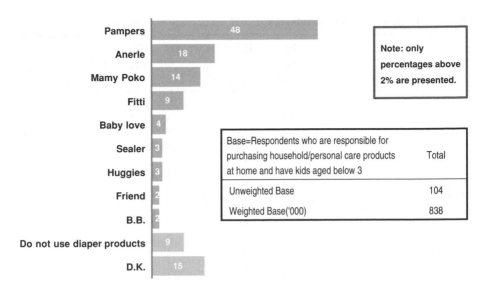

Source: CSFB research

Figure 15.4   Most consumed brands of diapers

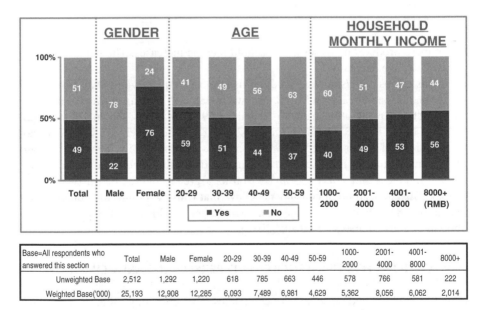

Source: CSFB research

Figure 15.5   Respondents use of skin care/cosmetic products

Table 15.1 Most consumed brands of skin care/cosmetic products by city (%).

	Total	BJ	SH	GZ	SZ	SY	WH	CD	XA
Unweighted base	1221	207	156	186	123	149	139	131	130
Weighted base ('000)	12 219	3130	2864	1317	312	1307	1561	925	803
Olay	19	15	14	24	30	18	22	23	23
Dabao	13	22	4	2	5	16	15	15	13
Avon	5	4	1	10	9	3	6	7	6
Mininurse	4	5	2	4	3	4	6	8	5
L'Oréal	3	4	3	2	2	4	4	3	2
Aupres	3	8	1	1	1	4	4	2	1
Pond's	3	1	6	2	2	1	5	2	2
Amway	3	3	4	2	0	2	2	2	1
Johnson & Johnson	3	2	4	6	2	3	1	0	0
Maybelline	2	2	5	0	1	0	2	2	2
Nivea	2	2	4	3	0	1	1	0	1
Shiseido	2	1	2	3	2	3	1	0	1
TJOY	2	1	3	0	2	1	1	1	3
D.K.	12	8	14	18	15	6	17	11	15
Total	100	100	100	100	100	100	100	100	100

Base = respondents who use skin care/cosmetic products.

Note: only percentages above 2 % are presented.

Source: CSFB research

to use these products increases as household income increases. The percentage also increases as age decreases.

Brands of cosmetic/skin care products used most frequently are Olay from P&G (19 %) and Dabao (local brand, 13 %), shown in Table 15.1. Olay appears to have the strongest brand penetration in the 30–39 and 40–49 age brackets, shown in Table 15.2.

It was found that 33 % of all cosmetic/skin care product users are willing to pay more for foreign brands while 50 % are not, as shown in Figure 15.6. The former group of consumers attaches more value to foreign brands for their perceived better quality (65 %), mildness and safety (23 %) as well as a greater degree of trustworthiness (23 %). The latter group of consumers believe that Chinese brands are equally good in quality (38 %), that local products suit them better (23 %) while also perceiving an obligation to use domestic products (20 %).

IMPLICATIONS FOR HOUSEHOLD AND PERSONAL CARE COMPANIES[1]

Global household and personal care companies have great opportunities and have already had considerable success in the emerging markets. On average, the larger capitalisation household and personal care companies generate 25–30 % of sales

[1] Lauren Lieberman, Guillaume Dalibot, Yukiko Oshima and Michelle Yan contributed to this section.

Table 15.2   Most consumed brands of skin care/cosmetic products by age (%).

	Total	20–29	30–39	40–49	50–59
Unweighted base	1221	360	405	293	163
Weighted base ('000)	12 219	3594	3856	3068	1701
Olay	19	14	23	22	12
Dabao	13	7	13	14	19
Avon	5	6	4	5	4
Mininurse	4	6	3	3	5
L'Oréal	3	5	3	2	2
Aupres	3	4	4	3	1
Pond's	3	4	2	3	2
Amway	3	2	2	4	4
Johnson & Johnson	3	2	2	3	2
Maybelline	2	4	2	2	1
Nivea	2	4	1	1	1
Shiseido	2	3	2	1	1
TJOY	2	2	2	1	3
D.K.	12	10	10	12	22
Total	100	100	100	100	100

Base = respondents who use skin care/cosmetic products.

Note: only percentages above 2 % are presented.

Source: CSFB research

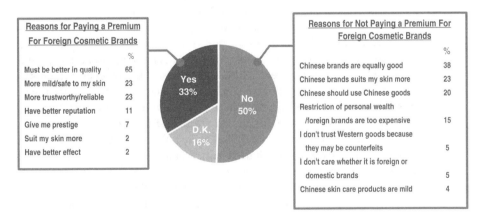

Reasons for Paying a Premium For Foreign Cosmetic Brands	%
Must be better in quality	65
More mild/safe to my skin	23
More trustworthy/reliable	23
Have better reputation	11
Give me prestige	7
Suit my skin more	2
Have better effect	2

Yes 33%
No 50%
D.K. 16%

Reasons for Not Paying a Premium For Foreign Cosmetic Brands	%
Chinese brands are equally good	38
Chinese brands suits my skin more	23
Chinese should use Chinese goods	20
Restriction of personal wealth /foreign brands are too expensive	15
I don't trust Western goods because they may be counterfeits	5
I don't care whether it is foreign or domestic brands	5
Chinese skin care products are mild	4

Base=Respondents who use skin care/cosmetic products	Total	Willing to pay a premium	Unwilling to pay a premium
Unweighted Base	1,221	402	627
Weighted Base('000)	12,219	4,077	6,147

Source: CSFB research

Figure 15.6   Willingness to pay a premium for foreign brands of cosmetic products and reasons

from the emerging markets compared with 10–15 % only for the food manufacturers. China is the next great frontier, although it currently represents less than 5 % of sales for the larger US companies in the household and personal care space. Procter & Gamble has the largest absolute presence in China, with approximately US$2bn of revenues. In some categories like shampoo and hair care it already dominates with a ~50 % market share.

Key determinants of a company's success in China will be branding, distribution and scale, in our view. Today, the global household and personal care companies face more competition from local manufacturers rather than from each other, with sudden brand proliferation pressuring manufacturer price points. Strong branding and understanding of the local Chinese consumer will allow companies to differentiate their products and provide some protection versus deflationary trends. Expanding distribution beyond the Tier 1 cities (which currently account for 15 % of industry revenue) is likely to be costly and local distributors are known to play manufacturers off each other, bargaining for the best price. We believe that companies with the greatest scale, in terms of portfolio breadth, will be advantaged in working with these distributors.

We believe Procter & Gamble (P&G) is best positioned in China today among the US companies and sets the gold standard for local execution. P&G first entered China in 1988 via a joint venture with Hutchison Whampoa. (Earlier this year, P&G bought out Hutchison's remaining 20 % stake in the JV.) The company's first entries were with top brands in major cities (in other words, Tier 1) to establish a foothold in the country and to learn the intricacies of the wholesaler/distributor system. More recently, P&G has expanded its reach into Tier 2 and 3 cities while also expanding its portfolio with additional categories and additional products. We believe that P&G's scale (in other words, breadth of product offerings) has been and will continue to be a competitive advantage in working with distributors to get into more rural areas and lower-tier cities. Over the past two years, the company has added lower price points to its product portfolio in a number of key categories like oral care and laundry detergent.

Colgate is the other large US company in this sector with a significant presence in China. Colgate first entered the country in 1992, and it currently accounts for about 3 % of total sales. In contrast to P&G, Colgate's first entry was solely in oral care and included rural markets where it used its 'tried and true' oral health education programmes to build awareness and per capita usage. Today, Colgate's business is still predominantly in oral care, potentially accounting for more than 80 % of sales in the country. We believe there is still room for Colgate to grow the overall oral care market with its educational programmes but emphasise that branding and marketing will be essential to maintain share versus the many local players. In addition, we believe Colgate will need to broaden its portfolio in China to include other lead products like fabric softeners, shampoo and liquid soaps to gain scale, which can be leveraged with distributors and media agencies.

Thus far, Procter & Gamble has manoeuvred through the challenges of bringing its brand names into lower segments of the market without diluting its brand image.

According to Tom Doctoroff, North East Asia Director and Greater China CEO for J Walter Thompson, P&G's success in China has been built around the theme of family protection. He cites the example of Safeguard soap, which has maintained a 20–30 % market share for the past 10 years using as part of its strategy advertisements focusing on the risks from germs. It is noteworthy that P&G has according to our survey the leading position in both women's cosmetics (via Olay) and babies' diapers (via Pampers). Notwithstanding the one-child policy, baby diapers is one area in which growth can be expected to continue going forward, with 9 % of the respondents saying they do not use diapers for their babies. Hengan's Anerle brand remains a solid number two in the baby diapers market with an 18 % share (in line with estimates given by the company). It is also the only local brand within the top three brands. Unicharm's Mamy Poko brand ranks third. We believe the innovative nature of the brand is well recognised among Chinese consumers and that the product will remain attractive to wealthier parents residing in metropolitan areas.

Our survey indicates that skin care and cosmetics products are attractively positioned from a demographic perspective with usage higher in higher income and younger age groups. We find that 76 % of females already use skin care/cosmetics products in China. With consumption rising as household income increases and younger generations spending more on these products, the market for skin care and cosmetics looks set to continue expanding from hereon. Other than P&G's Olay product, Shiscido's strength is evident. Its Aupres brand and Shiseido brand together account for 5 % of skin care and cosmetics consumption. These are premium brands and their healthy sales have been supporting Shiseido's high profit margin (approximately 20 %) in China. Currently, department stores are the main sales channel for cosmetics (especially for premium products) but new channels such as speciality stores are likely to emerge as a force in the future. This is clearly something that the Hong Kong based cosmetics retail chain Sa Sa is banking on, as it prepares to embark on its first retail store in China.

Among the European companies we would highlight L'Oréal. Although L'Oréal's revenue exposure to China is only around 2–3 % currently, the group has made no secret of its intention to make China a large revenue and profit contributor in the medium term. To this end the group is implementing a strategy based on three pillars:

• The introduction of its portfolio of global brands
• The Mininurse acquisition
• The Yu Sai acquisition

L'Oréal first entered the Chinese market with its existing portfolio of brands. Given the complexity and risks of the traditional retail system, the group's distribution was restricted to department stores and the just-implemented modern trade. Clearly this model quickly showed its limits as low-end brands such as Maybelline are sold in high-end department stores, preventing the group from building scale. In fact, to stimulate volume, management took what it described as a 'courageous decision' to reduce prices by 30 % across the board for Maybelline last year – a Maybelline

tube of mascara now sells at RMB 49/ US$5.9 in China, versus ¥1260/~US$12 at a
Seiyu superstore in Japan or a similar price in Hong Kong, even though they are all
manufactured at L'Oréal's Suzhou plant in eastern China.

In order to achieve scale and gain access to a wider mass-market distribution channel
L'Oréal acquired Mininurse in 2003. With a presence in 200 000 points of sales the
Mininurse deal is certainly a good starting point. It brings scale and ownership of
a local brand that is currently progressively being associated with Garnier, one of
L'Oréal's other mass-market brands not yet launched in China.

One important finding of our survey is that, in large part, Chinese consumers think
that local and foreign brands are equally good. Owning local brands or brands perceived as such seems therefore essential. The Mininurse/Garnier operation addresses
this issue in the mass market while the recent acquisition of Yu Sai probably fills the
gap in terms of high-end local brand offering.

With supermarkets/hypermarkets being ranked the best place to buy personal care
products (68 % of total), local companies such as Hengan potentially will see the
fastest shift in distribution from the traditional wholesaler network to direct selling to
retailers. Given Hengan's strong brand equity in local markets, we believe access to
modern retailer channels is easy relative to its local peers. The value migration issue
discussed under the 'food producers' and 'retail' sections of this book is in play here.
We expect the recent scandals involving rogue manufacturers producing paper-based
products from recycled industrial/ medical waste – which obviously raise concerns
on hygiene standards and consumer safety – will push consumers who can afford to
pay a little bit more towards the reputable branded products. Even if we disregard
these exceptional cases of irregularities, many local producers are still using low-cost
sugar cane waste to substitute for the more expensive pulp, which probably explains
some of the very low quality products we have come across in China. We are banking
on Chinese consumers growing more discriminating over time.

16
Luxury Goods

In the last three years, 27 % of survey respondents have purchased luxury goods (see Figure 16.1). No individual luxury goods brand has a large market share. Of those who made at least one purchase 48 % bought fashion/ready to wear. The brand with the largest market share is Pierre Cardin (5 %), shown in Table 16.1. Of all those who made a purchase 41 % bought premium perfumes and cosmetics. The brand with the largest market share is Christian Dior, shown in Table 16.1.

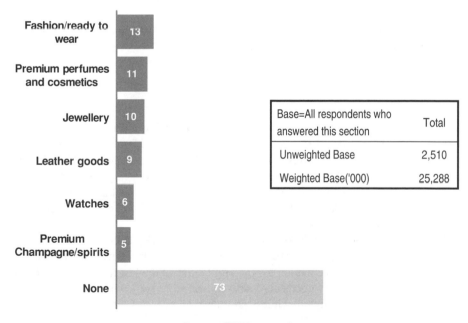

Source: CSFB research
Figure 16.1   Purchase of luxury goods in the last three years

Table 16.1 Most consumed brands of luxury goods in the last three years.

Fashion/ready to wear (%)		Premium perfumes/ cosmetics (%)		Jewellery (%)	
Unweighted base	343	Unweighted base	272	Unweighted base	258
Weighted base('000)	3385	Weighted base('000)	2695	Weighted base('000)	2556
Pierre Cardin	5	Christian Dior (CD)	15	Chow Tai Fook	13
Valentino	3	Lancome	11	Tse Sui Luen	10
Goldlion	3	Chanel	9	Chow Sang Sang	6
Ports	3	L'Oreal	6	Lao Mian Gold	5
Versace	2	Shiseido	6	Diamond	5
Lacoste	2	SK II	4	First Asia	2
Dunhill	2	Clinique	4	Leo Foo	2
Burberry	2	Estee Lauder	3	*Tiffany*	1
Gucci	1	Guerlain	2	*Bulgari*	*a*
Louis Vuitton	*a*	*Gucci*	2	D.K.	51
Hermes	*a*	Calvin Klein/CK	2		
Domestic suit		Elizabeth Arden	2		
brands mistaken		Biotherm	2		
for luxury goods	18	*Burberry*	*a*		
Leisure wear(such		Mass market brands			
as GAP, Esprit,		mistaken for			
Adidas, etc.)		luxury brands (e.g.			
mistaken for		Maybelline, Avon,			
luxury goods	8	Nivea, etc.)	20		
D.K.	48	D.K.	28		

Base = respondents who have purchased luxury goods in the category in the L3Y.

Note: only percentages above 2 % are presented except for brands of special concern (in italic font).

a Very small percentage.

Source: CSFB research

Of all those who made a purchase 37 % bought jewellery. The brands with the largest market shares are the Hong Kong originated Chow Tai Fook and Tse Sui Luen, shown in Table 16.1. Survey respondents view Dunhill, Valentino and Goldlion as the top three brands in luxury leather goods (Table 16.2). Omega is the top brand for luxury watches (Table 16.2). Remy Martin has the largest market share in premium champagne/spirits (Table 16.2). Burberry, Hermes, Louis Vuitton, etc., do not possess a large market share currently.

Total spending on luxury goods averages RMB 12 518 (US$1500) in total for the last three years (see Figure 16.2), which appears high relative to average income. The projected whole market for the eight cities in the last three years is RMB 86bn (US$10.4bn). Luxury goods purchases appear to be somewhat skewed towards younger consumers although much less so than in the case of electronic goods (see Figure 16.3).

Table 16.2   Most consumed brands of luxury goods in the last three years.

Leather goods (%)		Watches (%)		Premium champagne/ spirits (%)	
Unweighted base	215	Unweighted base	160	Unweighted base	147
Weighted base('000)	2142	Weighted base('000)	1589	Weighted base('000)	1175
Dunhill	6	*Omega*	17	Spirits	56
Valentino	6	Rolex	8	Remy Martin	35
Goldlion	6	Longines	7	Hennessy Cognac	16
Louis Vuitton	5	Rado	7	Martell	12
Pierre Cardin	4	Citizen	6	Courvoisier	2
Crocodile/Cartelo/		Tissot	5	Whisky	13
Lacoste (no		Tudor	4	Johnnie Walker	7
origin specified)	4	*Gucci*	3	Chivas Regal	5
Crocodile	4	*Cartier*	2	D.K.	33
Lacoste	4	Seiko	2		
Bally	2	Titoni	2		
Playboy	2	Domestic brands	3		
Versace	2	D.K.	26		
Burberry	a				
Coach	a				
Domestic leather					
goods brands	10				
D.K.	43				

Base = respondents who have purchased luxury goods in the category in the L3Y.

Note: only percentages above 2 % are presented except for brands of special concern (in italic font).

a Very small percentage.

Source: CSFB research

Of respondents 24 % plan to purchase luxury goods in the next year with similar percentages for intended purchases in each product category to the stated spending breakdown of the last three years (Figure 16.4).

Our respondents indicate that Crocodile is the brand most likely to be purchased for the fashion/ready-to-wear category and leather goods (see Tables 16.3 and 16.4). Christian Dior is the brand most likely to be purchased for premium perfumes and cosmetics (see Table 16.3). Chow Tai Fook is the brand most likely to be purchased for jewellery (see Table 16.3). Omega and Rolex are the brands most likely to be purchased for luxury watches (see Table 16.4). Remy Martin is likely to be the most purchased brand of premium champagne and spirits (see Table 16.4).

Personal budgets for spending on luxury goods are on average RMB 8026 (US$970) for the next one year, implying a potential acceleration in spending versus the annual average for the last three years. This figure allows us to project a total market of RMB 49bn (US$5.9bn) for the eight cities (see Figure 16.5).

Legend: RMB 0-2,000 · RMB 2,000-5,000 · RMB 5,000-10,000 · RMB 10,000-20,000 · RMB 20,000+ · Don't know

	RMB 0-2,000	RMB 2,000-5,000	RMB 5,000-10,000	RMB 10,000-20,000	RMB 20,000+	Don't know	Mean (RMB)	Estimated Market Size L3Y (RMB '000,000)
Total	9	16	14	13	14	33	12,518	86,487
BJ	7	13	15	17	15	30	14,475	25,172
SH	5	14	15	13	14	37	12,660	23,244
GZ	12	19	14	11	7	34	10,417	8,479
SZ	10	15	12	7	17	39	13,824	3,511
SY	7	15	14	12	17	33	14,107	11,624
WH	12	21	19	15	8	26	9,256	5,507
CD	10	24	11	10	20	27	13,989	6,225
XA	12	21	17	13	3	35	6,702	2,694

Base=Respondents who have purchased luxury good in L3Y	Total	BJ	SH	GZ	SZ	SY	WH	CD	XA
Unweighted Base	705	115	100	115	100	94	53	63	65
Weighted Base('000)	6,909	1,739	1,836	814	254	824	595	445	402

Source: CSFB research

Figure 16.2 Total spending on luxury goods in the last three years by city

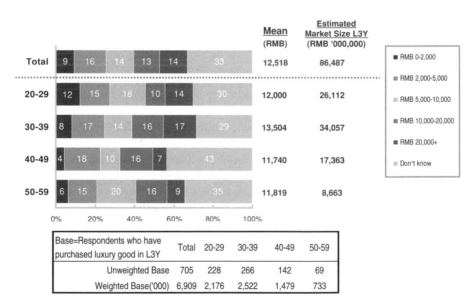

	RMB 0-2,000	RMB 2,000-5,000	RMB 5,000-10,000	RMB 10,000-20,000	RMB 20,000+	Don't know	Mean (RMB)	Estimated Market Size L3Y (RMB '000,000)
Total	9	16	14	13	14	33	12,518	86,487
20-29	12	15	18	10	14	30	12,000	26,112
30-39	8	17	14	16	17	29	13,504	34,057
40-49	4	18	10	16	7	43	11,740	17,363
50-59	6	15	20	16	9	35	11,819	8,663

Base=Respondents who have purchased luxury good in L3Y	Total	20-29	30-39	40-49	50-59
Unweighted Base	705	228	266	142	69
Weighted Base('000)	6,909	2,176	2,522	1,479	733

Source: CSFB research

Figure 16.3 Total spending on luxury goods in the last three years by age

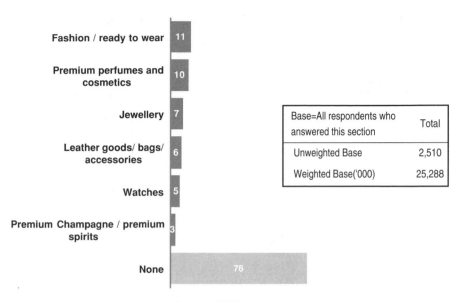

Source: CSFB research

Figure 16.4   Planned purchase of luxury goods in the next year

In order to gain information on the potential for counterfeit purchases we asked for attitudes to others purchasing counterfeit luxury goods. Of respondents, 42 % are opposed to others purchasing counterfeit luxury goods, while 52 % find this behaviour either acceptable or are indifferent (Figure 16.6). Aversion to counterfeit goods is highest in the 50–59 age bracket and lowest in the 20–29 age bracket (Figure 16.7).

IMPLICATIONS FOR LUXURY GOODS PRODUCERS[1]

During 2003 and 2004, China attracted increasing attention from observers of the luxury industry and the luxury goods companies themselves have been notably more inclined to discuss growth potential in this market.

We believe China represents a great opportunity for luxury goods companies. As explained in Section 1, the total value of urban household expenditure is set to grow by a CAGR of 17 % over the next 10 years. As the Chinese population ages over the coming years and becomes more affluent, we believe luxury goods companies will be strongly positioned to satisfy its needs, especially with product categories such as skin care and spirits. As the population grows older, the challenge for the luxury goods companies will be to retain the current customer base and extend the age range of their market as time goes by.

[1] Neville Pike contributed to this section but is no longer employed by CSFB as stock research coverage has been suspended currently for this sector.

Table 16.3   Brands of luxury goods most likely to be purchased in the next year.

Fashion/ready to wear (%)		Premium perfumes/ cosmetics (%)		Jewellery (%)	
Unweighted base	299	Unweighted base	264	Unweighted base	185
Weighted base('000)	2871	Weighted base('000)	2626	Weighted base('000)	1893
Crocodile	3	Christian Dior (CD)	10	Chow Tai Fook	21
Pierre Cardin	2	Shiseido	8	Tse Sui Luen	12
Ports	2	Lancome	8	Chow Sang Sang	8
Christian Dior (CD)	2	Chanel	8	Lao Mian Gold	5
Dunhill	1	L'Oreal	5	Diamond	3
Valentino	1	Clinique	5	*Bulgari*	2
Crocodile/Cartelo/		SK II	4	First Asia	2
Lacoste (no		Biotherm	2	Leo Foo	2
origin specified)	1	Calvin Klein/CK	1	*Tiffany*	1
Goldlion	1	Estee Lauder	1	Temple 1st	1
Lacoste	1	Boss	1	D.K.	59
Givenchy	1	Givenchy	1		
Louis Vuitton	1	Elizabeth Arden	1		
Hermes	[a]	Borghese	1		
Burberry	[a]	Nina Ricci	1		
Domestic suit		Adidas	1		
brands mistaken		*Gucci*	[a]		
for luxury goods	9	Mass market brands			
Leisure wear(such as		mistaken for			
GAP, Esprit, Adidas,		luxury brands			
etc.) mistaken for		(e.g. Maybelline,			
luxury goods	4	Nivea, etc.)	11		
D.K.	74	D.K.	52		

Base = respondents who intend to purchase luxury goods of the category in the N1Y.

Note: only percentages above 1 % are presented except for brands of special concern (in italic font).

[a] Very small percentage.

Source: CSFB research

Other important trends include: (a) the growth of consumerism among the new young generation who not only have the propensity to buy status goods but also the means, as their incomes are higher than the previous generation, and (b) the increase in income and wealth inequality discussed in Section 1. Our global outlook for the luxury goods sector as a whole in coming years is for more stable albeit lower growth. We believe that, in the longer term, China may well offer a sustainable platform for growth to mitigate effects of any slowdown in growth in Japan or in the US.

The key difference between China and other more developed markets (Japan, US or Europe) is that, as demonstrated by this survey, China is a volume and not a margin market. Analysis of the data shows that the number of households earning over US$5000 will rise more rapidly than the average income of the US$5000+

Table 16.4   Brands of luxury goods most likely to be purchased in the next year.

Leather goods (%)		Watches (%)		Premium champagne/ spirits (%)	
Unweighted base	156	Unweighted base	116	Unweighted base	98
Weighted base('000)	1527	Weighted base('000)	1161	Weighted base('000)	794
Crocodile/Cartelo/		*Omega*	14	Spirits	42
Lacoste (no		Rolex	12	Remy Martin	23
origin specified)	7	Rado	4	Martell	15
Louis Vuitton	4	Citizen	4	Hennessy Cognac	11
Pierre Cardin	4	Longines	4	Courvoisier	7
Crocodile	3	Tissot	3	Absolut Vodka	5
Lacoste	3	Swatch	3	Whisky	7
Bally	2	*Cartier*	3	Chivas Regal	4
Valentino	2	*Bulgari*	2	Johnnie Walker	3
Goldlion	1	Giorgio Armani	1	Jack Daniel's	1
Christian Dior (CD)	1	Titoni	1	Louis XIII	2
Dunhill	1	Tudor	1	D.K.	48
Satchi	1	Casio	1		
Playboy	1	TITUS	1		
Mont Blanc	1	D.K.	49		
Polo Ralph Lauren	1				
Cartelo	1				
Giorgio Armani	1				
Gucci	a				
Domestic leather					
goods brands	3				
D.K.	67				

Base = respondents who intend to purchase luxury goods of the category in the N1Y.

Note: only percentages above 1 % are presented except for brands of special concern (in italic font).

a Very small percentage.

Source: CSFB research

households, but most new consumers passing the hurdle will only just meet the income criteria.

In our view, LVMH, Swatch and Burberry are best positioned to capture Chinese spend at an earlier stage in the development of personal disposable wealth in China as they offer 'luxury' products at lower price points compared with, say, the super premium leather businesses of Hermès or the high jewellery businesses of Bulgari and Richemont. They have, in our view, most to gain from the 'democratisation' of luxury rather than just focusing on a smaller (though still growing) high-income elite:

- LVMH has a broader range of 'access' products than its competitors, notably through DFS, its travel retail arm, which recently relocated its headquarters to Hong Kong, and through its wines and spirits business and particularly cognac and champagne.

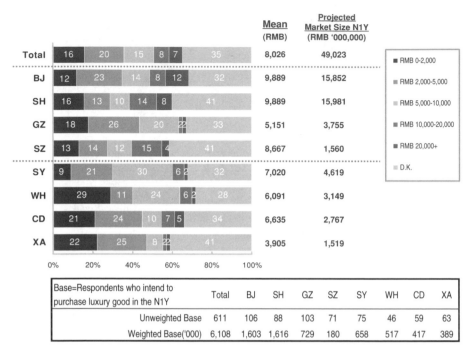

Base=Respondents who intend to purchase luxury good in the N1Y	Total	BJ	SH	GZ	SZ	SY	WH	CD	XA
Unweighted Base	611	106	88	103	71	75	46	59	63
Weighted Base('000)	6,108	1,603	1,616	729	180	658	517	417	389

Source: CSFB research

Figure 16.5   Planned budget for spending on luxury goods in next year

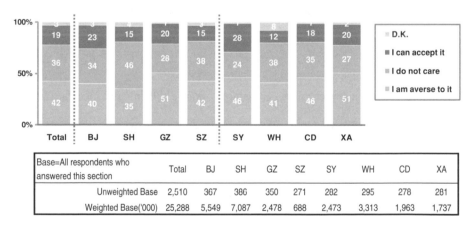

Base=All respondents who answered this section	Total	BJ	SH	GZ	SZ	SY	WH	CD	XA
Unweighted Base	2,510	367	386	350	271	282	295	278	281
Weighted Base('000)	25,288	5,549	7,087	2,478	688	2,473	3,313	1,963	1,737

Source: CSFB research

Figure 16.6   Attitudes towards others purchasing counterfeit luxury goods by city

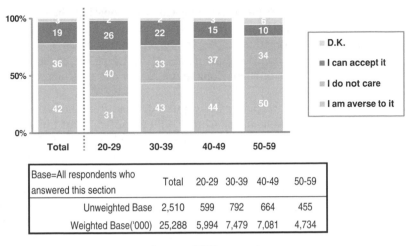

Base=All respondents who answered this section	Total	20-29	30-39	40-49	50-59
Unweighted Base	2,510	599	792	664	455
Weighted Base('000)	25,288	5,994	7,479	7,081	4,734

Source: CSFB research

Figure 16.7   Attitudes towards others purchasing counterfeit luxury goods by age

- Swatch Group's watch prices range from CHF 60 for a Swatch watch to above CHF 20 000 for a Breguet watch. The company entered the Chinese market over 40 years ago and has established brand awareness, especially with Omega, providing it with a considerable competitive advantage. Based on our survey, Swatch brands account for four out of the top six watch brands in mainland China over the last three years. Omega also has the highest reported incidence of purchase of any luxury brand.
- Burberry through its different lines is also in a position to offer accessible luxury apparel.

We expect jewellery markets in China to remain highly competitive. They are, in our view, less well positioned to benefit from the thickening of the household earnings tail around the US$5000 level because of the intensity of the local brands competition and the higher price point of the product. However, given the traditional preference for sometimes custom-made jewellery in materials like gold (increasingly incorporating diamonds too), it has, to date, been the smaller chains and independents in Hong Kong that have benefited most from the growing demand for jewellery among Chinese consumers rather than branded jewellery businesses.

If there is a note of caution for the sector as a whole in China, it is that, in our view, China's fourth-generation leadership of President Hu Jintao and Premier Wen Jiabao is prioritising rural poverty alleviation, environmental issues and financial sector reform. The previous government's focus had been on urban development and trade liberalisation which prompted rapid increases in income and wealth inequality. This change may imply a more difficult taxation environment for luxury goods companies in the future.

The overall market for luxury products among Chinese people is globally significant already. However, mainland China's contribution to the total remains limited. In the case of LVMH, for instance, Chinese people are said by the group to account for 10 % of global sales, but mainland China represents just 1 pp out of the total (1 % accounted for in Taipei, 4 % in Hong Kong and a further 4 % by Chinese travellers outside the region).

However, we believe the opportunity to capture demand from the mainland Chinese population is not just in mainland China. With the softening of Chinese travel regulations, the number of mainland Chinese people travelling to Hong Kong and to Europe and the US is set to continue growing substantially in the coming years. Some meaningful price differential for luxury goods between China domestically and overseas looks set to remain despite the reduction of import tariffs as part of China's entry into the World Trade Organisation (WTO). The price difference is easily 30–50 % today as a result of consumption tax, VAT and import tariff, meaning that those with the means to spend on luxury goods are likely to continue to buy these when they travel out of the country.

Against this background, our survey shows that the total spend per person on luxury goods over the last three years by Chinese residents (who indicated that they have purchased at least one luxury item) has been RMB 12 518 (mean average). Over the last three years, 27 % of survey respondents have purchased at least one luxury product over the period. Luxury goods consumers may have bought products from several categories. Out of respondents who made any purchase of luxury goods, we calculate that:

- 48 % of people purchased fashion and leather (13 % of 27 %);
- 41 % of people purchased perfumes and cosmetics (11 % of 27 %);
- 37 % of people purchased jewellery (10 % of 27 %);
- 33 % of people purchased leather (9 % of 27 %);
- 22 % of people purchased watches (6 % of 27 %);
- 19 % of people purchased champagne and spirits (5 % of 27 %).

It is important to point out that these data do not reflect the total number of purchases (for example, purchasers of cosmetics are more likely to have done so on more than one occasion than, say, purchasers of jewellery), nor do they give any indication of the total value of these purchases.

On the basis of the survey we would also make the following observations. The fashion and ready-to-wear segment is highly fragmented, with a predominance of access fashion brands. The penetration of European luxury goods brands appears particularly low and, in our view, the number of local and leisure names mistaken for luxury products shows lack of brand awareness.

In contrast, the perfumes and cosmetics segment shows high penetration by high-end and luxury brands. We believe the opportunity in this segment is especially in cosmetics as perfume consumption in China is generally lower. We note that the first five brands have particular strength in skincare products and in particular anti-ageing creams, which we believe could represent an important source of growth over the coming years as China's population ages.

In our view, a key factor explaining the poor penetration of luxury brands such as Cartier and Bulgari is that they have a higher average price point. We believe the weak presence of Tiffany is due to the focus of Chinese consumers on gold jewellery and precious stones in general rather than just diamonds, whereas the company is strongest in diamond engagement rings and silver jewellery.

Similar to the fashion and ready-to-wear segment, leather is also highly fragmented with a focus towards access fashion brands. We believe things may shift rapidly as companies such as Louis Vuitton have been making extensive PR efforts in China over recent months.

The watches segment is highly penetrated by European luxury brands and especially by Swatch. Adding the shares of the Omega, Longines, Rado and Tissot brands gives a total of 36 % penetration for the Swatch Group. We believe that the success of Swatch also reflects the public relation efforts undertaken by the company in this market. Omega will be the official timekeeper of the Beijing 2008 Olympic games and recently unveiled a special 'countdown' clock in Tiananmen Square in Beijing. The clock will count down the time remaining until the Games of the XXIXth Olympiad are opened.

Similarly to watches, the spirit segment is highly penetrated by European luxury brands. We believe that this mainly reflects the strength of cognac in China versus whisky.

Looking at the year ahead, our survey shows that 24 % of respondents intend to purchase luxury goods over the period compared with just 27 % in total over the last three years. Over the next year alone we estimate that the average spend per person on luxury goods will be around RMB 8026, implying acceleration in spending compared with the RMB 12 518 total of the last three years. From this we project a total market in the next year of RMB 49bn (US$5.9bn) for the eight major Chinese cities included in the survey.

The pattern of purchases between segments appears similar to that of the last three years. In relation to the results showing the brands of luxury goods most likely to be purchased in the next year by segment two things are worth noting:

- The survey results give qualitative information but cannot be extrapolated in the future as the question refers to a one-year period compared with three years previously.
- The number of respondents who do not have an opinion about intended brand purchases is much higher than that given when looking at the last three years, as indicated by high 'don't know/other brands' (D.K.) percentages. This statistic in itself suggests to us that there is, as yet, no clear leadership in brand positioning in China. While there is evidently an appetite to increase spend, the question is: what to buy?

On the basis of the survey results we make the following observations:

- The fashion and ready-to-wear segment seems set to remain highly fragmented, with a persisting predominance of access fashion brands. The key change for European luxury goods brands is the appearance of Christian Dior with 2 % of the respondents willing to purchase a product of the brand over the next year and the reduction in appetite for Pierre Cardin.
- We believe there are no significant changes on the perfumes and cosmetics segment.
- On jewellery, 2 % of respondents said they intend to purchase Bulgari products over the next year. In contrast, the percentage of respondents having bought a Bulgari product over the last three years was too low to be significant.
- Regarding the leather segment, Louis Vuitton remains at a similar percentage to that achieved over the last three years but moves ahead of Dunhill (down to 1 % versus 6 % over the last three years). However, access fashion brands remain predominant.
- The watches segment remains highly penetrated by brands of the Swatch Group: Omega, Rado, Longines and Tissot. Interestingly, 3 % of respondents said they intended to purchase a Swatch watch over the coming year whereas the percentage was insignificant over the last three years. We believe this is due to recent changes in quota limitations which, since 2002, are based on value rather than number of units and therefore have enabled the Swatch Group to launch the Swatch brand more aggressively.
- The spirit segment also remains highly penetrated by luxury brands. However, Remy Martin and Hennessy (LVMH) appear to lose ground against Martell and Courvoisier.

Our survey shows that 42 % of people are opposed to others purchasing counterfeit luxury goods, while 52 % find this behaviour either acceptable or are indifferent. Worryingly, aversion to buying counterfeit goods is lowest in the youngest age groups where income growth tends to be highest. However, in our view, the bigger threat is not that of counterfeits within China but that of Chinese counterfeiters exporting to Western Europe markets. We believe that all the luxury goods companies have increased efforts to combat counterfeiting at source, rather than targeting vendors in 'night markets' in China. This is illustrated by the announcement in late 2004 by Tiffany that it had obtained a US$600 000 judgement against Katz Imports, which had sold counterfeit Tiffany jewellery on the web.

17
Telecom Equipment

Among our survey respondents, the overall handset penetration rate has reached 81 % for the eight cities surveyed (Figure 17.1). The highest is Beijing with 91 % and the lowest is Wuhan with 70 %.

Household income levels strongly influence ownership of handsets. The penetration rate increases from 60 % for lower-income households (RMB 1000–2000) to 96 % for higher-income households (RMB 8000+). Mobile phone handset penetration is highest in the 20–29 age bracket (92 %) and lowest in the 50–59 age bracket (59 %), shown in Figure 17.2.

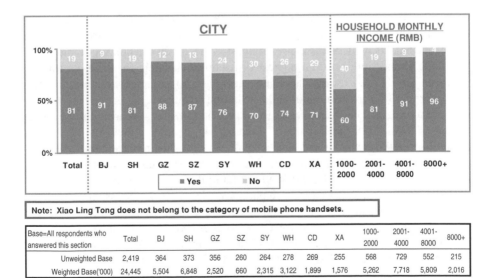

Note: Xiao Ling Tong does not belong to the category of mobile phone handsets.

Base=All respondents who answered this section	Total	BJ	SH	GZ	SZ	SY	WH	CD	XA	1000-2000	2001-4000	4001-8000	8000+
Unweighted Base	2,419	364	373	356	260	264	278	269	255	568	729	552	215
Weighted Base('000)	24,445	5,504	6,848	2,520	660	2,315	3,122	1,899	1,576	5,262	7,718	5,809	2,016

Source: CSFB research

Figure 17.1 Handset ownership and penetration rate by city and income

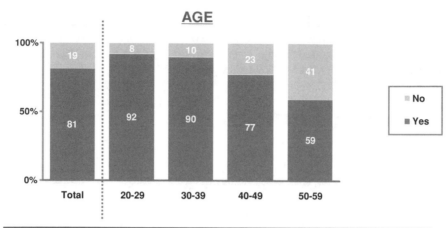

Base=All respondents who answered this section	Total	20-29	30-39	40-49	50-59
Unweighted Base	2,419	575	762	642	440
Weighted Base('000)	24,445	5,670	7,346	6,875	4,554

Source: CSFB research

Figure 17.2   Handset ownership and penetration rate by age

In terms of current handsets owned, Nokia (25 %), Motorola (22 %) and Samsung (15 %) have the largest market shares (see Table 17.1). Motorola is strongest in the 50–59 age bracket while Samsung is strongest in the 20–29 age bracket (Table 17.2).

Mobile phone stores are the biggest distribution channels for handsets (40 %), shown in Table 17.3. Electrical appliance stores (16 %) and telecommunication network stores (13 %) are also important distribution channels.

Current owners intend to replace their current handset in 1.4 years with an average budget of RMB 2138 (see Figures 17.3 and 17.4). Among nonowners, 20 % want to purchase in the next year and have a smaller budget than replacers of RMB 1384 (US$167) (see Figures 17.5 and 17.6). The total market in the eight cities next year is estimated to be RMB 7.2bn (US$0.9bn) (Table 17.4).

For handset nonowners intending to purchase, Nokia (16 %), Samsung (11 %) and Motorola (9 %) are the top three brands most likely to be purchased. Samsung and Motorola positions are reversed for current handset owners and intended handset owners (Table 17.5). This is a signal that Samsung may overtake the current position of Motorola in the future. Unlike in the case of private cars, consumers are aware of the origin of their handsets (see Figure 17.7). Over 70 % of all current foreign brand handset owners know the origin of their phone's brand.

Table 17.1 Most consumed brands of handsets by city (%).

	Total	BJ	SH	GZ	SZ	SY	WH	CD	XA
Unweighted base	1944	332	302	312	225	200	194	198	181
Weighted base('000)	19 794	5020	5545	2209	572	1754	2179	1398	1119
Nokia	25	31	25	31	30	21	14	20	17
Motorola	22	24	24	19	18	16	16	27	20
Samsung	15	12	13	16	22	23	20	11	19
Siemens	5	4	7	4	1	6	4	6	2
Sony Ericsson	3	2	4	4	4	1	2	4	2
TCL	3	1	2	1	3	3	5	7	2
Panasonic	2	5	2	2	1	1	1	1	2
Philips	2	2	1	4	1	6	2	1	6
Bird	2	2	2	1	1	3	4	2	3
Ericsson	2	2	1	2	1	1	2	2	1
Alcatel	2	2	2	3	1	1	2	0	1
D.K.	5	2	7	4	7	2	8	5	4
Total	100	100	100	100	100	100	100	100	100

Base = respondents who own and use handsets.
Note: only percentages above 2 % are presented.
Source: CSFB research

Table 17.2 Most consumed brands of handsets by age (%).

	Total	20–29	30–39	40–49	50–59
Unweighted base	1944	522	677	487	258
Weighted base ('000)	19 794	5214	6602	5284	2694
Nokia	25	26	22	25	28
Motorola	22	19	22	24	24
Samsung	15	18	17	13	11
Siemens	5	5	4	5	6
Sony Ericsson	3	5	2	3	1
TCL	3	2	2	3	4
Panasonic	2	2	3	2	3
Philips	2	3	3	1	1
Bird	2	2	3	2	2
Ericsson	2	1	2	2	2
Alcatel	2	2	2	1	2
D.K.	5	1	4	7	10
Total	100	100	100	100	100

Base = respondents who own and use handsets.
Note: only percentages above 2 % are presented.
Source: CSFB research

Table 17.3 Distribution channels for handsets (%).

	Total	BJ	SH	GZ	SZ	SY	WH	CD	XA
Unweighted base	1944	332	302	312	225	200	194	198	181
Weighted base('000)	19 794	5020	5545	2209	572	1754	2179	1398	1119
Mobile phone store	40	45	28	51	50	27	47	47	43
Electrical appliance store	16	22	20	4	6	12	4	18	17
Telecommunication network store	13	15	9	13	7	18	17	15	10
Department store	8	3	12	7	5	16	8	4	9
Gift from friends/family members, etc.	7	5	9	6	9	8	8	4	7
Electronics market	4	1	6	4	5	4	5	2	5
Electronics specialty store	3	2	1	3	4	4	4	7	6
Supermarket/hypermarket	3	—	5	2	6	4	3	1	2
Second-hand market	1	1	—	0	—	1	1	1	0
Others	2	0	2	6	5	—	2	1	0
D.K.	3	4	5	3	2	2	2	2	1
Total	100	100	100	100	100	100	100	100	100

Base = respondents who own and use handsets.
Note: only percentages above 1 % are presented.
Source: CSFB research

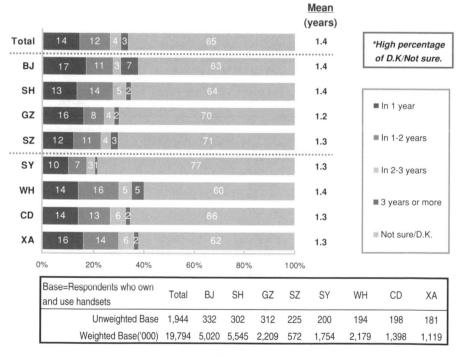

Source: CSFB research
Figure 17.3 Time to replace the current handset

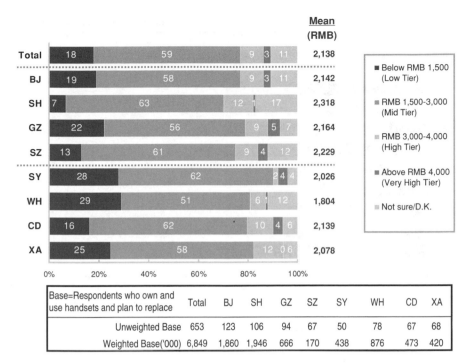

Mean (RMB)			
Total	2,138
BJ	2,142
SH	2,318
GZ	2,164
SZ	2,229
SY	2,026
WH	1,804
CD	2,139
XA	2,078

Legend:
- Below RMB 1,500 (Low Tier)
- RMB 1,500-3,000 (Mid Tier)
- RMB 3,000-4,000 (High Tier)
- Above RMB 4,000 (Very High Tier)
- Not sure/D.K.

Base=Respondents who own and use handsets and plan to replace	Total	BJ	SH	GZ	SZ	SY	WH	CD	XA
Unweighted Base	653	123	106	94	67	50	78	67	68
Weighted Base('000)	6,849	1,860	1,946	666	170	438	876	473	420

Source: CSFB research

Figure 17.4 Planned budget for spending on handsets from the base of respondents already owning handsets

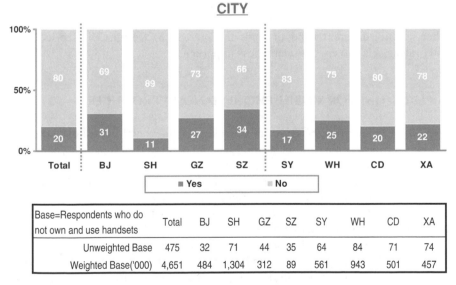

Base=Respondents who do not own and use handsets	Total	BJ	SH	GZ	SZ	SY	WH	CD	XA
Unweighted Base	475	32	71	44	35	64	84	71	74
Weighted Base('000)	4,651	484	1,304	312	89	561	943	501	457

Source: CSFB research

Figure 17.5 Purchase intentions in the next year of respondents not currently owning a handset

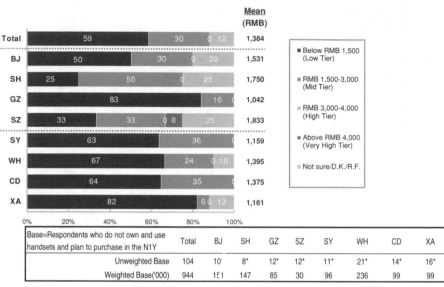

Source: CSFB research

Figure 17.6   Planned budget for spending on a handset from the base of respondents not currently owning a handset

Functionality (55%) and quality (42%) are the principal concerns of consumers when selecting different brands of handsets (Figure 17.8). Design (31%), price (25%) and branding (20%) are considered less important.

IMPLICATIONS FOR MOBILE PHONE HANDSET PRODUCERS[1]

Overall, we believe that the survey of Chinese consumers highlighted two main conclusions for the mobile handset sector. First, we observe that demand dynamics are changing – while unit growth has historically been very much driven by continued net additions growth, with Tier 1/2 cities largely penetrated, we expect incremental subscriber demand to now come from Tier 3/4 cities. Given that such cities tend to be smaller and have lower income, this would suggest that net additions may be close to peaking in China. Furthermore, replacement cycles of 1.4 years for the consumers surveyed are comparable with behaviour in developed markets, suggesting that replacements should continue to rise in the medium term. As shown in Table 17.6, we assume that as a percentage of the base, replacements should rise from 12.8% in 2004 to 14.6% in 2005.

[1] Kulbinder Garcha and Mike Ounjian contributed to this section.

Table 17.4 Estimated handset market within the next year.

		Total	BJ	SH	GZ	SZ	SY	WH	CD	XA
Noncurrent owners	Total size ('000) (a)	4651	484	1304	312	89	561	943	501	457
	Percentage intend to buy N1Y (%) (b)	20	31	11	27	34	17	25	20	22
	Size of intenders N1Y ('000) (c = a × b)	930	150	143	84	30	95	236	100	101
	Potential growth of penetration rate (%) (d)	5	3	3	4	5	5	11	7	9
	Budget per person (RMB) (e)	1384	1531	1750	1042	1833	1159	1395	1375	1161
	Total market size from intenders (RMB '000) (f = d × e)	1 287 397	229 711	251 020	87 778	55 467	110 534	328 871	137 775	116 727
Current owners	Total size ('000) (g)	19 794	5020	5545	2209	572	1754	2179	1398	1119
	Percentage intend to replace N1Y (%) (h)	14	17	13	16	12	10	14	14	16
	Size of intended replacers N1Y ('000) (j = g × h)	2771	853	721	353	69	175	305	196	179
	Budget per person (RMB) (k)	2138	2142	2318	2164	2229	2026	1804	2139	2078
	Total market size from replacers (RMB '000) (i = j × k)	5 924 398	1 827 126	1 671 278	763 892	153 801	354 550	550 220	419 244	371 962
Combined	Total potential market size N1Y (RMB '000) (m = f + i)	7 211 795	2 056 837	1 922 298	851 670	209 268	465 084	879 091	557 019	488 689

Note: market size is calculated only with a population aged 20–59 and low-income households excluded.
Source: CSFB research.

Table 17.5   Brands of handsets most likely to be purchased by nonhandset owners (%).

	Total	BJ	SH	GZ	SZ	SY	WH	CD	XA
Unweighted base	106	10[a]	8[a]	13[a]	12[a]	11[a]	22[a]	14[a]	16[a]
Weighted base('000)	962	151	147	92	30	96	247	99	99
Nokia	16	20	13	15	17	0	23	14	19
Samsung	11	20	0	0	8	36	0	21	13
Motorola	9	10	25	0	17	9	0	7	19
Ericsson	4	0	13	8	0	0	5	0	0
Siemens	1	0	0	0	8	0	5	0	0
Lenovo	1	0	0	0	0	0	5	0	0
Amoi	1	0	0	0	0	0	5	0	0
Sony Ericsson	1	0	0	0	0	0	0	7	0
None	1	0	0	8	0	0	0	0	0
D.K.	53	50	50	62	50	55	55	50	50
Total	100	100	100	100	100	100	100	100	100

Base = respondents who do not own and use handsets and plan to purchase in the N1Y.
Note: only percentages above 1 % are presented.
Samsung has shown a tendency to overtake the position of Motorola. [Shown in box]
[a] Small base.
Source: CSFB research

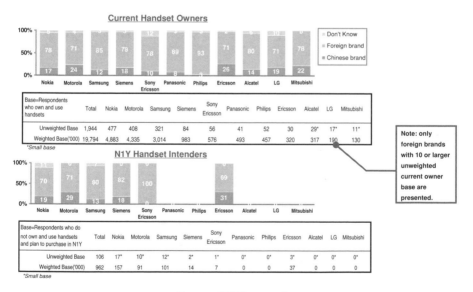

Source: CSFB research
Figure 17.7   Brand perception on whether foreign mobile handset brands are viewed as local

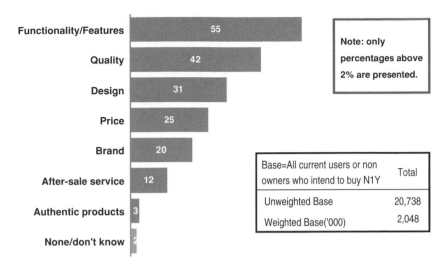

Source: CSFB research
Figure 17.8   Reasons for considering certain brands when purchasing a handset

Second, from a vendor perspective we believe that consumers seem to be demonstrating a stronger-than-expected preference for foreign brands, namely Nokia, Motorola and Samsung. We believe that, combined with a rising replacement rate and improved distribution, this could bode well for the top two vendors. In fact, we would argue that market share for vendors such as Nokia and Motorola could in fact begin to rise over the coming years (see Table 17.7).

Based on the above we arrive at several company implications/conclusions. Overall, while China is an important market for the handset industry, we estimate that it accounts for 6 % only of Nokia's shipments in 2004. On the positive side, we note that Nokia's brand preference of the installed base (25 %) is encouraging, especially as replacement continues to rise. This combined with an unrivalled focus on distribution as well as an improving product portfolio all suggest that Nokia's share could modestly recover. However, we believe that such encouraging implications have to be tempered by our concerns on the overall Chinese market in which net additions could begin to decline and a shift to Tier 3 and Tier 4 cities is taking place, where Nokia's share tends to be lower (we believe that Nokia has a share of 20 % in GSM in Tier 1 cities compared with 16 % in Tier 3/4 cities). In addition to continued concerns on the level of Chinese handset inventory (which could be as high as a 20–25m excess), even if this is mainly domestic vendors' inventory, the risk is that sell-in growth could be limited. Overall, we believe that near-term demand in the handset industry could surprise on the upside. Our concern remains that unit growth will slow in 2005 to low single digits from over 20 % in 2004.

Table 17.6 CSFB China handset model – looking for rising replacement to drive unit growth of 13 % medium term in thousands, unless otherwise stated.

Total China	2002	2003	2004E	2005E	2006E	2007E	2008E	CAGR 03-08E
Mobile subscribers ('000)	206 610	268 693	331 418	376 902	414 902	456 243	498 248	13.1%
Change (%)	43	30	23	14	10	10	9	
Penetration (%)	16.09	20.74	25.40	28.67	31.32	34.18	37.05	
Penetration gain (%)	4.71	4.66	4.65	3.27	2.65	2.86	2.87	
New subscribers	61 810	62 083	62 725	45 484	38 001	41 341	42 005	-7.5%
Change (%)	4	0	1	-27	-16	9	2	
Percentage of handset market (%)	109	99	87	60	47	41	36	
Extra SIM/recycling factor (%)	19	18	18	17	16	15	15	
Handsets relating to new subscribers (B)	50 214	51 048	51 449	37 563	31 762	35 024	35 874	-6.8%
Change (%)	5	2	1	-27	-15	10	2	
Percentage of handset market (%)	89	81	72	50	39	35	31	
Churned subscribers	20 714	27 709	36 007	42 499	47 120	57 303	70 558	
Annual churn rate (%)	11.8	11.7	12.0	12.0	11.9	13.2	14.8	
Churn unit sales (C)	16 828	22 784	29 534	35 098	39 385	48 547	60 261	
Gross subscriber additions ($D = B + C$)	67 041	73 833	80 982	72 662	71 147	83 571	96 135	
Change (%)	14	10	10	-10	-2	17	15	

Upgrade units (E)	7 414	8 264	12 897	19 885	26 383	33 192	36 499	
Change (%)	86	11	56	54	33	26	10	
Percentage of subscriber base (%)	5	4	5	6	7	8	8	
Percentage of handset market (%)	13	13	18	26	32	33	32	
Replacement market $(F = C + E)$	24 241	31 049	42 431	54 984	65 768	81 739	96 760	25.5
Market growth (%)	62	28	37	30	20	24	18	
Percentage of handset market (%)	43	49	59	73	81	82	84	
Replacement cycle	71.7	79.9	76.0	72.3	68.8	60.9	56.6	
Replacement units (%)	43	49	59	73	81	82	84	
Percentage of subscriber base (%)	11.7	11.6	12.8	14.6	15.9	17.9	19.4	
Previous year subscriber base (%)	17	15	16	17	17	20	21	
Mobile handset market pre-secondhand deflator	74 455	82 097	93 880	92 547	97 530	116 763	132 635	
Market growth (%)	19	10	14	−1	5	20	14	
Secondhand adjustment (%)	24	23	24	19	17	14	13	
Secondhand adjustment (units)	17 964	19 229	22 110	17 293	16 154	16 554	17 377	
Mobile handset shipments ('000)	56 491	62 868	71 769	75 254	81 376	100 209	115 258	12.9%
Market growth (%)	13	11	14	5	8	23	15	

Source: CSFB research

Table 17.7 Top two foreign handset vendors' exposure to the Chinese market (units in millions, unless otherwise stated).

	Total units 2004E	China units 2004E	Market share 2004E (%)	China as % of units	China as % of handset revenues	China as % of Group revenues
Nokia	203.3	11.9	17	6	9	8
Motorola	99.5	11.2	16	11	15	12

Source: CSFB research

While China remains an important market for Motorola, we continue to believe that the company's unit and handset revenue mix will tend to shift away from China over the next few years, particularly as 3G shipments to Europe increase. However, we believe the following trends highlighted in our survey point to Motorola's handset market share in China stabilising:

- Accelerating replacement rates as evidenced by expectations for a replacement cycle of 1.4 years among consumers surveyed. We believe higher replacement rates will continue to shift unit mix towards the mid range and high end, where Motorola has been more successful in the last several months.
- Focus on functionality and design as the key parameters for handset selection, which we believe favours vendors with strong product portfolios.
- Preference towards Western brands, including Motorola, and a strong presence in the installed base, which are likely to influence replacement purchase decisions.

We would also highlight the fact that Samsung appears better positioned than Motorola among consumers who do not currently own a handset, which we believe points to continued share loss at the low end of the market. However, we expect the company to continue to benefit from a shift in unit mix towards the high end in 2005 (both in China and globally), which combined with ongoing cost reductions should result in further margin improvements.

Our analysis highlights a trend that we have already seen developing over the course of 2004 with Tier 1 cities now almost fully penetrated and future unit demand now depending much more on Tier 3 and Tier 4 cities. Furthermore, it is clear that the replacement cycle in larger and more highly penetrated Chinese cities is demonstrating the maturity seen in many developed markets. However, we believe that over the course of 2005, with less penetration potential in Tier 3 and Tier 4 cities (smaller population and lower GDP per head), net additions will contract, which we believe will be offset by rising replacement, resulting in an overall unit growth of merely 5 %.

Among our respondents, overall handset penetration rate has reached 81 % for the eight cities surveyed. The highest is Beijing with 91 % and the lowest is Wuhan with 70 %. This would suggest that incremental unit demand and penetration potential will come from Tier 3 and Tier 4 cities over time. Given that Tier 3/4 cities tend to have a smaller population and lower GDP per head, this would suggest that the current rate of monthly net additions of 5m may be more difficult to sustain over time. As a result we see limited unit growth in the Chinese market in 2005 of only 5 %, mainly as a result of declining net additions. Meanwhile, the penetration rate increases from 60 % for lower-income households (RMB 1000–2000) to 96 % for higher-income households (RMB 8000+).

Our survey shows that current owners intend to replace their current handset in 1.4 years with an average budget of RMB 2138. Among nonowners, 20 % want to purchase a handset in the next year and have a smaller budget than replacers of RMB 1384. Applying these budgets to our net additions estimate (41 % of unit demand) as well as replacement forecast suggests a market average selling price (ASP) closer to RMB 1832 in 2005. This compares with a GSM ASP today of RMB 1500. However, we believe that while this suggests some price stabilisation in the Chinese market from a demand point of view, we overall still assume that ASPs will decline in China given three factors: (a) we believe the sample is based on higher-end consumers in the survey; (b) the increasing importance of Tier 3/4 cities, which have lower income, mean that ASPs will have to fall for penetration to significantly increase (potentially affecting handset vendors' operating margins); and (c) the excess inventory in China, which stands on some estimates as high as 20–25m units, is likely to put near-term pressure on prices.

Despite continued concerns regarding the low-end preference of Chinese consumers, the survey in fact found that functionality (55 %) and quality (42 %) are the principal criteria of consumers when selecting different brands of handsets. Design (31 %), price (25 %) and branding (20 %) are considered less important.

Overall, despite continued concerns that Chinese domestic vendors have unlimited potential to increase share in the market, we found that according to the survey the brand preference for Western vendors was surprisingly resilient. In terms of current handsets owned, the survey suggests Nokia (25 %), Motorola (22 %) and Samsung (15 %) have a dominant position. Of course, such penetration of the installed base is important in the replacement cycle, as historical patterns in developed markets tend to highlight the fact that consumers are most likely to replace with the same brand. Given that actual market shares for Nokia (15.5 % in October 2004), Motorola (13.6 %) and Samsung (11.6 %) (see Table 17.8) are lower than the share of the installed base, a rising replacement rate could put an upward bias on shares medium term for all developed market vendors.

Our survey finds that in terms of handset nonowners, Nokia (16 %), Samsung (11 %) and Motorola (9 %) are the top three brands likely to be purchased. Samsung and Motorola positions are reversed for current handset owners and intended

Table 17.8   China market share of top five handset vendors (%).

	Jan/04	Feb/04	Mar/04	Apr/04	May/04	Jun/04	Jul/04	Aug/04	Sep/04	Oct/04
Nokia	15.3	15.5	15.6	15.7	15.6	15.5	14.8	14.7	15.4	15.5
Motorola	15.7	15.3	15.4	15.5	15.2	14.1	14.0	14.5	14.0	13.6
Samsung	8.5	9.0	9.7	10.5	10.0	11.2	11.9	11.9	12.2	11.6
Bird	7.5	7.0	7.0	7.2	7.6	7.3	6.8	6.2	6.5	7.0
TCL	6.7	6.3	6.5	6.2	6.7	6.3	6.2	6.1	5.7	5.3

Source: Sino-MR and CSFB research

handset owners. This could be a signal that Samsung may overtake the current position of Motorola in the future. Over the past few years, developed market vendors
(notably Nokia and Motorola) have sought to improve distribution channels, especially as domestic vendors such as TCL were able to increase market share substantially (domestic vendors accounted collectively for less than 20 % in 2000 of the
Chinese market compared with 40–45 % currently). Indeed, the survey shows that
most mobile devices are being purchased through speciality mobile stores (mobile
phone stores are the biggest distribution channels for handsets at 40 %. Electrical appliance stores (16 %) and telecommunication network stores (13 %) are also important
distribution channels).

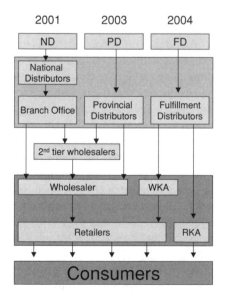

Source: Company data and CSFB research
Figure 17.9   Nokia's changing approach to Chinese distribution

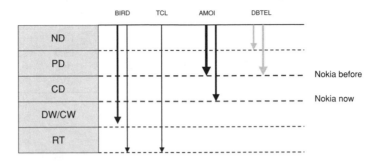

Local Brands are shifting focus from PD to CD to
further de-layer the channel

NOTE: ND – National Distributor, PD – Provincial Distributor,CD – City Distributor,
DW – Distribution Wholesaler, CW – County Wholesaler, RT - Retailer

Source: Company data and CSFB research
Figure 17.10   Nokia distribution versus key domestic competitors

From a vendor perspective, we therefore believe that the distribution channel will
continue to have a core competitive advantage. Nokia for instance now claims to
have 50 sales offices, with 4000 individuals in 380 cities focusing on 17 000 retail
accounts. Such continued evolution in distribution may be a key competitive advantage
to moving forward. We show Nokia's approach to distribution in Figures 17.9 and
17.10.

18
Tobacco

Our survey indicates that 29 % of respondents smoke; 54 % of males smoke and only 4 % of females (see Figure 18.1).

Smoking is most prevalent in the 30–39 and 40–49 age brackets (33 % and 32 %, respectively) and least prevalent in the 20–29 age bracket (see Figure 18.2). Moreover, younger people smoke on average significantly fewer cigarettes than older people (9.8 on average for those who do smoke in the 20–29 age group versus 14.5 on average for those in the 50–59 age group (see Figure 18.3)).

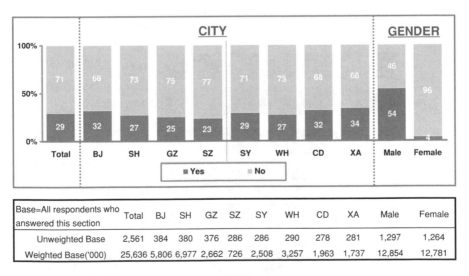

Base=All respondents who answered this section	Total	BJ	SH	GZ	SZ	SY	WH	CD	XA	Male	Female
Unweighted Base	2,561	384	380	376	286	286	290	278	281	1,297	1,264
Weighted Base('000)	25,636	5,806	6,977	2,662	726	2,508	3,257	1,963	1,737	12,854	12,781

Source: CSFB research

Figure 18.1 Prevalence of smoking by city and gender

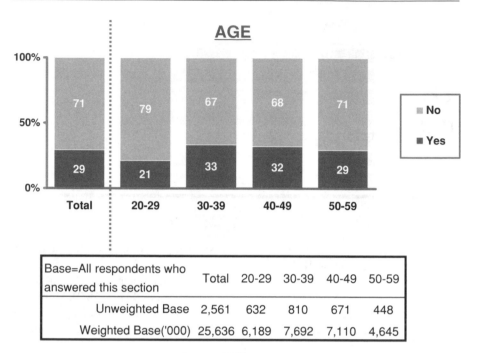

Base=All respondents who answered this section	Total	20-29	30-39	40-49	50-59
Unweighted Base	2,561	632	810	671	448
Weighted Base('000)	25,636	6,189	7,692	7,110	4,645

Source: CSFB research

Figure 18.2   Prevalence of smoking by age

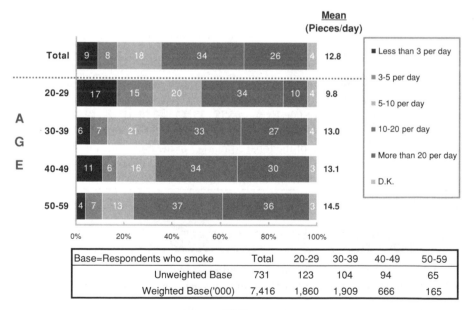

Base=Respondents who smoke	Total	20-29	30-39	40-49	50-59
Unweighted Base	731	123	104	94	65
Weighted Base('000)	7,416	1,860	1,909	666	165

Source: CSFB research

Figure 18.3   Amount of tobacco smoked daily by age

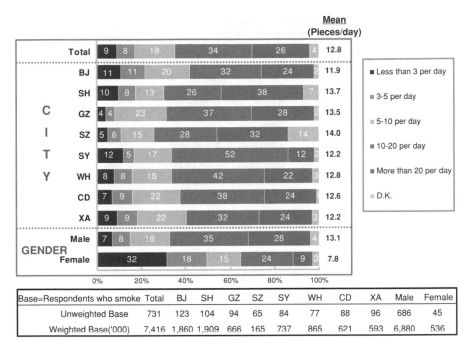

Base=Respondents who smoke	Total	BJ	SH	GZ	SZ	SY	WH	CD	XA	Male	Female
Unweighted Base	731	123	104	94	65	84	77	88	96	686	45
Weighted Base('000)	7,416	1,860	1,909	666	165	737	865	621	593	6,880	536

Source: CSFB research

Figure 18.4   Amount of tobacco smoked daily by city and gender

We find that an average smoker smokes 12.8 cigarettes per day (Figure 18.4): 13.1 cigarettes for males and 7.8 for females. Smokers spend RMB 181.5 (US$22) each month on cigarettes.

Chinese brands are most frequently smoked by our survey respondents (85 % of smokers mostly use Chinese brands versus 6 % of smokers purchasing mostly foreign brands), as shown in Table 18.1. However, among respondents who smoke mostly Chinese brands we find that State Express 555 (25 %) and Marlboro (9 %) would be preferred by smokers if they had to smoke a foreign brand (see Table 18.2).

The projected market size of the tobacco market in the eight cities is RMB17.3bn (US$2.1bn) annually, shown in Figure 18.5. Taste (53 %) is the most important criterion for our respondents in choosing cigarette brands (see Figure 18.6). Of secondary importance are branding (22 %) and price (20 %).

IMPLICATIONS FOR TOBACCO PRODUCERS[1]

The Chinese tobacco sector is one that holds substantial potential for international tobacco companies. Per capita consumption of cigarettes in China is approximately

[1] Pieter Vorster, Andrew Conway, Shuichi Shibanuma and Marisa Ho contributed to this section.

Table 18.1   Most consumed brands of tobacco (%).

	Total	BJ	SH	GZ	SZ	SY	WH	CD	XA
Unweighted base	731	123	104	94	65	84	77	88	96
Weighted base('000)	7416	1860	1909	666	165	737	865	621	593
Chinese brand	85	87	88	87	72	83	92	81	71
Double Happiness (Shanghai)	12	0	48	0	3	0	0	0	0
Hongtashan	6	21	3	1	5	0	0	2	0
Hong Jin Long	6	0	1	0	0	0	48	0	0
Zhongnanhai	6	20	1	0	2	4	0	0	0
Yunyan (Hongyun/ Baiyun)	5	4	1	1	3	10	4	19	6
Double Happiness (Guangzhou)	5	0	1	49	9	0	0	0	0
Honghe	4	9	0	0	0	6	4	9	3
Baisha	4	6	0	5	14	1	1	1	21
Hongmei	3	7	0	4	0	4	3	0	3
Shanghai	3	0	12	0	0	0	1	0	0
Mudan	3	1	10	0	0	0	0	0	1
Huang He Lou	2	0	0	0	0	0	21	0	0
Jiao Zi	2	0	0	0	0	0	0	22	1
Furongwang	2	2	2	1	11	0	0	0	4
Foreign brand	6	8	6	10	6	11	5	1	1
State Express 555	2	3	2	5	0	6	2	0	1
D.K	7	5	3	5	11	14	6	9	13
Total	100	100	100	100	100	100	100	100	100

Base = respondents who smoke.
Note: only percentages above 2 % are presented.
Source: CSFB research

20 times that of the US (Table 18.3). It represents some 35 % (1.7tn cigarettes) of global cigarette consumption, yet the market share of foreign brands is currently only 3 %. The balance of 97 % is held by the China National Tobacco Corporation (CNTC) operating a number of different brands via subsidiary entities. Since 1993, new joint venture manufacturing plants have been banned and quotas limit imports. We estimate the compounded annual growth rate of China's cigarette consumption over the last five years is around 1 %. We also estimate that China holds a 31 % global volume share and 12 % of the profit pool.

Over time we expect the tobacco industry to liberalise as China complies with conditions related to its entry into the WTO. Following China's entry into the WTO, cigarette duty is expected to drop from 70 % in 2001 to 20 % by 2004. Tobacco leaf duty will also be cut from 40 % to 10 %. The removal of the special retail licence for imported tobacco by the end of 2003 – simplifying previous requirements for tobacco retailers to maintain two separate licences for domestic and foreign-made cigarettes – should also help expand sales of imported cigarettes. However, although

Table 18.2 Brands of foreign tobacco most likely to be purchased (%).

	Total	BJ	SH	GZ	SZ	SY	WH	CD	XA
Unweighted base	451	108	85	71	40	34	16	48	49
Weighted base('000)	4917	1633	1561	503	102	298	180	339	303
State Express 555	25	19	32	30	10	21	6	21	35
Marlboro	9	15	4	6	7	12	13	8	2
Camel	2	6	0	0	0	3	0	2	0
Mild Seven	2	2	1	0	12	6	0	0	2
Hilton	1	2	0	1	0	0	0	2	4
Davidoff	1	0	4	0	0	0	0	0	0
Kent	1	1	0	3	2	0	0	2	0
None	3	3	2	11	2	0	6	0	0
D.K.	4	5	0	6	15	3	25	4	2
Don't smoke foreign cigarettes	50	46	56	35	47	50	44	60	53
Total	100	100	100	100	100	100	100	100	100

Base = respondents who most often smoke Chinese brand.
Note: only percentages above 1 % are presented.
Source: CSFB research

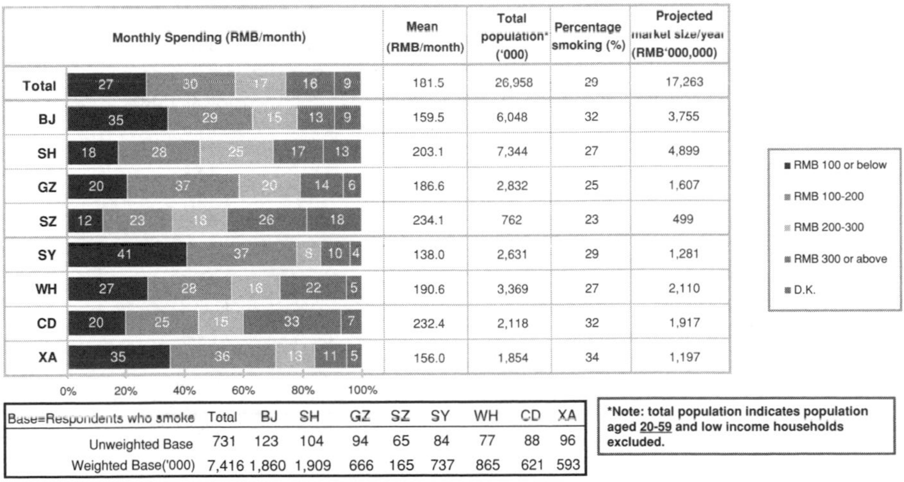

Source: CSFB research
Figure 18.5 Estimated tobacco market within the next year

Beijing has seemed to cast a more welcoming eye on foreign tobacco companies in recent times, tobacco remains a 'strategic' and closely guarded industry in China (tobacco companies are among the top corporate taxpayers in China). We estimate that the Chinese state-run monopoly CNTC generated around US$11bn in tax revenue, representing 10 % of the total government revenue in 2002. As a result, there remain significant restrictions on foreign tobacco companies' activities in China.

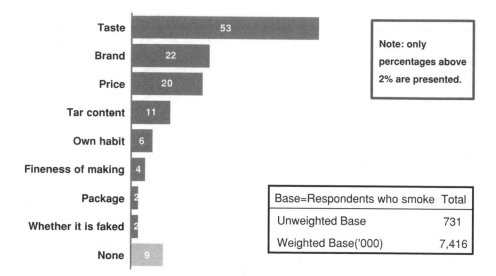

Note: only percentages above 2% are presented.

Base=Respondents who smoke	Total
Unweighted Base	731
Weighted Base('000)	7,416

Source: CSFB research
Figure 18.6   Factors considered when choosing a tobacco

Table 18.3   China versus US cigarette per capita consumption.

Year	China per capita consumption	US per capita consumption
1992	2045	134.0
1993	2049	120.7
1994	2044	127.3
1995	2060	124.1
1996	2009	123.4
1997	1998	120.8
1998	1981	114.4
1999	1952	108.8
2000	1930	98.8

Source: CSFB research

Under the CNTC umbrella, China's tobacco industry, like many others, is fragmented (with more than 2500 brands) and highly regional. Even the eight most competitive producers have a combined 26.4 % market share only. As a response, the State Tobacco Monopoly Administration (STMA) began to groom a 'Big Three' of domestic tobacco producers to produce seven key brands of cigarettes in an effort to fend off growing foreign competition. The first step of the consolidation game plan is to establish major flagship provincial firms, possibly followed by plans to set up national giant(s). Four provinces – Anhui, Guangdong, Hunan and Zhejiang – were selected as pilots and these will see a separation of their 'commercial' and 'industrial' operations. The separation process is deemed a necessary step to go round the 'commercial' restriction – in other words, the long-standing monopoly trading system. All separated tobacco producers will be put into a 'newco', with the provincial tobacco industrial company buying into other tobacco producers. Finally, these provincial companies will be merged into three to five groups. We note that Yunnan province's absence from the pilot scheme is probably intentional, with Yunnan province being the most prestigious tobacco-producing area in China, housing also Hongtashan, the country's largest and most prestigious tobacco group (also a top tax payer). China's state tobacco monopoly maintains that it will not abolish the current monopoly trading system. However, some industry watchers believe China will go down the same route as Japan and Korea in ultimately abolishing the monopoly.

Towards the end of 2003, Gallaher and Imperial Tobacco entered into cooperation agreements with Shanghai Tobacco and Yuxi Hongta, respectively. Gallaher's involves a reciprocal arrangement whereby Shanghai Tobacco manufactures and distributes Memphis and Gallaher manufactures and distributes Golden Deer in Russia. Hongta produces and distributes West on behalf of Imperial Tobacco. These agreements currently involve very limited volumes. *Time Asia Magazine* reported that Philip Morris was planning a cooperation with the Longyan cigarette factory for the production of Marlboro.

In July 2004, BAT announced that it had approval from the Chinese central government for a joint venture in China, which eventually would involve the manufacture and distribution of 100bn cigarettes in the premium segment and a total investment of $800m. However, the State Tobacco Monopoly Administration (STMA) said that it had not approved any new manufacturing joint venture agreements and it appears it would be years rather than months before any major new international manufacturing joint ventures might be approved. Once this happens, we believe the results of this survey support our view that BAT is potentially best placed in China over the longer term.

China also provides great opportunities for Altria, although it is one of the most tightly regulated markets in the world. Other than the China National Tobacco Corporation (CNTC) state-run monopoly advertising is restricted from television, radio, newspapers and magazines. In an effort to improve its quality and technology related to tobacco production, the CNTC signed an agreement with Altria's international tobacco business. We believe this strategic alliance will be pivotal when China's state-run monopoly eventually privatises.

For the tobacco sector in particular, the results of our survey should be seen in the context of covering only the eight largest cities with disposable incomes substantially higher than the national average and the fact that 70 % of China's population lives in rural areas.

Perhaps the most striking result from the survey is the significant gender differential in smoking prevalence with 54 % of males smoking versus only 4 % of females. A large difference in smoking rates between males and females was previously evident in Japan but has narrowed over time. In our view, we can expect to see the gap shrink gradually over time in China too, although much will depend on the health message and regulation that the government may impose.

The results of this survey suggest that 6 % of consumers in the eight largest cites smoke mostly foreign brands, which suggests significantly higher penetration than the 3 % total market share commanded by foreign brands. A third of those smoking foreign brands choose State Express 555, BAT's key premium brand in China. Of respondents who smoked 2 % said they smoked State Express 555.

Probably more important than current consumption patterns are likely future consumption trends. Current consumers of mostly domestic brands were asked which brand they smoked when they bought foreign brands. Some 50 % of respondents did not smoke foreign brands at all. However, a substantial 25 % of consumers who smoked mostly domestic brands chose State Express 555 (BAT), followed by Marlboro (Altria/Philip Morris) at 9 %. Mild Seven (Japan Tobacco), still the leading foreign brand in Taiwan, has also carved out a position among the top three brands in China. The fact that Japan Tobacco (JT) has two of the three brands bodes well for its business in the post-deregulation era. Blending technology, including aromas, is critical for determining the taste of cigarettes. JT enjoys an advantage here because of its track record of launching products that appeal to the tastes of Taiwanese consumers. Other BAT brands included Hilton (1 %) and Kent (1 %). The only other European company brand that featured was Davidoff at 1 %.

One conclusion from the survey that we were somewhat concerned about is the fact that only 2 % of respondents seemed to care whether the cigarettes they bought were counterfeit. We view this as one of the most important challenges faced by international tobacco manufacturers in China as the market starts opening up.

19
Transport and Travel

In our survey 47 % of respondents have travelled on an aircraft before, as shown in Figure 19.1. Guangzhou (63 %) and Shenzhen (59 %) have the highest percentages. Shenyang (36 %) and Wuhan (35 %) have the lowest percentages. Younger people are only slightly less likely to have flown before than older people (42 % of those in the 20–29 age group versus 50 % of those in the 50–59 age group – see Figure 19.2).

Most flights have been taken for domestic destinations while overseas flying experience is fairly limited, as shown in Figure 19.3. Of respondents 12 % indicated they

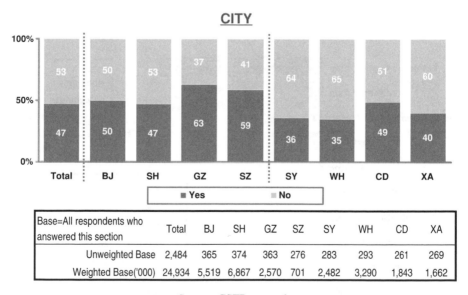

Source: CSFB research

Figure 19.1   Breakdown of respondents by whether they have taken a flight before by city

AGE

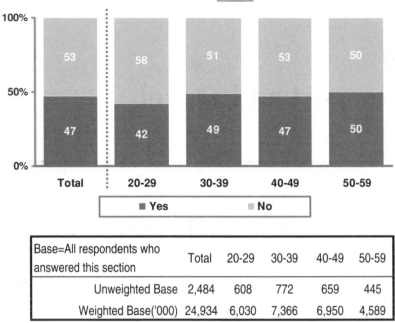

Base=All respondents who answered this section	Total	20-29	30-39	40-49	50-59
Unweighted Base	2,484	608	772	659	445
Weighted Base('000)	24,934	6,030	7,366	6,950	4,589

Source: CSFB research

Figure 19.2   Breakdown of respondents by whether they have taken a flight before by age

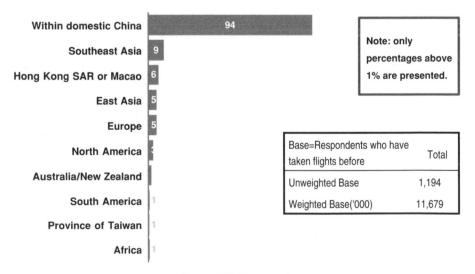

Base=Respondents who have taken flights before	Total
Unweighted Base	1,194
Weighted Base('000)	11,679

Note: only percentages above 1% are presented.

Source: CSFB research
Figure 19.3   Flight destinations

CITY

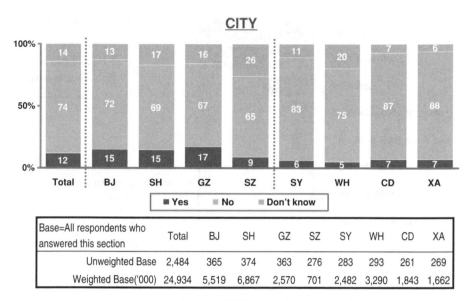

Base=All respondents who answered this section	Total	BJ	SH	GZ	SZ	SY	WH	CD	XA
Unweighted Base	2,484	365	374	363	276	283	293	261	269
Weighted Base('000)	24,934	5,519	6,867	2,570	701	2,482	3,290	1,843	1,662

Source: CSFB research

Figure 19.4   Intentions of taking flights abroad in the next year

are likely to take international flights within the next year (see Figure 19.4). Targeted top destinations are Europe (30 %) and Southeast Asia (25 %), shown in Figure 19.5.

When taking international flights, 26 % of flyers intend to choose foreign airlines. Of these, 63 % cite the better service offered; 47 % intend to choose Chinese airlines as they perceive Chinese airlines to offer better service (33 %), be more reliable (27 %) and to be safer (20 %); 21 % also feel Chinese people should travel on domestically owned airlines (Figure 19.6).

Singapore Airlines is the most well-known (65 %) and highest rated airline (43 % score in the Top 2 category weightings), as shown in Figure 19.7. Dragon Air (35 %) is the least well-known airline.

The number of respondents who have taken overseas holidays in the last three years is 8 % (see Figure 19.8). Most went to Southeast Asia (44 %), shown in Figure 19.9. East Asia (19 %), Europe (18 %) and Hong Kong/Macao (15 %) have also been popular destinations.

For the next year, 13 % intend to take an overseas holiday. The city with the highest percentage of respondents intending to travel overseas is Guangzhou at 21 % (see Figure 19.10) while Wuhan has the lowest at 3 %.

The most popular destinations intended for travel are Europe (29 %) and Southeast Asia (28 %), as shown in Figure 19.11. By contrast North and South America and Africa are much less favoured as potential travel destinations. This may well

Source: CSFB research

Figure 19.5   Planned flight destinations in the next year

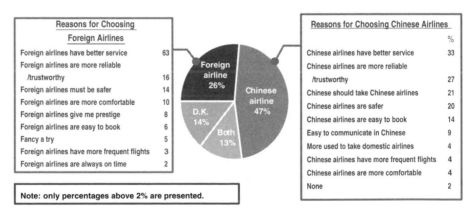

Source: CSFB research

Figure 19.6   Airline perception on whether foreign airline brands are viewed as local

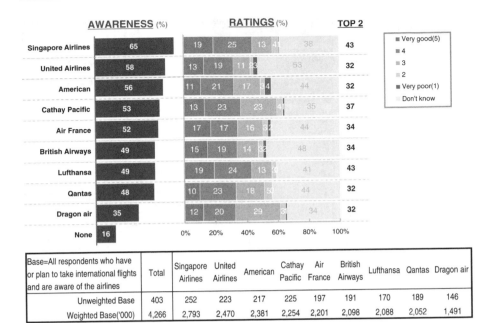

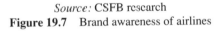

Source: CSFB research

Figure 19.7 Brand awareness of airlines

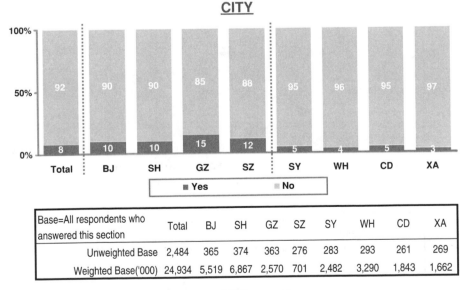

Source: CSFB research

Figure 19.8 Proportion of respondents having taken overseas holidays in the last three years

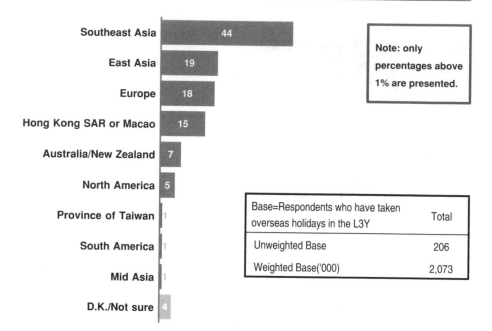

Note: only percentages above 1% are presented.

Base=Respondents who have taken overseas holidays in the L3Y	Total
Unweighted Base	206
Weighted Base('000)	2,073

Source: CSFB research

Figure 19.9   Destinations of overseas holidays in the last three years

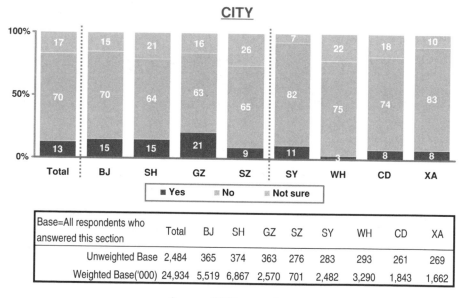

Base=All respondents who answered this section	Total	BJ	SH	GZ	SZ	SY	WH	CD	XA
Unweighted Base	2,484	365	374	363	276	283	293	261	269
Weighted Base('000)	24,934	5,519	6,867	2,570	701	2,482	3,290	1,843	1,662

Source: CSFB research

Figure 19.10   Intentions to take overseas holidays the next year

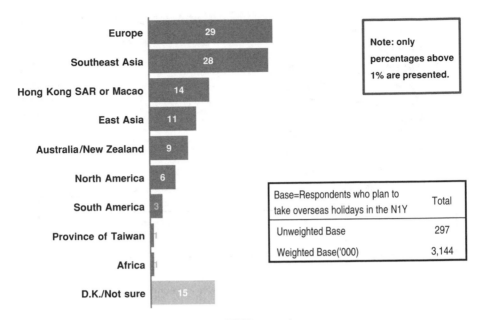

Source: CSFB research

Figure 19.11   Intended destinations for overseas holiday in the next year

be because of continued visa restrictions. Figure 19.12 provides projections for the likely size of the market for overseas holidays for the eight cities surveyed. The total projected spend is RMB 51bn (US$6.2bn).

Our survey suggests that resort-based holidays (62 %) and sight seeing (54 %) will form the majority of holiday types as shown in Figure 19.13. Less frequently mentioned types include: theme parks (30 %), sea cruises (23 %) or entertainment/gambling sites (21 %). Most people intend to go with an organised tour group (65 %) while 30 % will choose to create the trip by booking the component parts themselves, as shown in Figure 19.14.

IMPLICATIONS FOR AIRLINE AND HOTEL/LEISURE OPERATORS[1]

We believe that future growth from China is likely to represent a strong market opportunity for airlines and hotel/leisure operators. Our survey highlights the growth of leisure travellers and outbound traffic.

Currently, the penetration rate of previous flying experience is still relatively low in China at 47 % only. The majority of these respondents indicate that they have only flown domestically and not overseas to international destinations. Rising income

[1] Chris Reid, Karen Chan, James Higgins, William Drewry and Julia Pennington contributed to this section.

Personal Budget for an overseas holiday (/person)		Mean (RMB/person)	Total population* (000)	Percentage of intenders (%)	Projected market size N1Y (RMB '000,000)
Total	32 / 30 / 8 / 4 / 5 / 22	14,760	26,958	13	51,727
BJ	27 / 34 / 12 / 2 / 8 / 18	16,196	6,048	15	14,693
SH	27 / 30 / 4 / 9 / 4 / 27	15,305	7,344	15	16,860
GZ	50 / 24 / 4 / 19	10,635	2,832	21	6,325
SZ	16 / 24 / 32 / 0 / 12 / 12	21,429	762	9	1,470
SY	27 / 23 / 10 / 07 / 34	14,750	2,631	11	4,269
WH	20 / 40 / 0 / 10 / 30	17,857	3,369	3	1,805
CD	38 / 34 / 5 / 5 / 5 / 14	13,611	2,118	8	2,306
XA	43 / 26 / 5 / 0 / 10 / 14	14,583	1,854	8	2,163

0%   20%   40%   60%   80%   100%

■ Below RMB 10,000
■ RMB 10,000-20,000
■ RMB 20,000-30,000
■ RMB 30,000-40,000
■ Above RMB 40,000
□ D.K./No sure

*Note: total population indicates population aged 20-59 and have all low income households excluded.

Base=Respondents who plan to take overseas holidays in the N1Y	Total	BJ	SH	GZ	SZ	SY	WH	CD	XA
Unweighted Base	731	123	104	94	65	84	77	88	96
Weighted Base('000)	7,416	1,860	1,909	666	165	737	865	621	593

Source: CSFB research

Figure 19.12 Estimated market size for overseas holidays in the next year

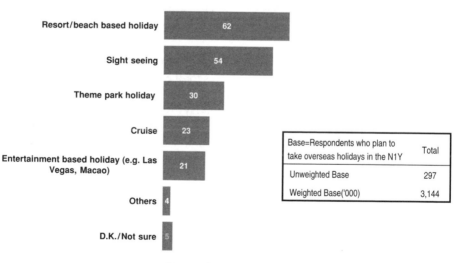

Base=Respondents who plan to take overseas holidays in the N1Y	Total
Unweighted Base	297
Weighted Base('000)	3,144

Source: CSFB research

Figure 19.13 Type of holiday intending to take

will tend to make airfares more affordable. The liberation and easing of individual travelling and visa application processes appears to have led to a shift in attitudes, with more opting for holidays to overseas destinations. Although 13 % only of the sample surveyed plan to travel overseas, it is still significant considering that only 8 % of the sample have taken overseas holidays in the last three years.

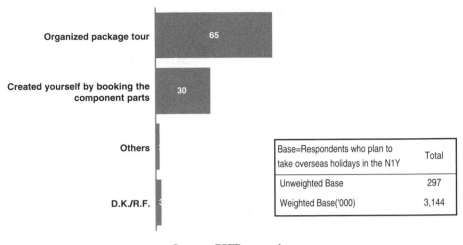

Base=Respondents who plan to take overseas holidays in the N1Y

	Total
Unweighted Base	297
Weighted Base('000)	3,144

Source: CSFB research

Figure 19.14   Format of booking overseas holiday

In the past, the growth of international traffic was mainly driven by business demand and in-bound traffic (in other words, overseas visitors). This along with the perception of foreigners that Chinese airlines are less safe and offer inferior services has led to foreign airlines gaining the majority of the demand. However, our survey indicates there is now a shift in the drivers of international traffic as demand is now increasingly for outbound traffic from China. This has been highlighted in the traffic flow during recent national holidays. Our survey shows that local people prefer to use domestic airlines and believe domestic airlines have better services (due to language, culture, airlines' sales network, etc.). This is a trend worth noting and we believe China Eastern Airlines, with larger international services, will be a major beneficiary. For example, our survey finds that 47 % of people taking international flights plan to choose Chinese airlines with only 26 % planning on choosing foreign airlines, primarily due to the better service they perceive as being offered by foreign airlines. We believe this is positive for the Chinese airlines, which can increase their market share of the international traffic.

However, our survey also shows good penetration of some non-Chinese airline brands into the Chinese market. We would highlight the US airlines' ability to connect Chinese gateways to US gateways and beyond as being a competitive advantage for them in gaining from this market. Although less than 5 % of their total revenues, Northwest and UAL are the incumbent US carriers in flights to mainland China, although American Airlines, Continental and Delta are all vying for some of the additional flights that are currently being competed.

What is also likely to benefit the US carriers, albeit less so than when they origi-nate Chinese travellers, will be passengers who fly Chinese carriers to US gateways and then hand them off to US airlines to complete their travel. On that front, UAL (allied with Air China) and Delta (partnered with China Southern) are relatively well positioned. China Eastern appears to be going it alone for now but we expect it will eventually choose either American, Northwest or Continental as a US partner. However, the choice of the latter two may be complicated by their alliance ties to Delta which, in turn, is allied with China Southern.

For European airlines the key issues are how many incremental passengers can be expected, and at what price the marginal traffic could be generated.

In general the overseas flying experience of our respondents is limited, as one would expect for a market at this relatively early stage of development. Only 6 % have flown internationally. The survey suggests that, of the 47 % Chinese who have taken a flight before, only 5 % have flown to Europe. Therefore the current penetration of Europe as an international destination is 2.4 % of the sample.

However, within the next 12 months, the survey suggests 12 % of the sample plan to fly internationally and that, given a Chinese individual's plans to fly internationally, there is a 30 % chance that he/she may fly to Europe. This implies that the penetration of Europe as an international destination is likely to rise to 3.6 % of the Chinese population. This in turn implies that in theory the volume of Chinese flying to Europe could rise by up to 50 % in the near term, positive news in general for the European carriers.

Brand awareness of European airlines is relatively strong. Of those flying internationally 49 % were aware of BA's brand, 49 % of Lufthansa and 52 % of Air France. Therefore it does not appear to us that a particular listed European flag carrier is occupying a stronger-than-average place in the hearts and minds of Chinese consumers currently.

In general the reasons cited by Chinese consumers to take overseas holidays were a resort/beach based holiday (62 %), sight seeing (54 %) or theme parks (30 %). Given Europe's relatively unfavourable resort/theme park holiday options versus other global international travel destinations, we believe that this means the major opportunity for European airlines to target China is sightseeing as well as business travel.

The most exposed listed European carriers, by current and planned revenues from Asia, are Lufthansa and Air France, where we estimate Asia/Pacific comprises 14 % and 22 % of current year revenues, respectively. While BA has 15 % of its revenues, from Asia/Pacific, we believe Lufthansa and Air France are most geared up for Asian growth, as they have already ordered the large-capacity A380 plane for delivery in 2007 and have ample airport and runway capacity in Charles de Gaulle, Frankfurt (and Munich). Heathrow, and for that matter we believe BA, is unlikely to see a significant alleviation of capacity until the opening of Terminal 5 in 2008–9.

While we can quickly conclude that the volume demand exists for passengers, the key issue remains the pricing of the marginal passenger. New routes to China typically increase average stage-length, require discounts to incentivise travel and with a lower cost of living in general dilute average price. However, European carriers must add significantly to their cost base in order to service these markets and, given that their cost base is significantly higher than the marginal revenue, we are still unconvinced of the overall argument that a strong and growing Chinese market will inevitably drive a much-needed increase in European flag carrier profitability. While Air France would be our preferred airline to play the dynamic, overall we would rather play the prospect of significantly rising volumes with the more defensive, price-protected airports, specifically Fraport and BAA.

Our preferred local airline to benefit from the likely increase in overseas travel is China Eastern Airlines based in Shanghai, although more people in Guangzhou (21 %) indicated in our survey that they are planning an overseas holiday than those in Shanghai and Beijing. However, China Southern may not benefit the most since Guangzhou is close to Hong Kong. People could prefer to travel to Hong Kong and transit to overseas destinations afterwards. Individual travelling to Hong Kong is much easier now.

It is a surprise that Dragon Air has the lowest awareness score among the foreign airlines and is below Cathay, although it has the largest market share of China's international traffic compared to the foreign peers. This may be because it mainly focuses on the business market and inbound traffic. The carrier plans to develop its regional network by competing directly with Cathay in order to attract the growing outbound traffic. However, it is likely to lose its niche position in the China market when Cathay increases its network and frequencies to China and has closer ties with Air China, the parent of CNAC/Dragon Air. We expect it would be a loser on this trend and therefore prefer Cathay.

The survey indicates an opportunity for Disney and the Macau casino operators. The Hong Kong government has recently announced that the opening of the Hong Kong Disneyland park will be on 12 September 2005. From the survey 13 % of respondents indicated that they are likely to take an overseas vacation next year and 30 % of these individuals indicated that they are targeting a theme park holiday. Given the success of Hong Kong in attracting mainland Chinese shoppers in recent years it seems likely that Hong Kong Disneyland will be an attractive destination to these travellers. Meanwhile, we believe that Disney will continue to outperform its peers in terms of earnings growth rate and that it will be the ultimate stock performance driver over the next 12 months, as it ultimately has been in 2004.

We were somewhat surprised that of those Chinese consumers who intended to take a holiday, some 23 % of respondents indicated the intention to take a cruise. This level of penetration, if it were to materialise, is far more significant than cruising achieves in Europe (for example, UK 1.5 % and Germany 0.5 % of cruise passengers as a percentage of vacationers) and even in the US, where adoption of cruising has historically always been highest (3 % penetration).

We would see this as a potentially positive feature for Carnival which has clearly identified Asia as a target market, with key focus specifically on China, Japan and India. The key dilemma with which Carnival is currently wrestling is identification of the optimum packages for Chinese clientele, both in terms of how far ideally they wish to travel to embark on a cruise and the appropriate selection of destinations to incorporate in a cruising itinerary in the region.

Further support for cruising in this survey is also inferred from a separate question, to which 65 % of respondents indicated that they intended to take an organised package tour compared to 30 % creating a holiday with individual component parts booked themselves. We would regard this response as entirely consistent with a population just emerging as a source of overseas travellers, where an organised package provides perceived ease of booking, ease of participation, security, and quality guarantee. Booking a cruise offers, in effect, the ultimate all-inclusive low-maintenance package where, from stepping on board, all means of travel, entertainment, dining, gambling, etc., are literally on the doorstep.

We see the results of our survey as positive for Millennium & Copthorne and InterContinental. These companies generate approximately 40 % and 10 % of EBIT, respectively, in Asia by our estimates, the largest exposures to the region of any public hotel companies. From their perspective we would see it as positive that, of intended destinations for overseas holidays by Chinese customers next year, some 28 % identify South East Asia as their likely destination, Hong Kong and Macao a further 14 % and East Asia and Taiwan totalling a further 12 %. As a growing proportion of the Chinese population in future years begin to travel overseas it is logical to expect their first trip to take place within Asia, rather than, for example, leaving the country for the first time and flying straight to the US. Although Europe and to a lesser extent the US are likely to grow proportionately as destinations for Chinese travellers, with the growth in first-time travellers the absolute numbers travelling within Asia is potentially very significant. Moreover, with Millennium & Copthorne and InterContinental having established reputations in the local Asian market it is logical that the US and European arms of these companies will be among the greatest beneficiaries of increasing travel of the Chinese outside Asia.

Kuoni, as a specialist travel operator, is perhaps best placed of the travel companies to benefit from growth in demand for holidays from the Chinese. The company's incoming and Asia business (a large proportion of which provides services in respect of Asians visiting Europe and the US) represents already approximately 18 % of turnover and Kuoni has recently clearly identified China (along with India) as possibly the greatest growth opportunity going forward. The evidence from within this survey for an increasing proportion of Chinese to travel to Europe in particular is a source of potentially significant benefit to Kuoni.

Appendix A: PPP Convergence Model

Our modelling of exchange rates is rooted in the traditional academic literature on PPP. This supports our key assumption of nonlinearity in the mean reversion process: 'the rate of convergence to PPP is faster when initial deviations are large' (Rogoff, 1996). Emerging economics and developed economies were modelled separately. A key assumption is terminal convergence of the actual exchange rate to the PPP level (that is, a conversion factor of 1.0 following the 'law of one price').

Our models were developed with the help of CSFB's Global FX Research team. The concept of nonlinearities in the adjustment of the real exchange rate towards its equilibrium levels is not new in economic literature. For example, Obstfeld and Taylor (1997) have investigated the nonlinear nature of the adjustment process in terms of a threshold model, which allows for a transactions cost band within which no adjustment takes place. Outside the band, however, the process switches suddenly and the real exchange rate starts converging towards its equilibrium level. Taylor, Peel and Sarno (2001) adopt a slightly different approach, where the process of nonlinear adjustment is smooth rather than discrete. Their evidence is consistent with the notion that the real exchange rate adjusts towards its equilibrium level in every period but that the speed of adjustment varies with the extent of the deviation from parity.

The emerging economies were modelled via simple ordinary differential equations where the rates of convergence to the PPP level of each exchange rate are dependent upon the amounts of deviation from the PPP level but also the average GDP and population growth rates over a significant historical time period. This allows us to calculate trends in real GDP per capita growth, which in the academic literature is found to be correlated with appreciation towards the PPP level. Typically, emerging market countries' exchange rates begin the convergence process from a situation of structural undervaluation versus the PPP level as most governments have followed models of export-led growth.

The significant time period was calculated via spectral analysis and the strongest signals from the Fourier transforms were used. The cycle length, which we analysed to be significant, was approximately 12 years. The average GDP growth rate was used as a proxy for probability and speed of revaluation.

The solutions of the differential equations take the form

$$p = A \exp(-kt) + c$$

The boundary conditions are: $t = 0$, $p = p_0$; $t = \infty$, $p = 1$; $t = T$, $p = \Omega$. By applying these conditions, the above A, k and c were calculated giving

$$p = (p_0 - 1) \exp \left\{ \left[\ln \left(\frac{\Omega - 1}{p_0 - 1} \right) \right] \left(\frac{t}{T} \right) \right\} + 1$$

where

$p_0 =$ initial PPP conversion factor to official exchange-rate ratio
$\Omega =$ defined PPP conversion factor after a time period, T
$T =$ time period at which the PPP conversion factor converges to Ω

The dependency upon the average growth rate is calculated from the Fourier transform described above and the time period T was scaled down accordingly.

For the developed economies, separate base-case scenarios were taken. This is owing to the cyclical nature of the relationships between actual and PPP exchange rates. In these countries, exchange rates are influenced by the monetary and fiscal stance adopted as well as by the business cycle. In most developed countries, convergence to the PPP level is found to be rapid, with a half-life of four years, supported by the work of academics such as Frankel and Rose's (1995) panel data analysis as well as Wei and Parsley (1995). Since the PPP ratio deviates above and below the unit value, the unit was taken as the ongoing trend. Stochastic solutions incorporating random walk models have been deemed inadequate by the academic consensus. They were not used in this exercise.

REFERENCES

Frankel, J. and Rose, A. (1995) A panel project on purchasing power parity: mean reversion within and between countries, NBER Working Paper 5006.
Obstfeld, M. and Taylor, A. (1997) Nonlinear aspect of goods–market arbitrage and adjustment: Heckscher's commodity points revisited. *Journal of the Japanese and International Economies*, **11**.
Rogoff, K. (1996) The purchasing power parity puzzle. *Journal of Economic Literature*, **34**.

Taylor, M., Peel, D. and Sarno, L. (2001) Non-linear mean-reversion in real exchange rates: towards a solution to the purchasing power parity puzzles. *International Economic Review*, **42**.

Wei, S. and Parsley, D. (1995) Purchasing power parity during the floating rate period: exchange rate volatility, trade barriers and other culprits, NBER Working Paper 5032.

Appendix B: Global Consumption Function

For each country the share of household consumption as a percentage of GDP is modelled in a similar manner to the exchange-rate model assuming convergence to the PPP level. We assume that household consumption as a percentage of GDP will increase at a rate proportional to its deviation away from the long-term developed world average of 60 % (65 % for the US and UK). Figure B.1 shows the global values

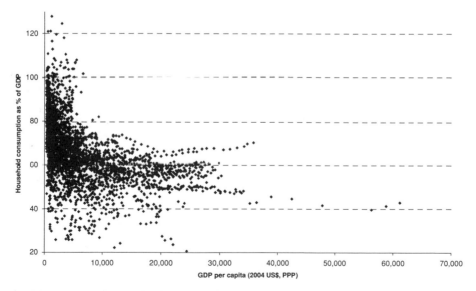

Source: World Bank and CSFB research

Figure B.1   Global household consumption as a percentage of GDP versus GDP PPP per capita, 1975–2002

for the share of household consumption as a percentage of GDP versus GDP PPP per capita from 1975 to 2002. The values seem to converge at 60 % for nearly all countries at high GDP levels. The exceptions are the US and the UK, which we converge to the previously mentioned 65 % level (implying a 5 % fall in consumption spending relative to GDP in the US in the next 10 years).

Using similar formulae to the above, the following solutions for differential equations were found:

$$h = (h_0 - 60)\exp\left\{\left[\ln\left(\frac{\Pi - 60}{h_0 - 60}\right)\right]\left(\frac{\text{GDP}}{T}\right)\right\} + 60 \quad \text{for nearly all countries}$$

$$h = (h_0 - 65)\exp\left\{\left[\ln\left(\frac{\Pi - 65}{h_0 - 65}\right)\right]\left(\frac{\text{GDP}}{T}\right)\right\} + 65 \quad \text{for the US and UK}$$

where

h_0 = initial household consumption as a percentage of GDP
Π = defined consumption as share of GDP after a time period, T
T = time period at which the consumption as share of GDP converges to Π

The solutions for household consumption spending to GDP are shown in Figure B.2. The values of GDP PPP per capita for each country were projected using IMF

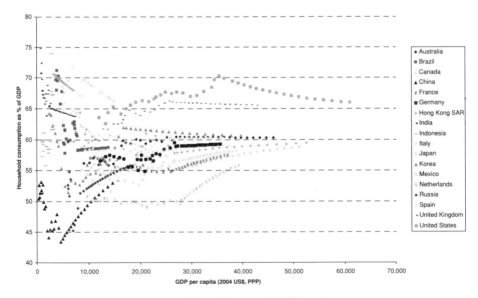

Source: IMF, World Bank and CSFB estimates

Figure B.2 Household consumption as a percentage of GDP versus GDP PPP per capita projected using the above model and CSFB estimates of trend growth in GDP PPP per capita

forecasted growth rates and CSFB economists' forecasts for GDP and population growth rates where available. For each country, the product of household consumption spending as a percentage of GDP and the value of US$ GDP projected using the PPP convergence model described above give the US$ consumption spending projections discussed in the main text.

Appendix C: Methodology of Product Category Projection

Annual product ownership numbers and hence CAGRs for several product categories have been calculated for 15 larger developed and emerging economies. These data then allowed market shares to be calculated. The economies were chosen for their relevance either globally or as comparative historical and cultural references for China (for example, Korea, Hong Kong SAR and Japan). China has arguably been following a similar high investment spend / export-orientated growth model to that used historically by Korea. Hong Kong SAR and Japan are arguably culturally most similar to China from the consumption viewpoint.

Our technique of modelling has taken into account GDP per capita, GDP growth rates and population growth of the selected countries using as a starting point historical product density values from the IMF World Economics Outlook publication and the World Bank World Development Indicators database. The related product densities were found by finding solutions to differential equations that converged to the historically observed trends of the countries used in this exercise. Since these densities were per capita, the forecast growth of each country's population was also used to calculate absolute ownership figures for each product category. The product category densities were also capped to avoid solutions where the ownership of items is infinitely proportional to GDP.

We have used the estimates of our global economics and demographics teams and, in China's case, Asian Demographics projections. The market shares and CAGRs have been graphed from the data in the calculation of absolute numbers.

Figures C.1 to C.7 show the product category density and GDP per capita relationships for all 15 countries that were used in the estimation of the values given in the main text. They also show the product density functions used.

Televisions

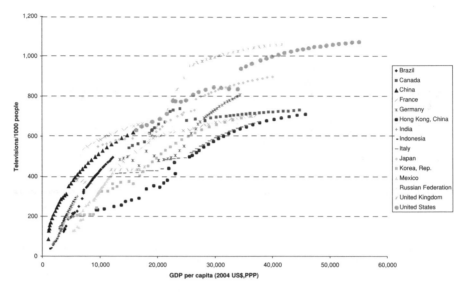

Source: IMF, World Bank and CSFB estimates
Figure C.1   Televisions per thousand people against GDP per capita, PPP, 1980–2020E

Mobile handsets

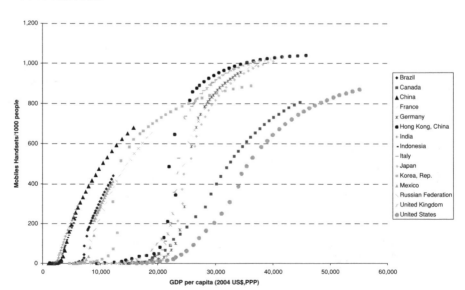

Source: IMF, World Bank and CSFB estimates
Figure C.2   Mobile handsets per thousand people against GDP per capita, PPP, 1990–2020E

Fixed-line telephony

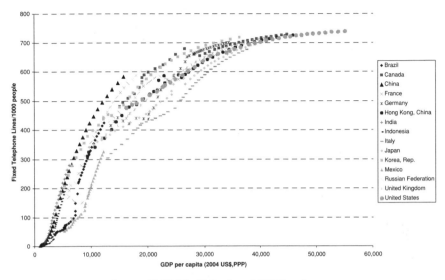

Source: IMF, World Bank and CSFB estimates
Figure C.3 Fixed telephone lines per thousand people against GDP per capita, PPP, 1980–2020E

Personal computers

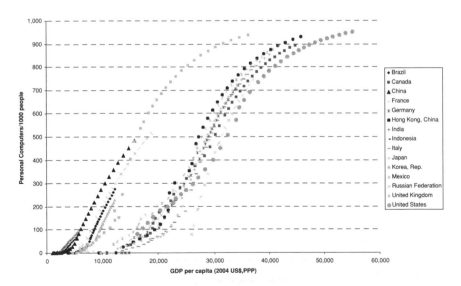

Source: IMF, World Bank and CSFB estimates
Figure C.4 Personal computers per thousand people against GDP per capita, PPP, 1985–2020E

Radios

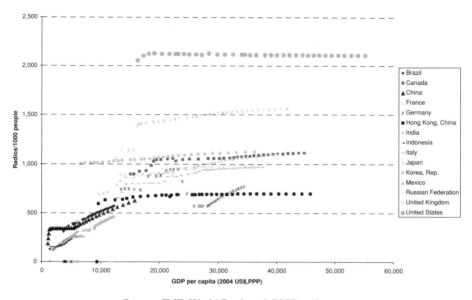

Source: IMF, World Bank and CSFB estimates
Figure C.5   Radios per thousand people against GDP per capita, PPP, 1980–2020E

Autos

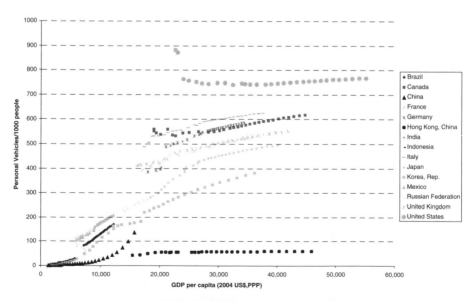

Source: IMF, World Bank and CSFB estimates
Figure C.6   Passenger cars per thousand people against GDP per capita, PPP, 1990–2020E

Air travel

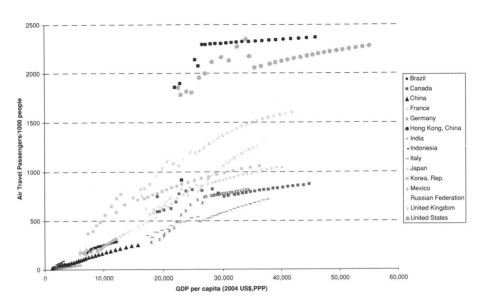

Source: IMF, World Bank and CSFB estimates

Figure C.7 Air travel passengers per thousand people against GDP per capita, PPP, 1990–2020E

Bibliography

ADB (Asian Development Bank) (1999) *Key Indicators of Developing Asian and Pacific Countries*, Oxford University Press, Oxford.

Alasuutari, P. (1995) *Researching Culture Qualitative Method and Cultural Studies*, Sage Publications, London.

Alden, D. *et al.* (1999) Brand positioning through Asia, North America and Europe: the role of global consumer culture. *Journal of Marketing*, **63**(1), 75–87.

Asian Demographics Limited (2004a) *Population Model*.

Asian Demographics Limited (2004b) *Household Income and Expenditure Model*.

Balassa, B. (1964) The purchasing power parity doctrine: a reappraisal. *Journal of Political Economy*, **72**, 584–96.

Barro, R. (1997) *Determinants of Economic Growth*, MIT Press, Cambridge, M.A.

Booth, W. *et al.* (2003) *The Craft of Research*, The University of Chicago Press, Chicago, Illinois.

Borden, N. (1965) The concept of the marketing mix, in *Science in Marketing* (ed. G. Schwartz), John Wiley & Sons, Inc, New York.

Boze, B. and Patton, C. (1995) The future of consumer branding as seen from the picture today. *Journal of Consumer Marketing*, **12**(4), 20–41.

Bradburn, N. *et al.* (1982) *Asking Questions: The Definitive Guide to Questionnaire Design – For Market Research, Political Polls, and Social and Health Questionnaires*, Jossey-Bass Inc., San Francisco, California; Revised edn, 2004.

Buzzell, R. (1968) Can you standardize multinational marketing? *Harvard Business Review*, **46**(6), 102–13.

Chandler, A. (1962) *Strategy and Structure: Chapters in the History of the Industrial Enterprise*, MIT Press, Cambridge, Massachusetts.

Chandler, A. (1977) *The Visible Hand: The Managerial Revolution in American Business*, Harvard University Press, Cambridge, Massachusetts.

Chandler, A. (1990) *Scale and Scope: The Dynamics of Industrial Capitalism*, Harvard University Press, Cambridge, Massachusetts.

Chen, Y. and Penhirin, J. (2004) Marketing to China's consumers. *The McKinsey Quarterly*, Special edn, 63–73.

Choudhri, E. and Khan, M. (2004) Real exchange rates in developing countries: are Balassa–Samuelson effects present?, IMF Working Paper 04/188.

Cui, G. and Liu, Q. (2000) Regional market segments of China: opportunities and barriers in a big emerging market. *Journal of Consumer Marketing*, **17**(1), 55–72.

Cui, G. and Liu, Q. (2001) Executive insights: emerging market segments in a transitional economy: a study of urban consumers in China. *Journal of International Marketing*, **9**(1), 84–106.

Czinkota, M. and Ronkainen, I. (2003) An international marketing manifesto. *Journal of International Marketing*, **11**(1), 13–27.

Diamond, J. (2005) *Collapse: How societies choose to fail or survive*, Allen Lane, pp. 358–78.

Dibb, S. (2000) Market segmentation, in *Oxford Textbook of Marketing* (ed. K. Blois), Oxford University Press, Oxford, pp. 380–413.

Dickson, P. and Ginter, J. (1987) Market segmentation, product differentiation and marketing strategy. *Journal of Marketing*, **51**(2), 1–10.

Dickson, M. *et al.* (2004) Chinese consumer market segments for foreign apparel products. *Journal of Consumer Marketing*, **21**(5), 301–17.

Economist, The (2001) The case for brands, 8 September, p. 9.

Economist, The (2004a) Luxury's new empire: conspicuous consumption in China, 19 June, p. 69.

Economist, The (2004b) The rich hit the road – China's car industry, 19 June, p. 70.

Edwards, S. (1989) Real exchange rates in the developing countries: concepts and measurement, NBER Working Paper 2950.

Eichengreen, B. *et al.* (2004) The impact of China on the exports of other Asian countries, NBER Working Paper 10768.

Ellen, R. (1984) *Ethnographic Research: A Guide to General Conduct*, Academic Press, London.

Engel, J. *et al.* (1995) *Consumer Behavior*, *8th edn*, The Dryden Press, Orlando, Florida.

Frankel, J. (2004) On the Renminbi: the choice between adjustment under a fixed exchange rate and adjustment under a flexible rate, Paper presented to the IMF Seminar on The Foreign Exchange System, Dalian, China, 27 May.

Frankel, J. (2005) On the Renminbi: the choice between adjustment under a fixed exchange rate and adjustment under a flexible rate, NBER Working Paper 11274.

Frankel, J. and Rose, A. (1995) A panel project on purchasing power parity: mean reversion within and between countries, NBER Working Paper 5006.

Gao, P. *et al.* (2003) Can Chinese brands make it abroad? *The McKinsey Quarterly*, Special edn, pp. 3–13.

Gilbert, N. (2001) *Researching Social Life*, Sage Publications, London.

Gill, J. and Johnson, P. (1997) *Research Methods for Managers*, 2nd edn, Paul Chapman Publishing, London.

Gilmore, F. and Dumont, S. (2003) *Brand Warriors China: Creating Sustainable Capital*, Profile Books, London.

Goldstein, M. (2004) Adjusting China's exchange rate policies, Institute for International Economics Working Paper 04/1.

Hannah, L. (1983) *The Rise of the Corporate Economy*, Methuen, London.

Hankinson, G. (2000) Brand Management, in *Oxford Textbook of Marketing* (ed. K. Blois), Oxford University Press, Oxford, 479–99.

Hankinson, G. and Cowking, P. (1993) *Branding in Action*, McGraw-Hill, Maidenhead.

Hofstede, F. *et al.* (1999) International market segmentation based on consumer–product relations. *Journal of Marketing Research*, **36**(1), 1–17.

Holz, C. (2003) Truth or consequences: China's GDP numbers. *China Economic Quarterly*, **3**, 30–40.

Hooley, G. *et al.* (1998) *Marketing Strategy and Competitive Positioning*, Palgrave, Basingstoke.

Hsieh, M. (2004) Measuring global brand equity using cross-national survey data. *Journal of International Marketing*, **12**(2), 28–57.

IMF (International Monetary Fund) (2004) *World Economic Outlook: The Global Demographic Transition*, Washington.

Inter Press News Service (2004) Development China: consumer powers corners multinationals, 21 June.

Isard, P. (1995) *Exchange Rate Economics*, Cambridge University Press, Cambridge.

Jin, Z. (2003) The dynamics of real interest rates, real exchange rates and the balance of payments in China, 1980–2002, IMF Working Paper 03/67.

Jobber, D. (1995) *Principles and Practice of Marketing*, McGraw-Hill, Maidenhead.

Kotler, P. (2003) Driving business strategy. *Brand Strategy*, p. 13.

Kotler, P. *et al.* (2004) *Principles of Marketing*, 4th European edn, Prentice-Hall, Harlow, Essex.

Krugman, P. and Obstfeld, M. (2003) *International Economics Theory and Policy*, 6th edn, Pearson Education, Boston, Massachusetts.

Leeflang, P. *et al.* (2000) *Building Models for Marketing Decisions*, Kluwer Academic Publishers, Dordrecht, Netherlands.

Levitt, T. (1983) The globalization of markets. *Harvard Business Review*, **63**(3), 92–102.

Li, Conghua (1998) *China: The Consumer Revolution*, John Wiley & Sons, Inc., New York.

Li, Y. (2004) Brand effect on consumer behaviour in China. *Fibres and Textiles in Eastern Europe*, **12**(2), 10–11.

Lieberthal, K. (2003) China in 2033: what will China look like in 30 years. *China Business Review*, **30**(2), 42–8.

Lieberthal, K. (2004) China tomorrow: the great transition, the hidden dragons. *Harvard Business Review*, **82**(2), 117–8.

Liu, X. and Shu, C. (2004) Consumption and stock markets in Greater China. *Applied Economics Letters*, **11**(6), 365–8.

Loeb, B. (1955) The use of Engel's law as a basis for predicting consumer expenditures. *Journal of Marketing*, **20**(1), 20.

Lofland, J. and Lofland, L. (1995) *Analyzing Social Settings: A Guide to Qualitative Observation and Analysis*, 3rd edn, International Thompson Publishing, London.

Lord, D. (2003) Targeting the individual: understanding consumer needs, drivers and marketing opportunities to 2010, in *Reuters Business Insight: Consumer Goods*.

Lucas R. (1988) In the mechanics of economic development. *Journal of Monetary Economics*, **22**(1), 3–42.

McKechnie, S. and Zhou, J. (2003) Product placement in movies: a comparison of Chinese and American consumers' attitudes. *International Journal of Advertising*, **22**(3), 349–74.

Maddison, A. (1997) Causal influences on productivity performance 1820–1992: a global perspective. *Journal of Productivity Analysis*, 325–60.

Maddison, A. (2001) *The World Economy: A Millennial Perspective*, OECD Development Centre, Paris.

Maddison, A. (2004) Contours of the world economy and the art of macro-measurement 1500 to 2001, Ruggles Lecture, Cork, Ireland.

Mallon, G. and Whalley, J. (2004) China's post accession WTO stance, NBER Working Paper 10649.

Marsden, D. and Littler, D. (1996) Positioning alternative perspectives of consumer behaviour. *Journal of Marketing Management*, **14**(1), 3–28.

Middleton M. *et al*. (1994) Small firms and clearing banks, in *Capital Markets and Corporate Governance* (eds N. Dimsdale and M. Prevezer), Clarendon Press, Oxford.

Modigliani, F. and Cao, S. (2004) The Chinese saving puzzle and the life-cycle hypothesis. *Journal of Economic Literature*, **42**(1), 145–70.

Morgan, R. (2000) A consumer-oriented framework of brand equity and loyalty. *International Journal of Market Research*, **42**(1), 65–78.

Muhlbacher, H. *et al*. (1991) *International Marketing: A Global Perspective*, Addison Wesley, Inc., Reading, Massachusetts.

National Bureau of Statistics of China (2002) *Measures for Fifth National Census*, China Statistics Press, Beijing.

National Bureau of Statistics of China (2004) *China Statistical Yearbook*, China Statistics Press, Beijing.

Nolan, P. (2001a) *China and the Global Economy*, Palgrave, Basingstoke.

Nolan, P. (2001b) *China and the Global Business Revolution*, Palgrave, Basingstoke.

Obstfeld, M. and Taylor, A. (1997) Nonlinear aspect of goods–market arbitrage and adjustment: Heckscher's commodity points revisited. *Journal of the Japanese and International Economies*, **11**.

Ogawa, N. (1988) Aging in China: demographic alternatives. *Asia-Pacific Population Journal*, **3**(3), 21–64.

Orr, G. (2004) The aging in China. *The McKinsey Quarterly*, Special edn, pp. 106–9.

Penhirin, J. (2004) Understanding the Chinese consumer. *The McKinsey Quarterly*, Special edn, pp. 46–57.

Penrose, E. (1995) *The Theory of the Growth of the Firm*, Oxford University Press, Oxford.

Peter, P. and Olson, J. (2001) *Consumer Behavior and Marketing Strategy*, 6th edn, McGraw-Hill, New York.

Porter, M. (1998) *The Competitive Advantage of Nations*, Macmillan Press, London.

Portes, R. and Santorum, A. (1987) Money and the consumption goods market in China, NBER Working Paper 2143.

Pralahad C. and Lieberthal, K. (1998) The end of corporate imperialism. *Harvard Business Review*, **76**(4), 68–79.

Prasad, E. (2004) China's growth and integration into the world economy, IMF Occasional Paper 232.

Quelch, J. (2003) The return of the global brand. *Harvard Business Review*, **81**(8), 22–3.

Quelch, J. and Hoff, E. (1986) Customizing global marketing. *Harvard Business Review*, **64**(3), 59–68.

Rawski, T. (2001) What's happening to China's GDP statistics? *China Economics Review*, **12**(4).

Rheem, H. (1996) International investing: who profits in China? *Harvard Business Review*, **74**(1), 10–11.

Rogoff, K. (1996) The purchasing power parity puzzle. *Journal of Economic Literature*, **34**.

Romer, P. (1994) The origins of endogenous growth. *Journal of Economic Perspectives*, **8**(1), 3–22.

Rugman, A. (1996) *The Theory of Multinational Enterprises: The Selected Scientific Papers of Alan M. Rugman*, Edward Elgar Publishing, Cheltenham.

Rugman, A. (2000) *The End of Globalization*, Random House Business Books, London.

Samuelson, P. (1964) Theoretical notes on trade problems. *Review of Economics and Statistics*, **46**, 145–54.

Shimp, T. (2003) *Advertising, Promotion, and Supplemental Aspects of Integrated Marketing Communications*, 6th edn, South-Western, Mason, Ohio.

Smith, A. (1776) *An Inquiry into the Nature and Causes of the Wealth of Nations*, University of Chicago. Reprint 1976, Chicago, Illinois.

Solow, R. (1956) A contribution to the theory of economic growth. *Quarterly Journal of Economics*, **70**(1), 65–94.

Solow, R. (1970) *Growth Theory: An Exposition*, Oxford University Press, Oxford.

Summer, R. and Heston, A. (1991) The Penn world table mark 5: an expanded set of international comparisons, 1950–1988. *Quarterly Journal of Economics*, **2**, 327–68.

Swan, T. (1956) Economic growth and capital accumulation. *Economic Record*, **32**(2), 334–61.

Tao, D. (2003) China: RMB/USD to hit 5 – the next global transition, Credit Suisse First Boston Emerging Markets Economics Research, 30 January.

Tao, D. (2004) China: RMB – ready . . . set. . . , Credit Suisse First Boston Emerging Markets Economics Research, 10 September.

Taylor, M., Peel, D. and Sarno, L. (2001) Non-linear mean-reversion in real exchange rates: towards a solution to the purchasing power parity puzzles. *International Economic Review*, **42**.

Tong, L. (1998) Consumerism sweeps the mainland. *Marketing Management*, **6**(4), 32–5.

UNCTAD (United Nations Conference on Trade and Development) (2004) World Investment Report: The Shift Towards Services, Geneva.

Underhill, P. (2000) *Why We Buy the Science of Shopping*, Texere Publishing, London.

US Census Bureau (2004) *Income, Poverty, and Health Insurance Coverage in the United States: 2003*, US Government Printing Office, Washington, DC.

Usunier, J. (1996) *Marketing Across Cultures*, Prentice-Hall, Harlow, Essex.

Wallis, K. (1979) *Topics in Applied Econometrics*, Basil Blackwell Publisher, Oxford.

Wang, F. (1998) Floaters, moonlighters and the underemployed: a national labor market with Chinese characteristics. *Journal of Contemporary China*, **7**(19), 466–7.

Wei, S. (1997) How taxing is corruption on international investors, NBER Working Paper 6030.

Wei, S. and Parsley, D. (1995) Purchasing power parity during the floating rate period: exchange rate volatility, trade barriers and other culprits, NBER Working Paper 5032.

Williamson, J. G. (1995) The evolution of global labour markets since 1830. *Explorations in Economic History*, **32**, 141–96.

World Bank (1993) *The East Asian Miracle: Economic Growth and Public Policy*, Oxford University Press, Oxford.

World Bank (2004) *World Development Indicators 2004*, World Bank, Washington.

Wright, L. and Crimp, M. (2000) *The Marketing Research Process*, 5th edn, Prentice-Hall, Harlow, Essex.

Yan, R. (1994) To reach China's consumers, adapt to Guo Qing. *Harvard Business Review*, **72**, 4–10.

Zhou, L. and Hui, M. (2003) Symbolic value of foreign products in the People's Republic of China. *Journal of International Marketing*, **11**(2), 36–58.

Index

Index compiled by Terry Halliday